METHODS FOR SOCIAL THEORY

This book constitutes a practical guide to the important skills of both theorizing and writing in social scientific scholarship, focusing on the importance of identifying relations between concepts that are useful for explaining social entities and of producing a text that convincingly advances the theory that has been constructed. Taking as its point of departure the distinction between the research process and the reporting process – between clarifying one's ideas to oneself and writing to express these ideas clearly to others – this volume concentrates on writing when theorizing as a way of thinking, emphasizing the series of relations that exist between ontology, epistemology and rhetoric upon which successful theoretical writing depends.

Richly illustrated with practical examples, the book is divided into two parts, the first of which presents techniques for theorizing based upon visualized and logical connections of ideas, concepts and empirical patterns in both free and systematic ways, and the second part providing techniques for structuring and presenting arguments in essays, papers, articles or books. As such, *Methods for Social Theory* offers a toolbox for the development and presentation of social thought, which will prove essential for students and teachers across the social sciences.

Jan Ch. Karlsson is Professor of Organization, Faculty of Business, Languages, and Social Sciences, Ostfold University College, Norway.

Ann Bergman is Professor of Working Life Science at Karlstad University, Sweden.

METHODS FOR SOCIAL THEORY

Analytical tools for theorizing and writing

Jan Ch. Karlsson and Ann Bergman

LONDON AND NEW YORK

First published 2017
by Routledge
2 Park Square, Milton Park, Abingdon, Oxon OX14 4RN

and by Routledge
711 Third Avenue, New York, NY 10017

Routledge is an imprint of the Taylor & Francis Group, an informa business

© 2017 Jan Ch. Karlsson and Ann Bergman

The right of Jan Ch. Karlsson and Ann Bergman to be identified as authors of this work has been asserted by them in accordance with sections 77 and 78 of the Copyright, Designs and Patents Act 1988.

All rights reserved. No part of this book may be reprinted or reproduced or utilised in any form or by any electronic, mechanical, or other means, now known or hereafter invented, including photocopying and recording, or in any information storage or retrieval system, without permission in writing from the publishers.

Trademark notice: Product or corporate names may be trademarks or registered trademarks, and are used only for identification and explanation without intent to infringe.

British Library Cataloguing-in-Publication Data
A catalogue record for this book is available from the British Library

Library of Congress Cataloging-in-Publication Data
Names: Karlsson, Jan, 1948- author. | Bergman, Ann (Professor in Working Life Science), author.
Title: Methods for social theory: analytical tools for theorizing and writing / Jan Ch. Karlsson and Ann Bergman.
Description: Abingdon, Oxon; New York, NY: Routledge, 2017. | Includes bibliographical references and index.
Identifiers: LCCN 2016021735 | ISBN 9781472472816 (hardback) | ISBN 9781472472847 (pbk.) | ISBN 9781315595115 (ebook)
Subjects: LCSH: Social sciences–Philosophy. | Social sciences–Authorship.
Classification: LCC H61.K274 2017 | DDC 300.1–dc23LC record available at https://lccn.loc.gov/2016021735

ISBN: 978-1-4724-7281-6 (hbk)
ISBN: 978-1-4724-7284-7 (pbk)
ISBN: 978-1-315-59511-5 (ebk)

Typeset in Bembo
by Sunrise Setting Ltd., Brixham, UK

CONTENTS

List of figures   *viii*
List of tables   *x*
Preface   *xii*
Acknowledgements   *xiv*

1 Theorizing and writing social theory   **1**
   Social theory   2
   Theorizing   5
   Writing   9
      Writing in the research process   10
      Writing in the reporting process   11
   Outline of the book   12
   References   15

PART I
Tools for theorizing in social science   **17**

   Graphic representations   17
   Displays and property spaces as preliminary endpoints   21
   References   23

2 Basics of displays   **25**
   What is a display?   26
   Building blocks of displays   29
   Putting a display together   32

vi Contents

    Summary 40
    References 41

3 The use of displays in theorizing   42
    Theorizing by extending 43
    Theorizing by mapping interaction 46
    Stepwise theorizing 49
    Summary 53
    References 54

4 Basics of property spaces   55
    Constructing a property space 56
    Hidden property spaces 57
    Housekeeping 60
    Labelling the types: terms 64
    Developing existing terminology 68
    Summary 71
    References 72

5 Reduction of property spaces in theorizing   74
    Rescaling 75
    Indexing 76
    Logic reduction 78
    Empirical reduction 79
    Theoretical reduction 82
    Pragmatic reduction 85
    Summary 87
    References 88

6 Expansion of property spaces in theorizing   89
    Substruction 89
    More properties of existing dimensions 91
    More dimensions 94
    Combining property spaces 96
    Inserting process arrows 97
    Creating scales 101
    Summary 105
    References 105

PART II
Tools for writing social science   **107**

    References 110

7 The Model of Argumentation: chain of reasoning, chains of argument and arguments — 111

The rhetorical situation 111
Purpose 112
Persona 113
Audience 114
Tone 114
The subject matter 115
The model 115
Summary 120
References 121

8 Examples of using the Model of Argumentation — 122

The process of writing a social science text: an example 123
The (preliminarily) finished structure of a text: an example 129
The structure of Chapter 4, 'Basics of property spaces' 129
Constructing a property space 130
Housekeeping 131
Moving the model down one level 132
Summary 132
References 133

9 Theorizing and writing — 134

Research process and reporting process 134
Displays 136
Property spaces 140
Writing 144
Summary 148
References 148

Appendix: from Bergman, Ann, Jan Ch. Karlsson and Jonas Axelsson (2010) 'Truth Claims and Explanatory Claims – an Ontological Typology of Futures Studies', Futures, 42(8): 857–65 150
Index 164

FIGURES

1.1	The research process	10
1.2	The reporting process	12
1.3	Connections between ontology, epistemology and rhetoric	13
I.1	Circle chart diagrams of gender segregation and sector among managers in Sweden	19
I.2	Symbols representing women's subordinated social position relative to men as a form of hierarchical gender segregation	20
I.3	Image of gender segregation	20
2.1	A basic form of a display as relata and relation	27
2.2	Basic forms of a display as relata and relations that either discover the answer of a question or verify a statement	28
2.3	Clusters separated by spatial distance	29
2.4	A separator as boundary between insider and outsider	30
2.5	Arrows as links	30
2.6	(a) A line-up showing stages of the writing process. (b) An unordered line-up showing stages of the writing process	31
2.7	Lines and arrows	31
2.8	A dichotomy of age	32
2.9	An ordered display of age	33
2.10	Steps between ages or phases of life	34
2.11	Continuum of age or life phases	34
2.12	Core and periphery	35
2.13	(a) Separate spheres between work and family. (b) Spillover from work to family. (c) Overlap/integration between work and family	36
2.14	Class society	37
2.15	Network in the form of a line-up as a one-to-one relationship	38

Figures ix

2.16	Linking many to many in a group	38
2.17	Network linking one to many showing a hierarchical and a democratic teaching style	39
2.18	Service work as three separate dyads	39
2.19	The triadic ensemble of the service triangle	40
3.1	Single-loop learning	44
3.2	Double-loop learning	45
3.3	Triple-loop learning	46
3.4	Segregation	47
3.5	The necessary structural constitution of gender segregation in working life	47
3.6	Simplified display and a synthetizing approach	48
3.7	Trade unions and employer organizations	49
3.8	Unions, employer organizations, capital and labour	50
3.9	Contradiction within labour and capital, respectively	51
3.10	Contradiction within labour and capital, respectively, and the contradiction between labour and capital	51
3.11	Trade unions placed between the contradiction within labour and the contradiction within capital	52
3.12	Trade unions as social weapons in relation to the contradiction between capital and labour	52
3.13	Contradictions and organizations on the labour market	53
6.1	Interpretation of Kolb's dimensions of learning as processes	98
6.2	Karasek's demand-control model with strain and activity developments	101
6.3	Management control and employee behaviour 2	103
6.4	Pattern of management control and employee behaviour at *Presswork*	103
6.5	Pattern of management control and employee behaviour at *Tech*	104
7.1	The Model of Argumentation for the reporting process	117
7.2	Detailed Model of Argumentation of the reporting process at different levels	119
9.1	Forecast and utopia	137
9.2	Two types of forecast	138
9.3	Two types of prediction	138
9.4	Two types of methodologies for studying predictions	139

TABLES

I.1	The quantitative dimension of gender segregation in different occupations	18
I.2	Property space of the relation between horizontal and vertical gender segregation in an organization	19
2.1	Concerns about the future in relation to age/life phase	35
4.1	Parts of a property space	56
4.2	Segmentation of a retail fashion market	58
4.3	Prediction and explanation in the social sciences	59
4.4	Two examples of twofold tables	60
4.5	Mechanisms behind attitudes to work	63
4.6	Attitudes to work, age and position	63
4.7	Attitudes to work, age, position and gender 1	64
4.8	Attitudes to work, age, position and gender 2	64
4.9	Dimensions in Wright's initial typology of class structure in the development of the concept of contradictory class locations	66
4.10	Wright's initial typology of class structure in the development of the concept of contradictory class relations	66
4.11	Wanted and not wanted change and no change	67
4.12	Interrelations among the concepts of flexibility, stability, instability and inflexibility	67
4.13	Exit and voice	69
4.14	Parties and value of rules	70
4.15	Types of workplace rules 1	70
4.16	Types of workplace rules 2	71
5.1	Commitment to work and position on the labour market	75

5.2	High and low commitment to work, and employee and small business owner	76
5.3	Numerical values and indices of text and melody of songs	77
5.4	Casino visits per week and income classes	78
5.5	The immediate producers and control of means of production and labour power	79
5.6	Types of power and types of involvement in organizations	80
5.7	Rank, pay, gender and ethnicity among members of a social science department at a large US state university (fictitious)	81
5.8	Labour's concerns	84
5.9	Capital's concerns	84
5.10	Developmental concerns	85
5.11	Logical possibilities of professional jazz groups' repertoire	86
5.12	Types of working repertoires of professional jazz groups	86
6.1	Intensity of (a) parent's exercise of authority and (b) children's acceptance of authority	90
6.2	Types of authority structures in families	91
6.3	Historical work forms based on the immediate producer's ownership of means of production and labour power	92
6.4	Historical work forms based on the immediate producer's ownership of means of production and labour power according to Cohen	92
6.5	The immediate producer's ownership of means of production and labour power	93
6.6	The immediate producer's ownership of instruments of production, raw materials and labour power	94
6.7	Absolute and relative attitude to work and position on the labour market	95
6.8	Combination of capital's and labour's concerns	97
6.9	Interpretation of Kolb's dimensions of learning	98
6.10	Karasek's demand-control model	100
6.11	Management control and employee behaviour 1	102
7.1	Example of the structure of an argumentation	118
8.1	Chain of argument$_1$ of Chapter 4	130
8.2	Chain of argument$_2$ of Chapter 4	131
8.3	Chains of argument of the section '*Housekeeping*' of Chapter 4	132
9.1	Explanatory claims and truth claims	142
9.2	Types of forecasts 1	143
9.3	Types of forecasts 2	143
9.4	Types of forecasts 3	146
9.5	The structure of the *Futures* article	147
A.1	Types of forecasts	152

PREFACE

There are many excellent books on methods, social theory and writing. Books on social theory usually describe, and perhaps compare, theories. Books on writing generally follow the writing process from start to finish. However, to our knowledge, there are not any books that combine these two dimensions and provide analytical and practical tools for both theorizing and how to present a theory to an audience through systematically structuring the argumentation. Thus, we intend this book as a resource for improving your skills to handle social theory in a creative and systematic way, whether you are a first year student, a PhD student or a professional researcher. The tools for theorizing that we present, which are displays and property spaces, can be used from the initial ideas about concepts at the first course in studying social science over theoretical development in a doctoral dissertation to producing a new theory as a senior researcher. The tools for writing, mainly the Model of Argumentation, are applicable from the first essay to the teacher at the first course over the doctoral dissertation to an article submitted to a high impact journal.

Thus, by bringing together the fruitful visual formats of unbound displays and more bound property spaces with a model of argumentation, we offer the reader tools to visualize and systematize theories and concepts when theorizing. We do so as we believe that the visualizing capacity of displays and property spaces are suitable to drag out and clarify fuzzy ideas and relationships in the research process, when the writing is mainly for the authors themselves. The Model of Argumentation is, on the other hand, a helpful tool in the reporting process, when arguments are laid out in texts that are produced for an external reader.

Although the book consists of different parts, there is an ontological and epistemological backbone to the book that has guided us in our writing and the tools presented. This backbone is as follows: social entities consist of relations and relations between relations; social theories are therefore constructed by relations between examined concepts; theorizing is in consequence trying to find relations between concepts that are fruitful for explaining social entities; and social science texts are as a result built up by systematic relations between arguments in order to convince an audience about the value of a theory. However, this rather abstract confession takes a broad range of manifest forms in the book.

There are different reasons why books are written. In this specific case, the book grew out of our teaching for many years at different levels in sociology, working life science and gender studies where we had to produce our own material as a result of the lack of course literature. Another source of inspiration is our experiences as researchers when it comes to theorizing and writing articles and books. All in all, this gave birth to the idea of putting together a book, which meant that we collected a wide range of notes for lectures, PowerPoint presentations and other types of slides, case studies and other material for workshops, memos to ourselves and students' course evaluations. As we point out in the book, writing for an audience means systematizing arguments and this has also inspired – or forced – us to read extensively in order to orientate in the literature on theorizing and writing social science. In sum, the writing process has been an enormous learning process for us and we definitely did not end up where we thought we would when we started. However, we hope that readers too will learn a few things from this product of that process and that they will have use for them in their own theorizing and writing.

As always when writing and rewriting we needed readers to spot what should be revised and developed. So, many thanks to Tora Dahl and Helena Lundberg for giving us critique on parts of Part I from a PhD student perspective at an early stage. It was very helpful and we could apply some of it also to other parts of the book. Thanks to Kristina Håkansson, who commented on an almost finished (we thought) version of the book. Thanks to Fanny Reinholtz for drawing all the figures that we were not skilful enough to manage ourselves. Thanks to Pia Renman who tracked original sources in order to collect permissions needed for reproducing figures and tables. All remaining deficiencies can only be blamed on us.

Karlstad, April 2016
Jan Ch. Karlsson and Ann Bergman

ACKNOWLEDGEMENTS

Permission has been granted for select use of material from the following:

Barton, Allen H. (1965) 'The Concept of Property-Space in Social Research', pp. 30–53 in Paul F. Lazarsfeld and Morris Rosenberg (eds), *The Language of Social Research*. New York: Free Press, Table 11, p. 52. Reprinted by permission of Simon & Schuster.

Bélanger, Jacques and Paul Edwards (2007) 'The Conditions Promoting Compromise in the Workplace', *British Journal of Industrial Relations*, 45(4): 713–34, Figure 1, p. 716. Reprinted by permission of Wiley.

Bélanger, Jacques and Christian Thuderoz (2010) 'The Repertoire of Employee Opposition', pp. 136–58 in Paul Thompson and Chris Smith (eds), *Working Life. Renewing Labour Process Analysis*. Basingstoke: Palgrave Macmillan, Figure 7.2, p. 149 and Figure 7.3, p. 151. Reprinted by permission of Palgrave Macmillan.

Bergman, Ann, Jan Ch. Karlsson and Jonas Axelsson (2010) 'Truth Claims and Explanatory Claims – an Ontological Typology of Futures Studies', *Futures*, 42(8): 857–65. Reprinted by permission of Elsevier.

Cohen, Gerald A. (1978) *Karl Marx's Theory of History: A Defence*. Princeton: Princeton University Press, Table 1, p. 65. Reprinted by permission of Princeton University Press.

Danermark, Berth, Mats Ekström, Liselotte Jakobsen and Jan Ch. Karlsson (2003) *Att förklara samhället*. Lund: Studentlitteratur, Figure 4.1, p. 124 and Figure 8.1 p. 310. Reprinted by permission of Studentlitteratur.

Edwards, Paul and Judy Wajcman (2005) *The Politics of Working Life*. Oxford: Oxford University Press, Table 5.1, p. 101. Reprinted by permission of Oxford University Press.

Edwards, Paul, Jacques Bélanger and Martyn Wright (2006) 'The Bases of Compromise in the Workplace: A Theoretical Framework', *British Journal of Industrial Relations*, 44(1): 125–45, Figure 1, p. 130, Figure 2, p. 131 and Figure 3, p. 132. Reprinted by permission of Wiley.

Etzioni, Amitai (1975) *A Comparative Analysis of Complex Organizations. On Power, Involvement, and Their Correlates*. New York: Free Press, Table, p. 12. Reprinted by permission of Simon & Schuster.

Faulkner, Robert R. and Howard S. Becker (2009) *'Do You Know...?' The Jazz Repertoire in Action*. Chicago: University of Chicago Press, Table, p. 171. Reprinted by permission of University of Chicago Press.

Jonsson, Dan (2007) 'Flexibility, Stability and Related Concepts', pp. 30–41 in Bengt Furåker, Kristina Håkansson and Jan Ch. Karlsson (eds), *Flexibility and Stability in Working Life*. Basingstoke: Palgrave Macmillan, Table 3.1 and 3.2, p. 34. Reprinted by permission of Palgrave Macmillan.

Karasek, Robert A. (1979) 'Job Demands, Job Decision Latitude, and Mental Strain: Implications for Job Redesign', *Administrative Science Quarterly*, 24(2): 285–308, Figure 1, p. 288. Reprinted by permission of Sage Publications.

Karlsson, Jan Ch. (2013 [1986]) *Begreppet arbete*. Lund: Arkiv, Figure 1, p. 63 and Figure 2, p. 65. Reprinted by permission of Arkiv.

Perfetto, Ralph and Arch G. Woodside (2009) 'Extremely Frequent Behavior in Consumer Research: Theory and Empirical Evidence for Chronic Casino Gambling', *Journal of Gambling Studies*, 25(2): 297–316, Figure 1, p. 302. Reprinted by permission of Springer.

Ragin, Charles C. (2000) *Fuzzy-Set Social Science*. Chicago: Chicago University Press, Table 3.3, p. 83. Reprinted by permission of Chicago University Press.

Wright, Erik Olin (1985) *Classes*. London: Verso, Table 2.1, p. 44. Reprinted by permission of Verso.

1
THEORIZING AND WRITING SOCIAL THEORY

This book provides you with the tools to help you, first, creatively play about with concepts to satisfy your own theoretical curiosity, then to creatively play around with arguments to arouse and satisfy other people's theoretical curiosity. It is a toolbox for theorizing and writing social science, whether it is in connection with your very first essay to your teacher or fellow students, your master or PhD thesis or an article to a prestigious journal in your later professional career as a social scientist. Naturally, the tools are used somewhat differently and with varying skill at the different levels, but they all come from the same toolbox. With the phrase 'social theory' we simply mean theories produced within the social sciences.

It is a tricky thing for us all to present the social theories we work with to our readers, be they undergraduate teachers or fellow students, postgraduate supervisors or examiners, or the social science community at large. It is equally tricky for us all to develop those theories in the first place. Both tasks require hard work and a lot of playing about with concepts and arguments. Still, you are dealing with two quite different processes and in this book we discuss how to handle both of them. In the research process, we concentrate on some tools – or tricks of the trade (Becker 1998) – that help you theorize through considering and playing about with concepts and terms. One of these tools is drawing up displays to explore possible relations between concepts, another is constructing property spaces (such as fourfold tables) in order to more systematically explore conceptual connections. This means that this is not a book *about* social science theories, their history and the people who produced them; instead, it is a book *in* developing such theories (cf. Turner 1989: 8–18), an endeavour that we call *theorizing*. Further, in the process through which you create *reports* – essays, papers, articles, books – about the results of the research process, we suggest a model for building up a systematic argumentation to present them to your audience. The model helps you to play about with arguments in relation to other arguments in order to construct a strong case for the theory you produced in the research process.

In this chapter, we introduce the themes of the book. First, we discuss what a social theory is, as theories and theorizing stand at the centre of the whole book. This includes what social theories are about, what characterizes their objects, concepts and terms. Then we provide you with some examples of theorizing that we think are inspiring and worth following, and we also offer some principles for theorizing. Following that, we go into differences in writing in the research process and the reporting process, respectively. This distinction motivates the book being divided into two parts: Part I on theorizing in the research process, Part II on constructing the argumentation in the reporting process in papers, articles and books, presenting what you found out in your research. Finally, we make an overview of the contents of the rest of the book.

Social theory

What social scientists work with, and work on, are social theories. Theories do not come from nothing, but are related to their forerunners. Many have pointed out that the central concept of 'theory' is fuzzy, unclear and impossible to define. Here are a few examples:

> The term *theory* is one of the most misused and misleading terms in the vocabulary of the social scientist.
>
> *(Mitchell 1968: 211)*

> Like so many words that are bandied about, the word theory threatens to become meaningless. Because its referents are so diverse – including everything from minor working hypotheses, through comprehensive but vague and unordered speculations, to axiomatic systems of thought – use of the word often obscures rather than creates understanding.
>
> *(Merton 1967: 39)*

> Few concepts have fared worse in the social sciences than that of theory.
>
> *(Bunge 1996: 113)*

We do not have the ambition to clean up this mess, but we take our point of departure in the fundamental idea that everything in social science studies is made up of relations and relations between relations (Danermark et al. 2002: Ch. 5). The objects of social science are what they are by virtue of the relations they enter into with other objects. At the same time, researchers can only think, talk and write about them through language, by putting words on these objects and relations. We simply regard a theory as interrelated statements that claim that a certain entity (thing, object, process) exists in the world and often what this entity can do, that is, which mechanisms it possesses. Social theories are, then, arguments or series of interrelated arguments about something existing in the social world and commonly what social mechanisms are parts of the entity. The latter characteristic is especially important as mechanisms are what social scientists refer to in explanations.

Theories are explanatory and what social science ultimately aims at is explaining the social world.

The statements or arguments of theories are specified in the form of concepts – concepts being units of meaning. All social science arguments include concepts, specifying what the argument is about. Using concepts in thought operations is the kernel of the work of social scientists from their first days as students to their heydays as professional researchers. But in opposition to everyday knowledge, social scientists not only think *with* concepts, but also *about* those concepts. Social theories are thereby examined conceptualizations (cf. Sayer 1992: Ch. 2). The work of doing such conceptualizations is also to build theory. When we talk about theorizing, we talk about examining and eventually changing social theories. To make it easier to think and communicate about entities in the social world, however, researchers put words on the concepts – called terms. A term is, then, a linguistic label on a concept.

In sum, there is a relation between a social theory, an entity in the world, a concept or a number of connected concepts as thought objects referring to that entity, and terms labelling the concepts:

> Social theories build upon concepts and relations between concepts. A concept refers to a particular body of thought, to a certain meaning. The concept must be distinguished from the term we use to express this meaning, and from the object or the properties in reality, to which the concept is supposed to refer.
> *(Danermark et al. 2002: 121)*

There is a parallel between social entities and social theories: social entities are composed of relations and relations between relations; social theories are constructed by relations between examined concepts. The correspondence is situated in the basic role of relations, but there are a few things that are important to note about these relations. To begin with, there are a number of different types of entities in the world (Fleetwood 2004, 2005) and social theories are concerned with only some of them. There are, in other words, limits to what social theories can be about. One type of entity is, of course, social objects such as organizations, genders and classes. The reason they are called social is that they are dependent on human activity for their existence – even though they, in their turn, influence human activities. Second, social entities must be distinguished from discursive entities such as language, ideas, symbols, beliefs – and concepts and theories. Third, we can talk about artefactual entities, which are made by human beings, for example houses, cars and meatballs. And fourth, material entities, which would exist even if there were no human beings on planet Earth, such as weather, mountains and the moon. Social theories can be about social and discursive entities, but not artefactual and material ones in themselves. Social theories can be used as explanations of why some organizations but not others require their employees to use their emotions in their relations with customers, why women perform the majority of domestic labour or the reasons for the income gap between the classes in the Western world having increased during recent decades. Social theories can also suggest explanations of why certain ideas flourish in connection with sports as compared to music or why Christianity has a different geography from Islam. Conversely, social theories cannot explain houses, cars and meatballs, which requires physics and chemistry, for example. Social theories can, however, explain social and discursive aspects of houses, cars and meatballs, such as the distribution of which social groups live in private houses and which live in flats or the coming and going of architectural fashions. And they can explain the social variation of ingredients in meatballs in different regions or which seasoning is considered tasty among which classes (or why there are no such variances). Social theories cannot explain the existence of weather, mountains or the moon, but why it seems politically impossible to stop negative human influence on the climate, why mountains are considered romantic places (or not) and why some states have spent so much money on going to the moon – or for that matter, why the moon has sometimes been believed to consist of cheese (if it ever has). In sum, social theories deal with social and discursive entities, but also with social and discursive aspects of artificial and material entities. This also means that many social theories span more than one type of entity.

Further, the relation in conceptualizing between the concepts of a social theory and the entity should not arbitrarily try to catch empirical patterns, but instead, what makes the entity what it is and not something else (Ackroyd and Karlsson 2014). Concepts are abstract – they specify properties that are essential for the entity, disregarding all other elements. This is what makes conceptualization such a crucial process in the work of social scientists. That is why we can spend two-hour seminars on discussing what the concept of class or work or gender or culture should mean. Conceptualization is to build theory and to form new concepts, which makes it possible to see new things. This also means that all knowledge social scientists produce by conceptualizing and forming theories can be wrong – it is fallible. A lot of the endeavours of social scientists go into improving existing theories or showing that they are false. But this is good rather than bad news, as it means that our knowledge can progress, our theories can be developed. Scientific knowledge is not only fallible – it is also corrigible.

While the relation between concepts and entities is such that concepts refer to specific properties or entities in thought, the relation between terms and concepts is often more arbitrary. A simple example is words in different languages: 'alienation' in English, 'Entfremdung' in German and 'främlingskap' in Swedish are different terms for the same concept. But a common criticism of social science, perhaps especially sociology, is that there is a strong inflation in terms: all researchers try to put forward their own terminology for concepts for which there already exist several sets of terms. The only thing we have to say about this is that, although they can be arbitrary, terms are important in communicating theoretical knowledge. Some terms simply transmit the thought content of a certain concept better than others do.

Finally, theories are not only used in explaining empirical patterns by referring to the mechanisms of entities that have produced them, they also guide empirical observations – observations which, in their turn, can corroborate a theory or concept or put them in doubt (Danermark et al. 2002: 124–48).

Theorizing

If social theory is constructed by relations between statements in the form of examined concepts, theorizing is experimenting and playing around with such relations in order to build theory. Conceptualizing and theorizing or developing theory is everything from the first guesses about the things that aroused your curiosity to the full-fledged and well-worked-out theory. We agree with this definition: 'the expression "to theorize" refers to what one does to produce a theory and to the thought process before one is ready to consider it final. While theorizing is primarily a process, theory is the end product' (Swedberg 2014a: 1). We would add that such end products are never really final. Theories can always be revised, even refuted by their originators or by someone else. Social science knowledge is, as we say, always fallible and thereby also corrigible. If social entities are made up of relations and social theories are relations between concepts, theorizing means playing around with different relations between concepts in search for those that you think are the most fruitful for explaining what you are curious about. Sometimes, theorizing is regarded in a rather romantic light as requiring inspiration and specific forms of creativity, but we want to put the main emphasis on this process as a craft – and as in all crafts it requires learning to handle tools. Therefore, one should 'regard theorizing as an integrated part of research methodology' (Danermark et al. 2002: 115). And as theories are there to explain, those who discuss theorizing agree that this activity is an explanatory endeavour (Danermark et al. 2002; Layder 1998; Swedberg 2014b).

There are several ways in which theory has been developed in the history of the social sciences – from the invention of new and revolutionizing theories to some modification of a single concept of an existing theory. In the following, we relate some examples of theorizing. There are no sharp boundaries between them, they often overlap and they can be combined. This little catalogue is far from exhaustive – we just want to give you an idea of what theorizing might mean in social science and perhaps inspire you to try it. One important lesson is, however, that theorizing, although the word might sound ambitious and grandiose, usually is a piecemeal activity. It advances in small steps such as changing a term of a concept or relating two formerly unconnected concepts. Therefore, this journey starts with the earliest reflexions on theoretical matters at the undergraduate level – and it never stops as long as you do academic work. Further, it is not only an activity that goes on during the whole research process (Layder 1998: 25), but is often strengthened by ideas you get when writing about the research for someone else.

The first step of theoretical development is often an empirical observation. The theory of aesthetic labour originated, for example, from a researcher noticing 'a number of job adverts in the UK press for the hospitality and retail sectors asking for potential employees who were "stylish", "outgoing", "attractive" or "trendy", and "well-spoken and of smart appearance"' (Warhurst and Nickson 2001: 17). The research group eventually formulated the theory of 'aesthetic labour', meaning corporeal dispositions in people that employers can commodify and exploit to their advantage when competing with other firms, and that these dispositions can be further trained and developed once the employee has been hired. The catch phrase is 'looking good and sounding right', while the theory is given precision in its conceptual structure by contrasting it with the theory of emotional labour and finding inspiration in the French sociologist Pierre Bourdieu (Witz et al. 2003). The theory has then been widely applied (for an overview, see Karlsson 2012) and further developed, for example, through the concept of 'athletic labour' (Huzell and Larsson 2012).

An example of theorizing by finding a new term is Erik Olin Wright's (1985, 1997) notion of 'contradictory class location'. An important difficulty in class analysis has long been how to deal with the growing number of people in modern capitalist societies who could not without difficulties be classified as capitalists, workers or petit bourgeois. Wright set out to solve this problem of the 'middle class' and he got a clue when someone at a seminar happened to use the phrase 'contradictory' in a discussion of the problem. Originally he referred to these positions as the following:

> [A]n 'ambiguous' class character, neither fish nor fowl. In a seminar discussion of the conceptual framework, the suggestion was made that this was not quite precise: such positions were really *both* fish and fowl, and therefore they should be seen as internally contradictory rather than ambiguous. . . . That shift in labels – from ambiguous locations to contradictory locations – was the crucial step in the development of the new concept.
>
> *(Wright 1985: 44)*

Wright tested the idea and finally suggested that there are a number of class locations that are put together by opposing characteristics and that therefore do not fit into the traditional class schemes. Instead of pressing them into these schemes, he claimed, it is more fruitful to take their inconsistent status seriously and analyse them as being contradictory. Among those locations are managers and experts who are employees but at the same time are agents of capital or master skills that are especially valuable to capitalists. On this basis, Wright presents his class scheme as twelve class positions, ordered in a combination of property spaces (1997: 25). This example also illustrates what we have said about the importance of finding a suggestive label – a term – for a concept. In Wright's case, he found the concept through the term contradictory instead of ambiguous.

Further, we can note Wright's (1985: 25) experience that 'conceptual innovations do not usually spring full-blown into the heads of theorists, but are built up through series of partial modifications and reformulations'. He illustrates his discussion of the development of the concept with a number of displays and property spaces, but it is easy to imagine Wright experimenting and playing about with many different displays and property spaces after that seminar as part of the research process, which led to the development of a new class theory that includes contradictory class locations.

Another way of theorizing in social science is to combine (traits of) two already existing theories. This is what Robert Karasek (1979; also Karasek and Theorell 1990) did in the very influential control-demand model for classifying good and bad work environments for employee health. Before this, there were two prominent but independent theories in the field of psychosocial effects of work environment on employees. One concentrated on work demands that led to stress while the other studied employee decision latitudes and influence in work. In each of these traditions there were, however, research results that seemed paradoxical and inexplicable. It was, for example, found that both assembly-line workers and executives had stressful work, which should have led to both groups having low job satisfaction. Such was not the case: executives were much more satisfied than workers. Another mysterious finding was that demands having to do with time pressure led to negative consequences for employees, but that was not the case for demands of an intellectual nature.

Karasek's theoretical development looks simple afterwards but it solved these problems. He combined high and low employee control with high and low demands in work, which resulted in a property space specifying different characteristics of four types of work environment, indicating that 'psychological strain results not from a single aspect of the work environment, but from the joint effects of the demands of the work situation and the range of decision-making freedom (discretion) available to the worker facing those demands' (Karasek 1979: 287). (We will return to this property space in Chapter 6.) The theorizing consisted of relating concepts from the two former theories to each other. In the same way as when it comes to Wright and the contradictory class locations, it is easy to picture Karasek trying out many displays and property spaces to depict the relations between the two former theories before arriving at the final model – the property space that was published in the first article that has attracted so many followers.

Our next example highlights how theory can be developed when a marginal concept in one study becomes the main conceptual tool in another. In a study of gender segregation in working life, Ann Bergman used a number of variables with an anchorage in a broader theoretical framework that she built on to understand quantitative segregation patterns (Bergman 2004). She identified certain mechanisms with importance for the reproduction and/or transformation of these patterns. For each of these mechanisms she used specific variables to measure whether they were activated or not in the data material. Among these variables there were a few that she used as indicators to measure what she defined as women's and men's temporal and spatial 'availability' towards work. Even though it proved to be a useful indicator in understanding gender segregation, it was just one small theoretical building block among many.

After the study was finished, Ann became curious about how to conceptualize the relation between work and family, without being caught in what she regarded as the subjective and consensus-impregnated concept of 'work–life balance'. She therefore turned back to her own concept of availability as she thought it could be a constructive tool to capture how women and men are accessible and responsive to the, often conflicting, needs of employer and family (Bergman and Gardiner 2007; Bergman and Gustafson 2008). She then, together with colleagues, continued to play about with the concept and developed it further in different ways.

Another way of theorizing is to use an already existing theory and model a new one on some of its concepts. One example is Anna Jónasdóttir's (1994) theory of 'love' and 'love power', which is a parallel to Karl Marx's concepts 'labour' and 'labour power'. What triggered Jónasdóttir's curiosity, or rather frustration, was the question of how the oppression of women in the present time of formal-legal equality can be so persistent in Western societies. Another driver was her critique of Marxist explanations of feminist questions. However, even if Jónasdóttir rejects the explanatory strength of Marx's theories when trying to understand the durability of the oppression of women, she finds his theoretical framework fruitful on an abstract and logical level. Thus, her point of departure is Marx's historical materialism, and his approach to understanding the reproduction of class and the capitalist system. But instead of seeing society as a web of relations between labour and capital, she sees it as a web of relations between the sexes, using the same relational logic when she develops her own theory. According to Marx, the exploitation of workers' labour power rests on the unequal socio-economic relationship between the worker and the capitalist: the latter harvests the fruits of the workers' labour. Jónasdóttir argues in line with this that the reproduction of men's exploitation of women's love power rests on socio-sexual circumstances within the partner relationship. Love should, in this case, be understood as socio-sexually relational and alienable practices and not only as an emotion. Jónasdóttir states that 'the core of male domination now lies in the sexual relationship itself' and by this she does not only refer to the intimate interactions within a partner relationship, but 'also to a similar unequal exchange of care and pleasure which occurs between men and women in other contexts – in work, within politics etc.' (1994: 35). Women have the right to give their love power to men of their free will, while their freedom to be empowered by men's love power is very restricted. Men, on the other hand, are legitimized to exploit women's love power for their own ends and they do not have to reciprocate. They are, in other words, empowered by women, while the women themselves are drained and alienated. Jónasdóttir argues that: 'if capital is accumulated alienated labour, male authority is accumulated alienated love' (1994: 37).

Sometimes the curiosity behind theorizing can come from personal or biographical experiences – even far back in the researcher's life. An example is Arlie Russell Hochschild's seminal theory of emotional labour. Her own story about this is well worth quoting at length:

> I think my interest in how people manage emotions began when my parents joined the U.S. Foreign Service. At the age of twelve, I found myself passing a dish of peanuts among many guests and looking up at their smiles; diplomatic smiles can look different when seen from below than when seen straight in. Afterwards I could listen to my mother and father interpret various gestures. The tight smile of the Bulgarian emissary, the averted glance of the Chinese consul, and the prolonged handshake of the French economic officer, I learned, conveyed messages not simply from person to person but from Sofia to Washington, from Peking to Paris, and from Paris to Washington. Had I passed

the peanuts to a person, I wondered, or to an actor? Where did the person end and the act begin? Just how is a person related to an act?

(Hochschild 2003 [1983]: ix)

When she later in life started studying social science she carried this curiosity with her. She read a number of theories dealing with persons, acting and emotions, but found them all wanting in one way or another for making her understand the questions from when she was twelve years old. She established terms such as 'feeling rules', 'emotional work' and 'emotional labour' as part of social science concepts for understanding modern life, especially how employers can utilize human feelings to their advantage.

We have mentioned a number of reasons behind theorizing in social science: empirical observations, the emergence of a new term, combination of existing theories, moving a marginal concept in one theory to the kernel of a new one, modelling new concepts on the meaning of an existing theory's concepts and building on the researcher's own biographical experiences. In all of the resulting strategies for constructing theory there are more detailed conceptual steps, 'series of partial modifications and reformulations' as Wright said. Social researchers try out, experiment with and play about with different concepts, relations between concepts and data, between concepts and other concepts, and between concepts and terms. And it is through doing this that you further develop your skill to do it even better: 'One becomes good at theorizing through practice' (Swedberg 2014a: 17). In this theoretical work, drawing up displays and constructing property spaces are important tools, as we will show in detail in Part I. At the same time, all this activity in the research process is to no avail if it stops there. It has to be written up in the reporting process and be launched to an audience to make a difference.

Writing

If social theories are made up of relations between concepts and theorizing means playing about with relations of that kind, writing research reports (essays, articles, etc.) is built on relations between arguments – arguments intended to convince an audience of the value of your theory. When reflecting on writing in social science, it is important to differentiate between two processes. On the one hand, the research process, and on the other, the reporting process. The difference of the types of writing involved is this: writing during the research process, you do for yourself as researcher or for your team of researchers; writing during the reporting process, you do for an audience outside the research process. We do not want to portray them as necessarily following each other in time – first the research process, then the reporting process. Instead, they tend to overlap (c.f. Turner 2014: 132): sometimes you write to elaborate your theoretical ideas in the research process, sometimes to present those ideas to a reader in the reporting process. It also happens that you get new theoretical ideas when writing for an audience, and therefore, temporarily abandon that task and return to theorizing. Or, in the middle of theorizing, you come to think of a chain of argument to convince readers, and for a while go to the reporting process to try it out in writing. The important thing is to be aware of in which process you write.

In the research process, writing is a way of thinking; in the reporting process, writing is a way of convincing people that your thinking is sound. You are thereby dealing with two qualitatively very different processes. The research process is working things out for yourself, the reporting process is laying things out for others. A social scientist has to master both processes, but do not mix them up! As Swedberg (2014b: 208) points out: 'Virtues at the stage of theorizing can become vices when one presents the research results, and vice versa.'

Writing in the research process

Often it is said that the research process is either inductive or deductive, going from data to theory or from theory to data. In practice, all research processes do both, in fact, most research processes are much more chaotic than portrayed in the methods literature and what most of us normally are prepared to admit (Figure 1.1). In elementary textbooks, it is usually said that there are two types of inquiries: one is inductive, starting with data and going to theory; the other is deductive and goes the

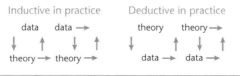

FIGURE 1.1 The research process

other way, from theory to data. This image is simplified to such a degree that it is deceptive. No social science research is done in that way. In more advanced textbooks, the interplay between inductive and deductive moments is recognized. There is a constant movement between inductive and deductive phases during the research process. It is also common that researchers describe their own research process in this way, such as in this example: 'During this study inductive and deductive analyses were combined. When a theme was identified inductively, the researchers then moved to verify or qualify the finding. This then set off a new inductive cycle' (Kitchener et al. 2000: 219). But even these more nuanced descriptions are simplified for the benefit of the reader's understanding of the process.

In reality, what researchers do is much more complicated. The research process is, it is often said, a creative adventure, involving new discoveries, some of them totally unexpected or serendipitous findings (Merton and Barber 2004). It contains, of course, a lot of systematic and logical thinking, but as it to a large extent deals with things that are not known in advance and ideas that have not been had before, it is by necessity somewhat chaotic (Townsend and Burgess [2009] provide good examples). Robert K. Merton once complained that we know little about the real research process, especially compared to the ideal one in textbooks on methods:

> The books on method present ideal patterns: how scientists *ought* to think, feel and act, but these tidy normative patterns, as everyone who has engaged in inquiry knows, do not reproduce the typically untidy, opportunistic adaptations that scientists make in the course of their inquiries. Typically, the scientific paper or monograph presents an immaculate appearance which reproduces little or nothing of the intuitive leaps, false starts, mistakes, loose ends, and happy accidents that actually cluttered up the inquiry.
>
> (Merton 1967: 4)

Writing in the research process is marked by the chaos Merton describes. It follows the 'intuitive leaps, false starts, mistakes, loose ends, and happy accidents' of that process. It is not intended to go further. It is not planned for an audience outside the research process. But this chaotic process reaches, when it is successful, answers to questions. In the research process you build theory through connecting concepts to each other and attaching terms to them. The end result is a *proposal* that a specific social object exists in the world, perhaps even what it can do (its mechanism or mechanisms) or at least a map of an empirical pattern. These are the results that researchers report to their audiences.

Writing in the reporting process

There is a specialism of the philosophy and sociology of science that is very interested in the real practice of research processes. If you are into that you might want to describe the chaos of your research process. If not, disregard *how* you reached the answers to your questions, just report the result in the form of the questions and the answers by arguing your proposal. You argue your proposal in three interrelated steps, starting with formulating the research question (or questions), which is the question you answered at the end of the research process – not always the one you started out with. Then you construct the arguments that lead up to the answer, and finally you state that answer. The steps of the reporting process are depicted in Figure 1.2. In reality, the steps interlock and overlap; further, you will surely find that you work on each of them at the same time. Still, it is helpful to think about the reporting process as steps in this order.

Of course, you write a lot of texts during the research process – actually our advice is to write constantly. But what you write during the research process, you write for your own or your research group's benefit. During that process you write to develop theoretical ideas and to make your ideas clearer to yourself. But during the reporting process, you want to make those ideas clear to your readers – and that is something quite different. In the research process, you try to find things out and formulate them systematically in theoretical terms so that you can answer your questions. In the reporting process you try to convince a reader that your questions are well motivated, your answers are reasonable and the way you reached them is defensible. Your job in the reporting process is to present a convincing argumentation by systematically offering your proposal, ?→!.

In the research process, analytical tools, such as displays and property spaces, are accompanied by texts – usually in the form of memos (Layder 1998) – discussing what they mean and in which way they can help in your theorizing. Some of those displays and property spaces survive into the reporting process, where you explain which theoretical arguments they illustrate. Those displays and property spaces look the same in both processes, but their function is quite different. Still, the two processes are related to each other in more complicated ways. Writing in the reporting process might suddenly turn into writing in the research process. While writing for an audience it happens that you get a new theoretical idea and start writing in order to make your thoughts clear about the possibilities of this new line of theorizing. And while doing this, you may start to arrange in a memo your argumentation for this idea in a way that can be used in the reporting process. Do not worry. It is all right as long as you know which process you are in at the moment.

Outline of the book

The basic idea behind this book is that there are connections between the nature of the social world (social ontology), theories about that world (social epistemology) and the way social scientists describe those theories for an audience (social rhetoric) (Figure 1.3). The entities or objects of the social world are what they are due to the

Arguing a proposal: ? → !
question to answer

FIGURE 1.2 The reporting process

Ontology →	**Epistemology** →	**Rhetoric**
(The nature of the social world)	(Theorizing to form theory about the social world)	(Convincing an audience of the value of the theory)
Social entities	Social theory	Social science reporting
Relations and relations between relations	Relations between examined concepts	Relations between arguments

FIGURE 1.3 Connections between ontology, epistemology and rhetoric

relations of which they are part. Social entities are made up of relations and relations between relations. Theorizing about entities of the social world means formulating statements about concepts trying to depict that world, ultimately constructing theories that can be used to explain what it is made up of and what happens there. The arrows in the figure should not be regarded as depicting a necessary relation. We do not intend to portray the steps from ontology to epistemology and from epistemology to rhetoric as being deterministic. Rather, the arrows indicate tendencies: as the nature of the social world is such that social entities are made up of relations and relations between relations, there is a tendency among social scientists to construct their theories by relations between examined concepts; and a tendency for social science reporting to build the texts through relating arguments to each other. In these cases, the concepts are thoroughly examined in the research process and placed in relation to each other to form theories. Writing in this process is a way of thinking, in which the researchers try to make clear to themselves which concepts to use, their meaning, relations between them and terms for them. When presenting the theory, the rhetoric they use in order to convince their audience that the theory is valuable and perhaps useful is quite different. In this reporting process, they carefully build systematic relations between arguments to make clear the theory to people they want to know about it.

After this introductory chapter, the book is divided into two parts according to the distinction we have made between the two processes involved in social research. The theme of Part I is tools for theorizing in the research process, while the theme of Part II is tools for arguing this theory to an audience in the reporting process. In the present chapter, we have stressed that the entities that social science research deals with are relational and that concepts and theories reflect this by being relational too. The rest of the book takes this relational theme quite seriously. In Part I – on the research process – we first present displays as ways of theorizing by creatively relating concepts to each other in the form of images of relata and relations. Then we discuss property spaces as ways of systematically and logically relating conceptual dimensions and properties to each other to formulate theoretical typologies. In Part II, which is about the reporting process, we suggest a model for systematically relating chains of reasoning, chains of argument and arguments to each other in order to convince an audience that the theoretical proposal you have formulated as the result of the research process is fruitful. Part I is about relating concepts to develop social theory, Part II deals with relating arguments to each other to present the theory to readers.

Part I discusses two types of tools for theorizing on each side of a continuum of more and less bound ways of playing around with concepts and relations between them. The less bound device is displays, the more bound property spaces. We start with a chapter (Chapter 2) that presents the basics of creating displays, defined as a 'graphic representation of relations and relata that answers one or more research questions or statements', as means to facilitate theorizing. Chapter 3 follows in which we present a number of examples of displays from which you can learn how to construct them and use them in order to theorize. Thereafter there are three chapters in which we discuss the second and more bound form of handling concepts, property spaces, which probably is the most common tool for elaborating social theory. In Chapter 4, we present the basics of constructing and using property spaces. We detail how they are built up, which in their simplest form – the fourfold table – means that two dimensions with two properties of each are combined, resulting in a typology with four outcomes. In Chapter 5 and 6, respectively, we exemplify how they can be reduced and expanded in order to refine theories. To reduce a property space means that you decrease the number of outcomes or types in it by combining two or more to one type in order to win better manageability if the property space has become to extensive. Expanding a property space is, of course, the opposite operation: you increase the number of types so you can cover a wider theoretical field.

The result of theorizing in the research process is a social theory. This theory should be presented to the world – or perhaps some smaller audience – something that is the result of writing in the reporting process. Part II discusses systematic writing in social science, completing the connections in the form of relations between social entities (ontology), theorizing and social theory (epistemology) and writing social theory (rhetoric). In writing social theory, you play around with arguments in order to convince an audience through relations between these arguments that the theory is valid. We start out in Chapter 7 with the problems of a specific social structure in the form of a rhetorical situation that every writer – including social science ones – has to handle. This includes such complications as which persona your text exudes, which tone you should try to achieve and for whom you write. You have to make yourself aware that the problems of the rhetorical situation exist so you can try to solve them – otherwise they remain problems. We continue the chapter by suggesting a model of argumentation, based on argumentation theory, for systematically writing social science theory for an audience. This tool is hierarchical and helps you to keep your argumentation for your proposal in order by systematically relating arguments at different levels to each other. At the same time, the model can also be used to dissect how other authors' argumentation is constructed in social science texts you read. In Chapter 8, we first exemplify how you can use the model when writing. Our case is our own writing and rewriting of Chapter 2 of this book and how we tried to find a sustainable chain of reasoning, built up by chains of arguments, which, in their turn, were constructed by a number of arguments. Our illustration of using the model when reading is Chapter 4 of this book. We show how the model can be applied as a tool to disclose the structure of the argumentation of the chapter.

Finally, we discuss in Chapter 9 ways in which the tools for theorizing and writing social theory can be related to each other. We start, however, by highlighting the importance of the researcher's curiosity as a driving force for playing about with thoughts, concepts and their relations when theorizing. Then we follow our own experience of using the tools we have presented in a research project on forecasts of working life. It is, then, a meta-theory study, examining theories about the future. We exemplify our way of applying displays and property spaces in theorizing, including how we related these tools to each other. Lastly, we show the use of the Model of Argumentation when (re)writing one of the articles from the project. Throughout this chapter, we illustrate our own research process of theorizing to clarify the nature of forecasting as well as our reporting process of writing an article presenting the theory.

References

Ackroyd, Stephen and Jan Ch. Karlsson (2014) 'Critical Realism, Research Techniques and Research Designs', pp. 21–45 in Paul Edwards, Joe O'Mahoney and Steve Vincent (eds), *Explaining Management and Organization Using Critical Realism: A Practical Guide*. Oxford: Oxford University Press.

Becker, Howard S. (1998) *Tricks of the Trade. How to Think about Your Research while You're Doing It*. Chicago: University of Chicago Press.

Bergman, Ann (2004) *Segregerad integrering. Mönster av könssegregering i arbetslivet*. Karlstad: Karlstad University Studies. Doctoral Thesis.

Bergman, Ann and Jean Gardiner (2007) 'Employee Availability for Work and Family: Some Swedish Case Studies', *Employee Relations*, 29(4): 400–14.

Bergman, Ann and Per Gustafson (2008) 'Travel, Availability and Work-Life Balance', pp. 192–208 in Donald Hislop (ed.), *Mobile Work and Technology*. London: Routledge.

Bunge, Mario (1996) *Finding Philosophy in Social Science*. New Haven: Yale University Press.

Danermark, Berth, Mats Ekström, Liselotte Jakobsen and Jan Ch. Karlsson (2002) *Explaining Society. Critical Realism in the Social Sciences*. London: Routledge.

Fleetwood, Steve (2004) 'An Ontology for Organisation and Management Studies', pp. 27–53 in Steve Fleetwood and Stephen Ackroyd (eds), *Critical Realist Applications in Organisation and Management Studies*. London: Routledge.

Fleetwood, Steve (2005) 'Ontology in Organization and Management Studies: A Critical Realist Perspective', *Organization*, 12(2): 197–222.

Hochschild, Arlie Russell (2003 [1983]) *The Managed Heart. Commercialization of Human Feeling*. Berkeley: University of California Press.

Huzell, Henrietta and Patrik Larsson (2012) 'Aesthetic and Athletic Employees: The Negative Outcome of Employers Assuming Responsibility for Sickness Benefits', *Economic and Industrial Democracy*, 33(1): 103–23.

Jónasdóttir, Anna (1994) *Why Women Are Oppressed*. Philadelphia: Temple University Press.

Karasek, Robert A. (1979) 'Job Demands, Job Decision Latitude, and Mental Strain: Implications for Job Redesign', *Administrative Science Quarterly*, 24(2): 285–308.

Karasek, Robert and Töres Theorell (1990) *Healthy Work. Stress, Productivity, and the Reconstruction of Working Life*. New York: Basic Books.

Karlsson, Jan Ch. (2012) 'Looking Good and Sounding Right: Aesthetic Labour', *Economic and Industrial Democracy*, 33(1): 51–64.

Kitchener, Martin, Ian Kirkpatrick and Richard Whipp (2000) 'Supervising Professional Work under New Public Management: Evidence from an "Invisible Trade"', *British Journal of Management*, 11(3): 213–26.

Layder, Derek (1998) *Sociological Practice. Linking Theory and Social Research*. London: Sage.

Merton, Robert K. (1967) *On Theoretical Sociology*. New York: The Free Press.

Merton, Robert K. and Elinor Barber (2004) *The Travels and Adventures of Serendipity. A Study of Sociological Semantics and the Sociology of Science*. Princeton: Princeton University Press.

Mitchell, G. Duncan (1968) *A Dictionary of Sociology*. London: Routledge and Kegan Paul.

Sayer, Andrew (1992) *Method in Social Science. A Realist Approach*. London: Routledge.

Swedberg, Richard (2014a) 'From Theory to Theorizing', pp. 1–28 in Richard Swedberg (ed.), *Theorizing in Social Science*. Stanford: Stanford University Press.

Swedberg, Richard (2014b) *The Art of Social Theory*. Stanford: Stanford University Press.

Townsend, Keith and John Burgess (2009) *Method in the Madness: Research Stories You Won't Read in Textbooks*. Oxford: Chandos.

Turner, Jonathan H. (1989) 'Can Sociology Be a Cumulative Science?', pp. 8–18 in Jonathan H. Turner (ed.), *Theory Building in Sociology. Assessing Theoretical Cumulation*. London: Sage.

Turner, Stephen (2014) 'Mundane Theorizing, *Bricolage* and *Bildung*', pp. 131–57 in Richard Swedberg (ed.), *Theorizing in Social Science*. Stanford: Stanford University Press.

Warhurst, Chris and Dennis Nickson (2001) *Looking Good, Sounding Right: Style Counselling in the New Economy*. London: The Industrial Society.

Witz, Anne, Chris Warhurst and Dennis Nickson (2003) 'The Labour of Aesthetics and the Aesthetic of Organization', *Organization* 10(1): 33–54.

Wright, Erik Olin (1985) *Classes*. London: Verso.

Wright, Erik Olin (1997) *Class Counts*. Cambridge: Cambridge University Press.

PART I
Tools for theorizing in social science

Social scientists are trained in expressing their results, analytical reasoning and thoughts in general in the graphical format of text. They write a lot – often with a tenacious feeling that they should write even more. Although the value of writing is indisputable, drawing is also helpful in the process of theorizing in social science, doing research and reporting research. By drawing, we mean using graphical formats other than text to visualize phenomena and represent, more or less systematically, preliminary theory or parts of a theory. Drawing can of course be done by hand as well as by computer.

Building blocks are needed to formulate social theory, and drawing and writing are two different ways of using building blocks for that purpose. In both cases, the building blocks are concepts and the material connecting the concepts are relations conceptualized or visualized in a more or less bound way. Displays (which we discuss in Chapters 2 and 3) are graphic representations that are less bound than property spaces (which we discuss in Chapters 4 to 6), which are more systematic than displays. Before we introduce displays and property spaces in theorizing, we provide some insight into how one can distinguish between different graphic representations.

Graphic representations

In social science, it is necessary to describe abstract phenomena such as concepts and relations between them. Sometimes the description is done in a textual format and sometimes in visual symbols or pictures. According to Engelhardt, 'A graphic representation is a visible artefact on a more or less flat surface, that was created in order to express information' (2002: 2). Information can be visualized in a number of ways and in a number of different graphic formats such as plain verbal text to pure visual pictures. Marcus Banks states accordingly that 'The distinction between text and image, as found in illustrated academic textbooks, is not absolute' (2001:24). Instead, one can talk about a continuum between a verbal text – 'a linear flow of language' – on the one hand and a more open-ended visual one such as a photograph or picture on the other. Banks places graphic representations such as tables in the middle of his continuum between verbal and visual because deciphering a table demands 'a combination of linguistic and visual reading skills'. To understand a table, you need to comprehend the layout and the units of written information. Closer to the open-ended part of the continuum we find another graphic format – diagrams. They are structured and have textual elements, such as labels, and a framework holds the elements together (cf. Richards 2002: 91); but they are more unpredictable and unbound than tables. Graphic modes such as symbols and signs are even closer than diagrams to the open end of the continuum, but they are not as open-ended as pictures or photographs.

In Banks's model, neither displays nor property spaces are included. Nevertheless, we find that his continuum has a pedagogical value in relating the verbal and the visual to each other. The visual makes complex things more comprehensible, and the verbal provides information needed to make the graphics understandable.

Different modes of graphic representation can, further, be distinguished by their structural composition of the verbal and the visual (cf. Varga-Atkins and O'Brien 2009: 55). We give examples of different modes of graphic representation using the concept of gender segregation. At the very bound and verbal end of Banks's continuum is text, which is what we ordinarily use to literally write down what we mean. The *Oxford English Dictionary* defines *segregation* as an 'action or state of setting someone or something apart from others'. By taking this characterization as our point of departure, *gender segregation* can be defined broadly as 'women's and men's different social positions and conditions'.

Taking the definition of gender segregation to the next step in the continuum, you can visualize it as in Table I.1. The table shows gender segregation as quantitative variables of the distribution of women and men. To decide whether an economic sector, an organization, an occupation and so on is gender segregated, you count the proportion of women and men – that is, you calculate the gender ratio. The table is a combination of visual drawings (the boxes around the text), a sign (%) and text, and it has a certain structure relating its different dimensions to each other.

In Table I.2, we present a property space as a fourfold table and show how to relate the two dimensions of horizontal and vertical segregation to each other – the table could provide information about an organization or the labour market as a whole. A property space can thus be seen as a table, but can also be placed on the continuum somewhere between a table and a diagram.

TABLE I.1 The quantitative dimension of gender segregation in different occupations

Segregation type in a specific occupation	Gender ratio in %
Non-segregated	60/40 women/men
Segregated by numerical domination of women	61–100 women
Segregated by numerical domination of men	61–100 men

TABLE I.2 Property space of the relation between horizontal and vertical gender segregation in an organization

		Horizontal segregation	
		Yes	*No*
Vertical segregation	Yes	Dually segregated	Vertically segregated
	No	Horizontally segregated	Non-segregated

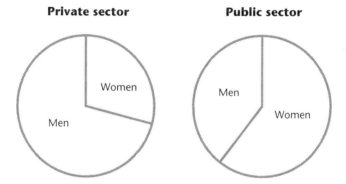

FIGURE I.1 Circle chart diagrams of gender segregation and sector among managers in Sweden

Source: Statistics Sweden (2014: 102).

A diagram, according to Banks, is closer to an image or picture than it is to a table as it contains less text and is more image-like. For example, a pie chart diagram that shows the gender segregation between men and women can be depicted as in Figure I.1. The diagram shows visually that managerial positions in the private sector are dominated by men and that the opposite is the case in the public sector. In a circular pie chart or a rectilinear stack bar chart, the proportional division can rest upon percentages of a quantitatively defined totality, and in a qualitative approach, the proportional division can represent the relative size of something.

Moving further towards the open-ended part of the continuum, we find symbols, which are graphical representations with even less use of words or numbers. They are instead abstract, and often iconic, signs representing something, as in Figure I.2. A symbol is an artificial sign, and it is 'produced or used to either designate a concept or to denote a non-conceptual item, such as an individual material thing or another symbol' (Bunge 1999: 280). In other words, a symbol is a perceptible entity that is socially constructed and culturally impregnated. For example, the symbol for being happy can be ☺, while the symbol for a euro is €; a triangle, Δ, can be a symbol for hierarchy as well as a symbol for the Greek letter delta or

20 Tools for theorizing in social science

FIGURE I.2 Symbols representing women's subordinated social position relative to men as a form of hierarchical gender segregation

FIGURE I.3 Image of gender segregation

the numerical value of four, or, as in mathematics, a symbol depicting change. In Figure I.2, the international symbols of female/woman and male/man are related to each other in a way that shows that women and men are separated and placed in a hierarchical order. Nevertheless, these same symbols have other meanings; for example, in astrology, they denote the planets Mars and Venus, and in alchemy, they denote copper and iron.

At the most open visual end of the continuum are pictures and images. In social science, this graphical format is not used as often (for arguments for using it more, see Becker 1998), but it can, of course, be used to represent empirical patterns and analytical schemes. In the representation in Figure I.3, gender income segregation is presented as a drawing.

In the light of Banks's (2001) continuum, we place displays closer to the open-ended extreme than property spaces since the latter usually contain more textual and literal information than displays. However, displays can also contain verbal information such as labels. While a property space often has the format of a fourfold table combining different dimensions, a display usually rests upon the format of diagrams and symbols. However, there are two things that unite displays and property spaces. First, their focus is on how various objects, dimensions or relata are related to each other. Second, they are simplifications of social phenomena and need to be accompanied and explained by literal text – the explicit theorizing.

Displays and property spaces as preliminary endpoints

In theorizing, there are no ready-made puzzles waiting to be organized in the right and final way. Instead, theorizing is often about constructing the puzzle itself by creating the shapes of the pieces and drawing the synthesizing picture. This construction work is done by reasoning, understanding, and playing with concepts and terms, sometimes in relation to empirical patterns and sometimes in relation to purely theoretical arguments. To theorize is to make some advancement in the understanding of social phenomena and patterns (Corley and Gioia 2011: 12). In performing this work, displays and property spaces are useful in different ways. Displays, as graphical formats, are valuable as tools to help visualize and drag into the open lurking and sometimes fuzzy thoughts and ideas about how relata and relations are connected to each other. Property spaces are graphical formats that are fruitful ways of systematically and logically relating conceptual dimensions and properties to each other in order to formulate theoretical typologies.

We are not the first ones to emphasize the role of displays and property spaces in social science theorizing. Verdinelli and Scagnoli (2013) state that displays are often used to organize, summarize, simplify or transform data in both quantitative and qualitative studies. In quantitative studies, displays often take the graphical format of tables and different diagrams such as charts, plots, stem leaf or bars (Nicol and Pexman 2010; Tufte 2001). In qualitative data analyses, common formats are different conceptual matrices, maps, or networks constructed to systematize data and depict patterns (Becker 1998; Slone 2009). In Miles and Huberman's seminal book on qualitative data analysis (1994: 93–4), displays fall within two major formats: (i) matrices, which are a combination of rows and columns; and (ii) networks, which are a series of nodes or points connected by links or lines. Wheeldon and Åhlberg (2012) draw attention to the usefulness of networks throughout the research process by suggesting mind maps and conceptual maps. However, their work mainly concerns the use of these maps in the research and writing process as a whole and not specifically in theorizing. In this book, we do not examine data analysis and will therefore leave the discussion about quantitative and qualitative data analysis to others. Instead, we focus on the development of social theory. Of course, theorizing is connected to data, since data are one of the cornerstones on which we build our theories; but since there is quite an extensive body of literature on data analysis, we take another path.

Still, it is not entirely clear what the distinction between displays and other graphical formats are. For example, in 'Data Display in Qualitative Research', Verdinelli and Scagnoli (2013) use displays, diagrams, and figures as synonyms, and they are not alone in adopting this strategy (Nicol and Pexman 2010; Wheeldon and Åhlberg 2012). In many cases, models and diagrams are used in a way that resembles our way of discussing displays, with no clear distinction of what is what. In Chapter 2, we offer a definition of a display that is related to how we understand a display in terms of its usefulness – its use as a tool with which to play with relations and relata. Our argument is that in theorizing, you need to work with a conceptual system or with discourses that cover the object of interest. One way to combine creativity and systematization is to use displays. The guiding principles for playing with displays are these: some curiosity has to be involved, manifested as a question or proposal, and the display has to be about relata and relations. In Chapter 3, we give examples of how these guiding principles can be used.

The composition of a display is strongly connected to theorizing by graphically revealing how questions and statements can be handled by visualizing relations and relata. The use of displays is more pragmatic than the use of property spaces and other more bound graphical formats such as various diagrams. The determining principle of the display is the purpose rather than the form itself. In most cases, in the process of theorizing, a display or a property space is a preliminary endpoint. In some cases, displays and property spaces last all the way through to the reporting process and are presented as a model or a typology. If the concept of display in general is a rather broad concept, property spaces has a clearer definition and the construction of property spaces follows given rules. Constructing property spaces is one of the most common tools – perhaps *the* most common tool – for theorizing in social science. Sometimes property spaces are explicitly described through a table or a figure; sometimes the author presents only the argumentation itself and you have to be a bit knowledgeable to notice that there is a property space behind it. In Chapters 4 to 6, we present different ways of using property spaces as tools for investigating relations between concepts and thereby organizing and generating concepts and theories. Property spaces are powerful tools for organizing ideas logically and systematically and for creatively developing new ideas. If displays are tools for playing around with conceptual relations and relata, property spaces are useful when doing some conceptual and theoretical housekeeping tasks as well as when theorizing.

In spite of the common practice of playing about with property spaces, there is a surprising shortage of meta-comments on these experiences. Masses of social scientists – too many to count – have used and currently use this tool, but very few – they can be counted on the fingers of one hand – have at any length reflected on its use. But there are some meta-comments, and we are strongly inspired by them. The first was published in 1937 by Paul F. Lazarsfeld; he and his colleague Allen H. Barton later wrote the classic texts in the field (Barton 1965; Lazarsfeld and Barton 1965 [1951]). There is also an excellent Swedish book by Johan Asplund (1969), which unfortunately has not been translated into English. Asplund emphasizes that the construction of property spaces is a type of *formalization* of social science analysis. The technique thereby transgresses the usual divide between qualitative and quantitative methods. Because property spaces can be used to systematize relations between concepts, they can be applied in *all* contexts in which researchers conduct a line of theoretical argumentation. Finally, there is a brilliant article by Colin Elman (2005) in which he discusses different ways of building property spaces and how they can be applied to various theoretical approaches. That is (to our knowledge) all when it comes to more comprehensive treatments. Of course, other scholars have made contributions in connection with discussing related matters; these include Bailey (1994) on typologies and taxonomies; Becker (1998) on tricks of the sociology trade; Collier et al. (2008, 2012) on typologies; Glaser (1978: 65–70) on theoretical sensitivity in Grounded Theory; and Stinchcombe (1968) on constructing social theories.

We take advantage of our precursors, and it is not our primary goal to say original things about property spaces as creative tools for social science theorizing. Still, we make a few contributions of our own to the field by elaborating on the terms for the parts of a property space and by distinguishing between different ways of reducing property spaces. Property spaces are a general logical tool to keep track of concepts and relations between concepts and to develop new concepts. In contrast to our predecessors, we concentrate on using property spaces to theorize.

In Chapters 2 and 3, we focus on displays, and in Chapters 4 to 6, we focus on property spaces. In Chapter 2, we start by presenting a definition of displays, and then we continue with a description of the basics of displays, their building blocks, and ways of putting them together into a meaningful whole when theorizing. Thereafter, we present the basics of property spaces and how to use them when theorizing, first by reducing them and then expanding them.

References

Asplund, Johan (1969) *Sociala egenskapsrymder. En introduktion till formaliseringsteknik för sociologer*. Uppsala: Argos.

Bailey, Kenneth D. (1994) *Typologies and Taxonomies. An Introduction to Classification Techniques*. London: Sage.

Banks, Marcus (2001) *Visual Methods in Social Research*. London: Sage.

Barton, Allen H. (1965) 'The Concept of Property-Space in Social Research', pp. 30–53 in Paul F. Lazarsfeld and Morris Rosenberg (eds), *The Language of Social Research*. New York: Free Press.

Becker, Howard S. (1998) *Tricks of the Trade. How to Think about Your Research While You're Doing It*. Chicago: University of Chicago Press.

Bunge Mario (1999) *Dictionary of Philosophy*. Amherst: Prometheus Books.

Collier, David, Jody LaPorte and Jason Seawright (2008) 'Typologies: Forming Concepts and Creating Categorical Variables', pp. 152–73 in Janet M. Box-Steffensmeier, Henry E. Brady and David Collier (eds), *The Oxford Handbook of Political Methodology*. Oxford: Oxford University Press.

Collier, David, Jody LaPorte and Jason Seawright (2012) 'Putting Typologies to Work: Concept Formation, Measurement, and Analytic Rigor', *Political Research Quarterly*, 65(1): 217–32.

Corley, Kevin G. and Dennis A. Gioia (2011) 'Building Theory. About Theory Building: What Constitutes a Theoretical Contribution?' *Academy of Management Review*, 36(1): 12–32.

Elman, Colin (2005) 'Explanatory Typologies in Qualitative Studies of International Politics', *International Organization*, 59(2): 293–326.

Engelhardt, Yuri (2002) *The Language of Graphics: A Framework for the Analysis of Syntax and Meaning in Maps, Charts and Diagrams*. Amsterdam: Institute for Logic, Language and Computation.

Glaser, Barney G. (1978) *Theoretical Sensitivity*. Mill Valley: Sociology Press.

Lazarsfeld, Paul F. (1937) 'Some Remarks on the Typological Procedures in Social Research', *Zeitschrift für Sozialforschung*, VI: 119–39.

Lazarsfeld, Paul F. and Allen H. Barton (1965 [1951]) 'Qualitative Measurement in the Social Sciences: Classification, Typologies, and Indices', pp. 155–92 in Daniel Learner and Harold D. Lasswell (eds), *The Policy Sciences*. Stanford: Stanford University Press.

Miles, Matthew B. and A. Michael Huberman (1994) *Qualitative Data Analysis*. Thousand Oaks: Sage.

Nicol, Adelheid A.M. and Penny M. Pexman (2010) *Displaying Your Findings*. Washington: American Psychological Association.

Richards, Clive (2002) 'The Fundamental Design Variables of Diagramming', pp. 85–102 in Michael Anderson, Bernd Meyer and Patrick Olivier (eds), *Diagrammatic Representation and Reasoning*. London: Springer.

Slone, Debra. J. (2009) 'Visualizing Qualitative Information', *The Qualitative Report*, 14(3): 489–97.

Statistics Sweden (2014) *Women and Men in Sweden 2014*. Stockholm: Statistics Sweden.

Stinchcombe, Arthur (1968) *Constructing Social Theories*. Chicago: University of Chicago Press.

Tufte, Edward R. (2001) *The Visual Display of Quantitative Information*. Cheshire: Graphics Press.

Varga-Atkins, Tünde and Mark O'Brien (2009) 'From Drawing to Diagrams: Maintaining Researcher Control during Graphic Elicitation in Qualitative Interviews', *International Journal of Research and Method in Education*, 32(1): 53–67.

Verdinelli, Susana and Norma I. Scagnoli (2013) 'Data Display in Qualitative Research', *International Journal of Qualitative Methods*, 12(1): 359–81.

Wheeldon, Johannes and Mauri K. Åhlberg (2012) *Visualizing Social Science Research: Maps, Methods, and Meaning*. London: Sage.

2
BASICS OF DISPLAYS

As mentioned in Chapter 1, the internal structure of this book is based on a number of statements about theorizing in social science; namely, that curiosity is a driver and that there are one or more questions to be answered, or a proposition to be verified, and the question or proposition has to do with different types of social relations and relata. The aim of social science is to create knowledge and in order to create knowledge, questions or statements must be expressed. Displays are facilitators in the sometimes messy process of trying to answer these questions or verify these statements.

Chapters 2 and 3 present tools in the form of displays, which are useful when theorizing during the research process. Displays are not necessarily built on systematic or logical procedures; instead, they visualize relations between concepts and other relata in ways that are more heuristic and therefore have a wide scope of use. A display connects things, logically or not; it does not have to be systematic and logical, but it can be so. Thus, in theorizing in social science, a display plays the role of a device or multi-tool that can be used in various ways. According to our definition, a display cannot be reduced to a picture, sign or symbol, but it can include these as vital parts. A display is a visual graphical format that helps us to see, depict and understand social relations in the process of theorizing. Some displays can be used in the research process to sort data or to structure disparate thoughts. Displays are useful for making comparisons, for tracing causal links and for summarizing the outcome of a study. Displays can also be presented to a wider audience and, when manifested in written scientific texts, have to be clear and relevant.

Our aim is not to give general guidelines for the best way to design a display. Instead, we focus on the principles and the usefulness of displays in relation to theorizing. Although this is not a book about scientific creativity in general, we believe that creativity and skill are needed to construct displays. At some stages, the creativity factor is more important than at others. For example, in the reporting process, the demands for transparency and clarity often have priority over creativity, whereas in the theorizing process, creativity is crucial. We argue that displays are a great help when throwing ideas, concepts, data, assumptions and questions into the sometimes bottomless box of what can potentially become social theory.

Although creativity is used when playing about with concepts and data, displays are not constructed with the aim to amuse or delight, but rather to describe, explain or inform their creator (Engelhardt 2002). At the end of the day, it is important to know why you use the display, what you use it for and how you use it (cf. Varga-Atkins and O'Brien 2009: 57). Since our intention is to focus on building blocks of displays and techniques to apply when using displays in the research process, and since we emphasize theorizing, we do not give much attention to method. Instead, we extend the use of displays to be a useful tool for theorizing irrespective of method (Verdinelli and Scagnoli 2013). Our intention is to show what a display is, what the different building blocks in a display are and how you can put a display together. Let us start by proposing a definition.

What is a display?

In the most basic sense, a display is a device to depict parts, patterns and processes in the objects of research. It is a tool to order, sort and connect things. A display can represent the unobservable and abstract, and it can help us to describe and understand complex social phenomena. Some displays, such as unsorted mind maps, are unbound or free, whereas others are more bound and systematic. A free display is often made from scratch, but a bound display rests upon certain assumptions or defined characteristics. To our knowledge, Miles and Huberman's (1994) seminal book on qualitative data analysis is the only one containing an exhaustive study of displays used in analysing qualitative data. They define a display as 'a visual format that presents information systematically, so the user can draw valid conclusions and take needed action' (1994: 91). We believe that they capture something quite essential in the phrase 'a visual format', and we agree with their statement that a display has to be informative. However, we want to broaden their premise to some extent, since we believe that displays can be useful also for other purposes in the research process. Presenting information systematically is one important way of using a display, and we agree with their claim that the display should help a user draw valid conclusions for further action. Still, we want to stress other characteristics that are important when the aim of using displays is not restricted to analysing a specific type of data but includes theorizing. Therefore, we would like to put forward a somewhat different definition: *a scientific display is a graphical representation of relations and relata that answers one or more research questions or statements* (see Figure 2.1).

The relata are dependent on relations and the relations are dependent on relata. For example, the relation of friendship is dependent on at least two related friends. Even though a display can take many different forms and be used in a great variety of ways, as we will show, it does not mean that 'anything goes'. As the definition indicates, two criteria must be fulfilled to turn a figure, sketch, matrix, diagram, mind map and so on into a scientific display and a useful device for theorizing. First, a display has to answer – in a graphic format – one or more questions, or it has to illustrate one or

FIGURE 2.1 A basic form of a display as relata and relation

more statements or assumptions. Second, it has to be relational; that is, it should connect two or more sets, or relata, to each other. The question can be of a descriptive character, for example, 'what are the characteristics of the respondents in this study?' To answer this question, the display could be a matrix where the relation between variables – for example, each respondent's age, gender, education and occupation (i.e. relata) – is systematized and described by the combination of two lists – columns and rows. Another way of framing the question is to make it analytical, which means that the relations and the relata in the display are of analytical or causal character, for example, 'how or why does this happen?' 'What are the causal powers behind this outcome?' 'How can we explain gender segregation through the concept of power?'

In some cases, a display can be transformed into a property space, and in others, it can be the result of one. However, one important aspect to take into account is the purpose of the display. What questions does it answer or what statement does it illustrate? Last but not least, what are the relevant relations and relata? Displays are tools for producing knowledge by graphically representing the abstract and thus non-visual, and they can be used at every stage of the research process – from trying to grasp and identify the area of interest to summarizing results. We focus mainly on theorizing, although this activity cannot be fully separated from other stages and activities in the research process.

Our last argument to support the use of displays is perhaps the most basic one and has to do with the visual dimension. We agree with Goldstone and Barsalou (1998) that human beings' perception is related to their cognition. We also support Podolny (2003: 173), who asks us to think about how often we have used the expression 'I see' to indicate that we have understood something. The visual format of a display – what we see – is what makes it valuable in addition to plain text. Since this and the next chapter is about how to theorize using displays, we find it quite suitable to mention that the concept of 'theory' comes from the Greek 'theoria', which has, among other meanings, the meaning of 'to look at'. At the same time, it is appropriate to consider O'Brien et al.'s statement that the works and endeavours of social scientists and philosophers show that 'vision' cannot be seen as one single thing (2012: 252), since 'it is layered with meaning that is personal, social, and historical and in ways that we are often barely conscious of'. Thus, displays are constructed graphical representations, metaphors or analogies of something; the construction is made by someone and coloured by the understanding of that someone. Therefore, it is always important to add a descriptive, clarifying text to the display. This is important to remember in the reporting process, but it is also something to pay attention to in the research process, which is often a collective activity in which understanding is not necessarily shared.

In Figure 2.1, we present one way of graphically visualizing a display in which the two ellipses represent the relata, and the line represents the relation between the relata. The characteristic of the relation is that it exists between two or more phenomena – the relata. The relata can be concepts, things, individuals, characteristics and ideas; but the essential thing about relata is that they are connected and correspond to each other in one way or another by a relation. The display in Figure 2.1 is not filled with any content, but it still functions as a descriptive and pedagogic device and shows what a display of a relation can look like. The display shows what constitutes a display according to our definition. Now, let us recall the example of friendship mentioned before. In Figure 2.1, the line in the display could symbolize a friendship relation and the two relata could symbolize the two friends – Thelma and Louise. Even though there is no sharp distinction between description and analysis, the display could be seen as a graphic device with the purpose of describing friendship; alternatively, if the purpose is theoretical or analytical, it could be seen as a graphic device showing how friendship is constituted.

Another way to describe a display in simple terms is presented in Figure 2.2. As you might recall, part of it was Figure 1.2 in the previous chapter, where it displayed the reporting process. A display has to answer a question or make a statement. As always, a display cannot stand by itself – there is a need for a written explanation as well. In this case, what needs to be clarified is that the first relatum, the question mark, symbolizes the question, and the second relatum, the exclamation mark, symbolizes the answer, while the relation between them connects the answer with the question. In the other case, the exclamation mark symbolizes the statement, and the question mark symbolizes the verification of it. In both cases, the display is ordered by time. In the first case, the relation between the question and the answer is ordered in such a way that the question precedes the answer. In the other case, an assumption about something precedes the search for the right questions to ask to verify the assumption.

By pointing this out, we want to illustrate the importance of being both playful and mindful when using displays. Relations are powerful devices in social science, and you have to be cautious and aware of what kind of relation you have in mind when you are working your way through the research process. Is it just something that shows a connection, or do you have a specific type of connection in mind? The connection could be related to time, power or causality. Let us therefore look more closely at what characterizes different types of displays and their building blocks.

FIGURE 2.2 Basic forms of a display as relata and relations that either discover the answer of a question or verify a statement

Building blocks of displays

Since there are no real conventions for using displays, our contribution takes as its point of departure an overview of what we think are useful basic building blocks. In the presentation, we leave different types of mathematical models and complex logical schemes out and instead shed light on how displays in general can be used as tools when theorizing in social science. Since our perception of the visual format is an important aspect of displays – remember the 'I see' expression – the use of different graphical or basic geometrical figures such as circles, different forms of squares or triangles, and arrows or lines is functional but of course not obligatory. However, there is a risk that a display can be extremely complicated and consist of a complex network of a variety of nodes, lines, circles, boxes and arrows. A guideline when constructing displays is not to overdo things, but rather to use them to make complexity understandable and to answer questions.

According to Engelhardt (2002: 32), one way to distinguish between different modes of graphic format is to take their structural compositions and relations into account. The basic formats he suggests are spatial clustering, separation by separators, linking, line-up and containment. Since we see his framework as a fruitful source of inspiration when working with displays, we briefly describe how he defines different graphical building blocks. To *cluster* is to show that some things have common characteristics or are related to each other in some way, both within groups and between groups. A cluster is usually defined by a spatial distance or separation of two or more relata that, in turn, contain subsets. Grouping things is a form of clustering as well as a form of categorization (see Figure 2.3). Separation in one way or another is always needed in order to group or cluster things (Engelhardt 2002: 32). To depict separation, you can use an empty space or a separator. In Figure 2.3, an empty space is used to separate the clusters from each other. The picture of gender segregation in Figure I.2 provided another example of using space as a separator.

A *separator* is often a 'line- or a band-shaped graphic object' (Engelhardt 2002: 34), a sort of dividing line that separates graphic objects – in this case relata – from one another. In other words, a boundary is a separator, and a relation can be illustrated as a separation between two entities, spheres and so on. In Figure I.2, we separated the symbols of woman and man to display gender segregation. In Figure 2.4, the circle can display a closed system, closure or an insider–outsider phenomenon. A separator can be straight or take some other form, but it can also be ordered by some principle (criterion

FIGURE 2.3 Clusters separated by spatial distance

or characteristic) or unordered. Think of a train timetable and the importance of being able to distinguish times and stations from each other. A timetable is ordered by time and place. In addition, a level is a separator, since it is used for vertical separation; and a matrix is a combination of horizontal and vertical separations (cf. p. 56). Table I.1, in which we illustrated different types of segregation indices, provides another example.

Linking is another way of graphically representing a relation. According to Engelhardt (2002: 40), a link has two components, nodes and connectors; and a connector can be an arrow or a line that connects or is attached to two or more objects (nodes). The shape can be a linear chain, a circle, a loop, a triangle, a tree or a network. The line can be directed, as an arrow is, or undirected, as lines or bars are. The horizontal arrow in Figure 2.5 can visualize a process in time or a movement in space, and the vertical arrow can display phenomena such as upwards mobility from social position A to position B. Networks are also a form of linking.

A *line-up* is an object-to-object relation in which all the objects, except the ones at either end, have two adjoining objects. The line-up can be ordered or unordered (Engelhardt 2002: 36), and it does not necessarily have to have a link between every object. In a table, there can be horizontal line-ups (i.e. rows) and vertical ones (i.e. columns), as in Table I.1 (which showed a gender segregation ratio) or Figure 2.6a, which shows different stages of the reporting process. Another way of depicting the reporting process is a line-up with a start and an end but considerably more unordered points between the start and end, as in Figure 2.6b.

Containment is a graphical object with content, which can be a symbol or written text. To enclose something is a form of containment. In the example in Figure 2.6a, the content of the containers are the labels of stages in the writing process.

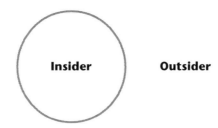

FIGURE 2.4 A separator as boundary between insider and outsider

FIGURE 2.5 Arrows as links

The containers are symbolizing how these different stages are related to each other in time; in other words, it is a line-up that is linked and ordered using the criterion of time. The different stages in this display are distinguished by separators that take the form of rectangles and their boundaries. Labels can have textual, pictorial or symbolic shapes.

When working with displays and visualizing relations, you need to be aware of, and reflect on, how to use lines and arrows as connectors. An arrow has to do with direction. Of course, what is directional varies with the purpose and content of the display. The direction can be one-way or two-way; and it can depict such phenomena as time, power, order or causality. If using a straight line, a dotted line or an arrow, you can designate different things, as shown in Figure 2.7. In that figure, the horizontal line *can* signify an equal relation, the dotted a weaker and more blurred relation and the arrow a direction. If an arrow is tilted up or down, it is usually to depict an increase or decrease of something. There is no scientific rule that the symbol of a line has a specific meaning depending on its shape; therefore, you need to specify the meaning in each case.

Often, simple displays, such as the displays in the examples just given, are building blocks used when putting graphical figures together to form a more complex pattern. In the research process, this step-by-step procedure is almost always present, whereas in the reporting process, what is usually shown is the final result of the construction work.

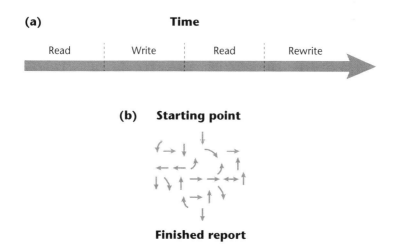

FIGURE 2.6 (a) A line-up showing stages of the writing process. (b) An unordered line-up showing stages of the writing process

FIGURE 2.7 Lines and arrows

Putting a display together

When defining a display, we do not specify the character of either the relata or the relation in terms of such things as strength or direction. However, in order to make use of the full potential of displays, you should use various means to differentiate the relata and the relations. How to do this, and visualize it, is dependent on whether the display is constructed in the research or in the reporting process. In the former case, you can be quite self-centred, innovative, artistic and experimental; but in the latter case, you need to be clear and convincing, since an audience has to be able to follow your thoughts and methods of reasoning.

When working with displays, there is no given rule about when to use a square, a circle and so on; making such decisions is up to the creator of the display. This is especially true during the research process, when displays are an informal matter and are used as tools for theorizing. The examples we present below are useful for showing how to work with displays in a creative and theoretically productive way. As we have mentioned earlier, there is a symbolic-cultural dimension to working with displays, and this dimension tends to play an important role in how we prefer to depict certain things and how we perceive certain formats. The examples below can therefore be seen as ethnocentric ways to graphically visualize social objects. So once again, in this part of the book, our main purpose is to stimulate your ideas and thoughts about concepts, objects, relata and relations in order to answer questions.

One fundamental characteristic of a display is that it shows how entities – in the form of terms for concepts – are related to each other. A display used in theorizing therefore involves clusters, boundaries and connections as line-ups and links between concepts. The displays in Figures 2.8 to 2.19 show parts in relation to each other and the constituents of each part. Despite their simplicity, their meaning and content can be theoretically sophisticated, and they can be an exceptionally useful tool for the producer of social theory. These kinds of simple displays can also be made into more detailed and complicated ones.

Even though a square or a rectangle divided into two parts appears to be a very modest display, it is useful. To divide or separate a whole or to visualize two mutually exclusive categories or parts can be one way to depict a dichotomy. Suppose our question is 'what constitutes the labour market?' We can visualize it as a divided rectangle to show that the labour market consists of employers and employees. They are two categories with different characteristics and logics but are still related to each other, and they are both necessary for the labour market to exist. Other examples are the more or less clear separation and relation between men and women, work and family, mind

FIGURE 2.8 A dichotomy of age

and body, or theory and practice. Tilly (1998: 47) argued that social relations are often categorical pairs; for example, parent/child, wife/husband and servant/master. In the ideal dichotomy, one phenomenon or characteristic cannot exist in two spheres at the same time. In Figure 2.8, age is displayed as a dichotomy consisting of young and old.

When using dichotomies, you have to be aware that the border or separator can be fuzzy. Some regard gender as a self-evident dichotomy, whereas others are critical of the distinction; according to them, gender is far too complex and cannot be dichotomized. Thus, when using dichotomies, you have to be cautious about defining the different categories and their content. You need to think about how the separation and the relation between the relata are constituted. Still, we regard a dichotomous display as a powerful tool when theorizing. It can be a starting point when you are scrutinizing the phenomenon of interest and asking what constitutes your empirical and theoretical material. In the next step, you might ask yourself how that comes about. In Figure 2.9, there is no indication of whether the dichotomy is ordered in any way. Ordering can be the next analytical step.

Depending on your object of interest, it is possible to use a more differentiated categorical division, as in a trichotomy or a classification with even more divisions. The rectangle is therefore a starting point for a basic table with two or more ordered columns (showing such phenomena as different age groups, or different levels of skills) that are separated but still adjoined, as in Figure 2.9. In the next step, the columns can be developed into a matrix or a table by adding rows that represent other relata to which you want to relate the first categories. Alternatively, it might be more fruitful to merge the categories, depending on where your theoretical reasoning leads you.

You can display the different relata by ordering them into different steps that indicate a direction. Ageing can for example be represented in different forms depending on how you frame your study and theoretical reasoning. In Figure 2.10 getting old is represented as steps or as a stair to show advancing age. Yet another way to display ages is as a continuum where the relata are not easy to separate from each other (Figure 2.11). Despite the blurriness in the continuum, the two ends or extremes are distinct. We all know that birth and death are the two ends of the continuum called life. There are various ways to pinpoint different stages in life by using age in years. Conversely, social scientists today tend to claim that different life phases are fuzzy and dependent on a number of factors. For example, when does the transition from youth to adult occur? In research, there are various ways to handle these two phases (relata), one of which has resulted in a new category, namely young adult. By studying this relation empirically and by trying to understand it theoretically, researchers have found that the concepts of

FIGURE 2.9 An ordered display of age

34 Tools for theorizing in social science

youth and adult are in some cases not enough to understand and explain the specific transition involved in becoming an adult (Furlong 2009). In Figure 2.10, the continuum is presented vertically as a stair display, but it can be presented in other ways depending on the purpose and content of the display.

Even if the displays are rather similar, they can have many different meanings depending on how you compose them. This has consequences for theorizing as displays of entities that are dichotomous or strictly separated from each other are different from displays of continua but also from depictions that have a specific direction, as in the example of the stair display. Thus, a display can be of great help when trying to answer questions such as 'what are the crucial parts of this entity, what are its characteristics, and to what is it related?' When theorizing, it is important to be as clear and specific as you can. If the study object is fuzzy or multi-layered, you have to be clear about that, too. However, to be clear about things takes time, so you have to be bold and creative along the way. You might start off with understanding age as the dichotomy young–old; then see it as more differentiated, as in Figure 2.9; then see it as a stair consisting of steps, as in Figure 2.10; and finally, understand it as a continuum, in which the stages and transitions are more fluent, as in Figure 2.11. Irrespective of which alternative you select, you need to know why you choose to understand age in the way you do.

A display can take the form of a matrix or a table in which the relations and relata are illustrated by separate, ordered rows and columns, as in Table 2.1. Here, the structure is a combination of horizontal and vertical separations, or a combination of horizontal and vertical line-ups. As mentioned in connection with the description of the display in Figure 2.9, this is an extended version in which one more factor is included. The question to be answered is 'what are the concerns of young adults and old people regarding the future?' The question can be answered by doing an

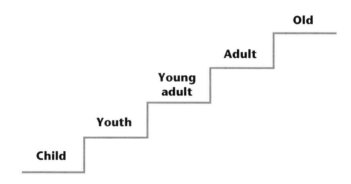

FIGURE 2.10 Steps between ages or phases of life

FIGURE 2.11 Continuum of age or life phases

TABLE 2.1 Concerns about the future in relation to age/life phase

	Concerns about the future
Young	
Adult	
Old	

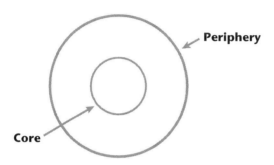

FIGURE 2.12 Core and periphery

overview of existing research, an empirical investigation, or both. The display can be a tool to test a statement or assumption, and you can add more rows and columns depending on the purpose of the display.

The next graphical figure to be presented is the circle (Figure 2.12). A circle and its border is in itself sometimes enough to visualize a relation; for example, a relation of insider and outsider or closure, as mentioned above. A circle can be used to divide one part into two or more parts to show the relative size of something, as in the pie chart diagrams of gender segregation in Figure I.1. The relative size does not necessarily have to be a quantitative measure, since displayed relative size can illustrate qualitatively how you understand the relation between two or more relata. Furthermore, circles and other graphical forms can be used to illustrate containment. Within a specific phenomenon, there can be one or more internal parts or subparts. For example, within an organization, there can be one or more subgroups. Within one defined culture, there can be one or more subcultures. The circle can exemplify a core–periphery relation, as, for example, in Atkinson's model of the flexible firm (1984, 1985). Atkinson divides the labour force into a core group that enjoys better working conditions than do groups in the periphery, which consists of employees with bad and insecure working conditions. A subgroup can be differentiated according to membership or some other shared characteristic. Here, the relata are not separated in the same way as in the case of a dichotomy or the other examples above; instead, one relatum contains the other. When trying to understand and explain social phenomena, this is an important analytical and theoretical distinction. In these endeavours, displays can be of great help. When testing various connections and relations, the effort of constructing a display is valuable theoretical or analytical footwork.

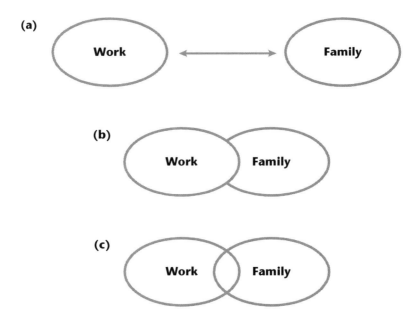

FIGURE 2.13 (a) Separate spheres between work and family. (b) Spillover from work to family. (c) Overlap/integration between work and family

As Figure 2.13 shows, you can use more than one circle to connect entities and concepts to each other in various ways. Figure 2.13 uses two circles to show how separate parts are united or overlap. As we have mentioned, it can often be a delicate task to decide how two or more phenomena are related. Sometimes two parts can be described as intertwined with each other, as are mind and body, or yin and yang. Yet another example is the relation between work and family life outside work: in some cases, there might be a distinct separation between the two spheres; in other cases, they might overlap. In their work on the concept of availability, Bergman and Gardiner (2007) argue that for some groups in our Western society, the demands of being temporally and spatially available for work and for family life tend to overlap more and more. Women's higher degree of labour market participation, the development of dual-earner families, men's increasing participation in unpaid work in the family and the growing use of information technology have changed the relation between work and family. As shown in Figure 2.13, how these spheres are related to each other can be visualized in different ways. In some studies, work and family are thought of as separate but related spheres (Lambert 1990); in other studies, one sphere, work, is thought of as spilling over into the other (Grzywacz et al. 2002); and in yet other studies, the two spheres are thought of as overlapping or integrated spheres (Ruppanner and Huffman 2014). In the first case, work is seen as one separate arena and the family another; work-related activities are carried out at work and family-related activities are carried out within the family and/or at home. This separation can be a result of how work and family life are organized. In the example of spillover, the relation between the two is more permeable, and individuals might bring work home with them and work in their free time. In the third example, the border between work and family is blurred and permeable; thus, a new sphere emerges in which both private matters and work-related matters are carried out. Once again, playing with the graphical layout of the display is a useful way of understanding phenomena and the relations between concepts. Trial and error is an indispensable strategy in this process.

The triangle in Figure 2.14 illustrates in another way of how the depiction of related parts can direct our thoughts to the nature of relations. In the triangle, there is a part that can be defined as a top and another part that can be defined as a bottom – the triangle is pyramid-like. Adding layers inside the triangle makes it not only more differentiated, but also more hierarchically stratified. Often, when describing various organizational forms, the triangle is the graphical format used to represent a hierarchical organization. It can be used to illustrate a society or a stratified system, for example a class society. In other words, a layered triangle is an example of a vertical line-up in which every level can contain a number of concepts, phenomena or characteristics that are related to each other and together create the specific characteristic of that particular level. Maslow's (1943) often-cited theory of needs is one well-known example, although Maslow did not present his theory other than literally. Maslow's argument is that individuals are motivated by a number of universal needs, which they strive to achieve in different ways, depending on their dispositions, resources and potentials. Maslow described his theory of needs as a hierarchy since the needs can be ranked from basic biological and physiological needs at the bottom to the need for self-actualization at the highest level. At every level, a number of specific needs are clustered together, but they are qualitatively separated from the needs at the other levels in the form of vertical line-up. When needs on one level are satisfied, other higher-level needs emerge (Maslow 1943: 375). To mobilize motivation and advance towards the satisfaction of higher-level needs, the individual's needs at the underlying levels have to be fulfilled. Maslow developed his theory by synthesizing

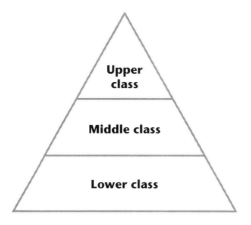

FIGURE 2.14 Class society

38 Tools for theorizing in social science

existing literature, sorting knowledge into specific clusters and then ranking the needs described in the literature in order to explain human needs and motivation.

Because linking concepts is important in theorizing, we now provide examples of how this can be done. Relations between relata do not necessarily have to be visualized as a straight line or as an arrow pointing from A to B; these relations can be visualized in more complicated ways. However, one common approach is to use different types of networks, which can be defined as sets of relations between different nodes – that is relata. Most of us can think of examples of networks: our social network of family and friends or our team at work. In network theory, the dyad or pair is the smallest possible entity. A network can be a chain, as shown in Figure 2.15. Thelma knows Louise, who knows Chris but Thelma and Chris do not know each other. Put differently, the latter two are indirectly linked to each other through Louise.

Theoretically and analytically speaking, both direct and indirect links are often very important in social life. In some cases, we can talk about mediators between different individuals or groups – in this case, Louise can be seen as the mediator or middle manager between Thelma, who might be the top manager, and Chris, who might be an employee on the shop floor. (In these examples, the network consists of individuals, but a network can comprise other types of objects or concepts as well.)

A network can be depicted in other ways. Figure 2.16 shows how different individuals constitute a workplace team or a group of friends. In this example, there is no specific hierarchical order, and this lack of hierarchical order can be the answer to a question raised or it can be a point of departure for the next question, such as one about another type of coordination between the individuals identified. For example, the same sort of depiction of a network could be used to show how different work tasks together constitute an occupation.

Links can be made from one to one, one to many, many to one or many to many. Figure 2.17 provides two examples of one-to-many linking, where the layout of the relata and relations shows that there are different types of relations in focus. In the first

FIGURE 2.15 Network in the form of a line-up as a one-to-one relationship

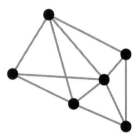

FIGURE 2.16 Linking many to many in a group

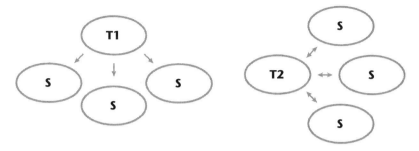

FIGURE 2.17 Network linking one to many showing a hierarchical and a democratic teaching style

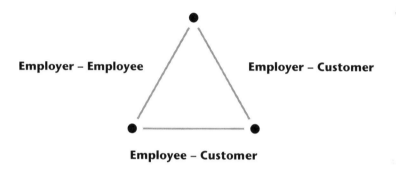

FIGURE 2.18 Service work as three separate dyads

display, the relata are ordered to depict a hierarchical order that is divided into two levels; for example, the relation between a teacher Thelma (T1) and the three different student groups (S) that she teaches. The display illustrates that Thelma (T1) has an authoritarian style of teaching based on one-way communication. Her colleague Louise (T2), on the other hand, has another type of relation to her student groups. Louise uses a democratic style of teaching based on two-way communication and dialogue. Of course, these displays can be developed and extended, but here we want to show how you can use networks. Once again, we stress the importance of describing in text what your displays represent.

In our final examples in this chapter, networks are displayed as triangles but are used differently from the way in which a triangle was used in Figure 2.14 to show a class society. Triangles can also be understood to represent a network in which all three relata or nodes are connected to each other by the links between the nodes. A triad displayed as a triangle consists of three dyads related to each other. Depending on the purpose of the display and its relations and relata, the triadic pattern can be understood in different ways. In Figure 2.18, service work is seen as three dyads and separate relations between employee and customer, between employer and employee and between employer and customer. The different dyads have their specific characteristics given the relata and the relation. For example, the customer and the employer can have

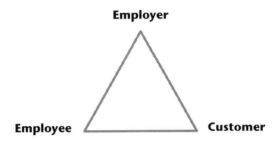

FIGURE 2.19 The triadic ensemble of the service triangle

a joint interest in the relation to the employee. Conversely, the employee and the customer can act in ways that are not in line with the employer's interests. In addition, the employee and the employer can share more or less explicit agreements concerning the customers. All three dyads have consequences for service work.

There have been attempts to capture these three sets of relations in service work by introducing the concept of a 'service triangle' (Albrecht and Zemke 1985). Nevertheless, there is still a need for a deeper understanding of how the different relata are related in service work. Jonathan R. Anderson claims that 'to date we do not yet understand the relationship between a manager's behaviour, employee perceptions, and customer outcomes on the triad level. This is one large shortcoming of current writings on the service sector' (2006: 505–6). One reason for this lack of understanding is that the service triangle has been used as a device for analysing relations to only one of its vertices at a time (i.e. managers *or* service workers *or* customers). Therefore, Kenneth Brown and Marek Korczynski (2010) go from the dyads to the triad in their analyses of service work (Figure 2.19). This way of reasoning is in line with Georg Simmel's (2009 [1908]) famous work on the differences between dyads and triads. He emphasizes that triads are important units in social science and he argues that even though a triad consists of three dyads, a triad cannot be reduced to its set of dyads, it is a qualitatively different social form. By analysing the set of relations and relata in the triad as an interactive whole, in accordance with Simmel's theory, further theorizing is possible.

Summary

The purpose of this chapter has been to show and define what a display is, what the different building blocks are and how a display can be put together to support theorizing. We have emphasized the graphical format of a display, its relational character and its usefulness when answering questions or statements about social phenomena. We have also presented various simple building blocks using different examples of graphical formats. Finally, to clarify how relational social phenomena can be visualized when theorizing, we have shown how these various graphical formats can be used to put together a display. In this chapter, we have given you only glimpses of the theorizing part while we focused more on the building blocks. In Chapter 3, we will give three examples of how to use displays when theorizing.

References

Albrecht, Karl and Ron Zemke (1985) *Service America! Doing Business in the New Economy*. Homewood: Dow Jones-Irwin.
Anderson, Jonathan R. (2006) 'Managing Employees in the Service Sector: A Literature Review and Conceptual Development', *Journal of Business and Psychology*, 20(4): 501–23.
Atkinson, John (1984) *Flexibility, Uncertainty and Manpower Management*. Brighton: Institute of Manpower Studies.
Atkinson, John (1985) 'The Changing Corporation', pp. 13–34 in David Clutterbuck (ed.), *New Patterns of Work*. Aldershot: Gower.
Bergman, Ann and Jean Gardiner (2007) 'Employee Availability for Work and Family: Some Swedish Case Studies', *Employee Relations*, 29(4): 400–14.
Brown, Kenneth and Marek Korczynski (2010) 'When Caring and Surveillance Technology Meet: Organizational Commitment and Discretionary Effort in Home Care Work', *Work and Occupations*, 37(3): 404–32.
Engelhardt, Yuri (2002) *The Language of Graphics: A Framework for the Analysis of Syntax and Meaning in Maps, Charts and Diagrams*. Amsterdam: Institute for Logic, Language and Computation.
Furlong, Andy (2009) *Handbook of Youth and Young Adulthood: New Perspectives and Agendas*. London: Routledge.
Goldstone, Robert L. and Lawrence W. Barsalou (1998) 'Reuniting Perception and Conception', *Cognition*, 65(2–3): 231–62.
Grzywacz, Joseph G., Daniel M. Almeida and David A. McDonald (2002) 'Work–Family Spillover and Daily Reports of Work and Family Stress in the Adult Labor Force', *Family Relations*, 51(1): 28–36.
Lambert, Susanne J. (1990) 'Processes Linking Work and Family: A Critical Review and Research Agenda', *Human Relations*, 43(3): 239–57.
Maslow, Abraham H. (1943) 'A Theory of Human Motivation', *Psychological Review*, 50(4): 370–96.
Miles, Matthew B. and A. Michael Huberman (1994) *Qualitative Data Analysis*. Thousand Oaks: Sage.
O'Brien, Mark, Tünde Varga-Atkins, Muriah Umoquit and Peggy Tso (2012) 'Cultural–Historical Activity Theory and "the Visual" in Research: Exploring the Ontological Consequences of the Use of Visual Methods', *International Journal of Research and Method in Education*, 35(3): 251–68.
Podolny, Joel M. (2003) 'A Picture Is Worth More Than a Thousand Symbols: A Sociologist's View of the Economic Pursuit of Truth', *American Economic Review*, 93(2): 169–74.
Ruppanner, Leah and Matt L. Huffman (2014) 'Blurred Boundaries: Gender and Work-Family Interference in Cross-National Context', *Work and Occupations*, 41(2): 210–36.
Simmel, Georg (Anthony J. Blasi, Anton K. Jacobs and Mathew Kanjirathinkal [eds]) (2009 [1908]) *Sociology. Inquiries into the Construction of Social Forms,* Vol. 1 and 2. Boston: Brill.
Tilly, Charles (1998) *Durable Inequality*. Berkeley: University of California Press.
Varga-Atkins, Tünde and Mark O'Brien (2009) 'From Drawing to Diagrams: Maintaining Researcher Control during Graphic Elicitation in Qualitative Interviews', *International Journal of Research and Method in Education*, 32(1): 53–67.
Verdinelli, Susana and Norma I. Scagnoli (2013) 'Data Display in Qualitative Research', *International Journal of Qualitative Methods*, 12(1): 359–81.

3
THE USE OF DISPLAYS IN THEORIZING

You now have an idea of what a display is and how various graphical parts can be put together to build a display. In this chapter, we will give examples of how to use displays when your aim is to theorize. The illustrations might help you to get started playing about with your own displays to make your thoughts clearer. There is often a gap between tentative thoughts and ideas, on the one hand, and written theoretical claims and explanations on the other. Displays are tools to drag sometimes lurking ideas and thoughts into the open daylight in order to be scrutinized and refined (cf. Kaplan 1964: 268–9).

Even if it is often hard work to develop and build theory, curiosity is an important ingredient and driver. In most cases, the ambition to investigate and explain something can be traced back to some form of curiosity manifested as a research question or proposal. The main reason to theorize is to explain the phenomena of interest and to understand them better. One way to use a display is as a sorting mechanism whereby you can map different theories and concepts and their relation to each other. In some cases, you might use displays to refine or modify existing theory, and in other cases, you might have the ambition to build a totally new theory. However, a display is in itself not a theory. While theories are tools to understand and explain reality, displays can only be a representation of the theory in whole or in part.

Sometimes, when working with displays, you might prefer to use paper and pen or sticky notes. At other times, you will work directly on your computer using available software tools. Our advice is to use whatever feels most convenient to start with. In the beginning, you might be impatient and use paper and pen; in the end, you can make the display look tidy with the help of computer software. Irrespective of how you work with displays and how much effort you put into constructing them, a display has no purpose of its own; it has to be useful for your purpose and for clarifying that which you are curious about. If you realize that the display does not work, try to understand why, and then modify it or discard it. It is appropriate to mention here that when doing research, discarding a display is not the same as being defeated. Instead, it might show that you are trapped in a dead end, that you do not have enough data to claim what you are claiming, or that there is something missing in the theoretical framework. This can be a painful experience, but at the end of the day, the display has done its job and some knowledge has been gained.

The examples in this chapter do not cover the entire range of possible uses of a display – your understanding and research problem are the only limits. Instead, we want to give three examples of working with displays that are a bit more elaborate than the examples in the previous chapter. The first example shows how to extend an already existing theory about learning; the second is the interaction of the necessary components of gender segregation in working life; and the third is a stepwise theoretical reasoning about labour market relations. The three examples are not exclusively separable as they have some common traits, but they illustrate three different ways to analytically move forward to a more elaborate understanding of the problem you are curious about. The chapter ends with a summary.

Theorizing by extending

Let us start with a well-known, widely used, revised and criticized theory of organizational learning developed by Argyris and Schön (1978) in their book *Organizational Learning: A Theory of Action Perspective*. Even though this book is sometimes described as the first real attempt to theorize organizational learning, the theory in the book was a result of extending an already existing theory. The curiosity and questions that triggered the development of Argyris and Schön's theory of organizational learning were first raised when they were writing an earlier book, *Theory in Practice*, published in 1974. In this earlier book, they developed a theory of action to understand human learning in situations of interpersonal interaction among professional practitioners. They focused on the individual practitioners and the conditions for learning in relation to being more competent and efficient. Here, they developed their first thoughts and the theory of single- and double-loop learning. Their main point was that it was important to distinguish between instrumental, routine based action and knowledge on the one hand, and more reflective action and learning patterns on the other. Argyris and Schön (1974) described single-loop learning as a process of identifying problems and then modifying and correcting these to minimize the discrepancy between expected and achieved outcomes. Single-loop learning can be seen as an instrumental response to existing goals, plans, norms and assumptions. The logic for the individual is as follows: this is what I should do. Can I do it or are there any problems? If there are problems, I have to identify them and correct my action in relation to them. In double-loop learning, the individual is able to modify and rethink goals, plans, norms and assumptions. In other words, there is awareness about the system and a capacity to subject it to critical inquiry. Argyris and Schön (1978) describe the two ways of learning like this:

> When the error detected and corrected permits the organization to carry on its present policies or achieve its present objectives, then that error-and-correction

44 Tools for theorizing in social science

> process is *single-loop* learning. Single-loop learning is like a thermostat that learns when it is too hot or too cold and turns the heat on or off. The thermostat can perform this task because it can receive information (the temperature of the room) and take corrective action. *Double-loop* learning occurs when error is detected and corrected in ways that involve the modification of an organization's underlying norms, policies and objectives.
>
> *(Argyris and Schön 1978: 2–3)*

We do not know if Argyris and Schön used displays in their research process, but let us imagine that they did. We can picture them sitting at a desk, drawing on sheets of paper, successively trying out displays to represent the different types of learning. The final versions could have been a series of extensions, each display extending the previous version in some way. We can illustrate this process in the following displays. In Figure 3.1, the process of learning is displayed as single-loop learning. The display shows the temporal dimension in the learning process and identifies separate steps that are given specific characteristics (i.e. it shows how the relata are related to each other in an ordered linking). Step one includes sensing, scanning and monitoring of the environment; step two, comparing the findings and information in relation to operating norms and goals; and step three, initiating and taking the best possible actions in the situation.

The display of double-loop learning in Figure 3.2, on the other hand, is created by adding a relatum and a set of relations to visualize a higher level of learning. By extending the learning process with step 2a, it is possible to emphasize a stage in the learning process when the individuals or groups question the assumptions, values and actions that are a result of the first loop. They might ask 'are we doing the right things?' This is a way to reflect on the situation, values, and existing norms and assumptions. Adding step 2a is an example of how to extend a theory by inserting another dimension to it.

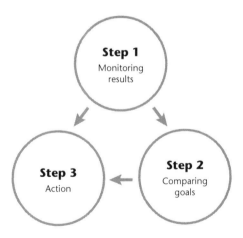

FIGURE 3.1 Single-loop learning

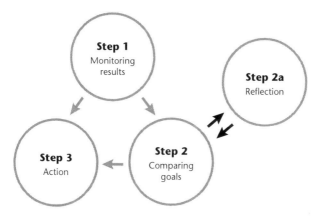

FIGURE 3.2 Double-loop learning

By using Argyris and Schön's (1974, 1978) theorizing, we have provided an example of how to use displays to depict the ways in which steps are related to each other, not only in terms of content and characteristics but also in terms of a time-ordered circular process. Their theory has influenced research on organizational learning and on phenomena such as management and control. It has also been the object of a lot of criticism, but criticism is an important trigger for theorizing and generating further contributions to the production of knowledge (cf. Arthur and Aiman-Smith 2001; Fiol and Lyles 1985; Miner and Mezias 1996; Senge 1990).

Theories about triple-loop learning are an example of how theorists can extend a theory even further by adding a third dimension, or another set of relations and relata. Argyris and Schön (1974, 1978) did not explicitly use the concept of triple-loop learning but according to Tosey et al. (2011: 302), the concept 'appears to be an attempt to expand Argyris and Schön's schema'. Even if Argyris and Schön did not develop the concept of triple-loop learning themselves, their theories generated curiosity and questions among other scholars in the field of learning and organizational learning, and these scholars extended the original theory. The concept of triple-loop learning is considerably more contested than the concepts of single- and double-loop learning; it also has more than one definition (see Tosey et al. 2011). However, Swieringa and Wierdsma (1992: 41–2) were among the first to use the concept, and they defined it as a form of learning that takes place 'when the essential principles on which the organization is founded come into discussion' and when new principles are developed 'with which an organization can proceed to a subsequent phase'. In this third loop, the question of *how* to decide what is right to do is crucial. Here, the context becomes important, and so do the power relations and the power to decide and define what the right thing to do is. The learning includes understanding why individuals, including oneself, groups and organizations, want to do certain things (see Figure 3.3). Thus, it includes an understanding of principles.

In this section about how to theorize through extending displays, we have used Argyris and Schön's (1974, 1978) theory of learning as an example. Theorizing can be

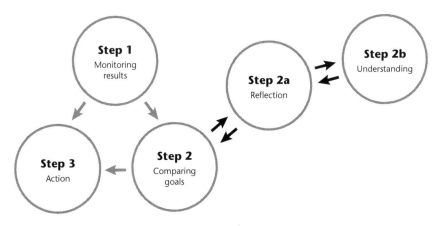

FIGURE 3.3 Triple-loop learning

accomplished by extending existing theory into different contexts or by adding more relata to it. When adding yet another set of relations and relata, new knowledge and theory are developed.

Theorizing by mapping interaction

Our next example is a display that Ann Bergman used to develop a theoretical starting point for understanding gender segregation; she first defined the components, relations and relata. The display dates back to her period as a doctoral student, when she was trying to find a relevant and fruitful way of understanding the mechanisms or forces behind the reproduction of gender segregation in three different workplaces in Sweden (Bergman 2004, 2006). Bergman can recall that she had a persistent feeling of despair over the fact that so many had written so much and so brilliantly about gender segregation in working life, and she felt that her contribution had no chance of adding anything of value to the field. However, after a while, her curiosity about the topic grew, and she started to think about what gender segregation in working life actually is and what the necessary components of it are. Her interest grew when she started to think of segregation both as a general phenomenon and as the specific form of gender segregation she was going to study.

In Part I, we presented a general definition of segregation from the *Oxford English Dictionary*: an 'action or state of setting someone or something apart from others'. This definition says nothing about who is segregated, or how, or where; it only specifies that something is set apart from something else. One way to display it is shown in Figure 3.4; the figure could represent any type of segregation, as there is no specific labelling of the categories involved.

To understand what gender segregation is and what generates its reproduction, the question Bergman asked at this stage was: 'Which structures are necessary for gender segregation in working life to be reproduced?' She regarded social structures as the invisible architecture of society; it was therefore important to identify those structures

FIGURE 3.4 Segregation

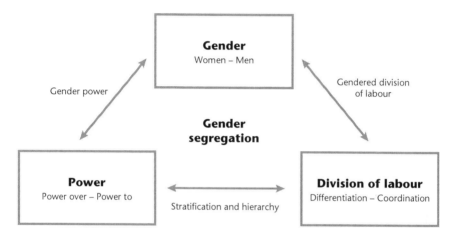

FIGURE 3.5 The necessary structural constitution of gender segregation in working life

to explain the empirical patterns in her study. Ann Bergman was strongly inspired by Mario Bunge, who stated: 'There are two main kinds of relations: those that make some difference to the relata and those that do not' (1999: 6–7). This means that when people – for example, women and men – enter a gender power relation, which is a social structure, they will be influenced by this differently. In most cases, the power relation will generate advantages for the men relative to the women.

The display in Figure 3.5 was a result of moving between theory and data. Working with the display was invaluable for Bergman because it forced her to be explicit when formulating assumptions about what generates gender segregation. Since gender segregation is a complex phenomenon and explanations are only partial and fallible, she was working from the point of view that her displays should simplify the phenomenon, showing what it consists of and how it functions. The delicate challenge in social science is that you see only the result and seldom the causes and never the relations (i.e. the structures).

The three structures she saw as necessary for gender segregation in organizations were gender, power and division of labour. We will not go into detail about the study itself but will briefly describe its building blocks. The most evident and important relatum to add to the display (Figure 3.5) was gender, since women and men are the categories that are set apart. Gender was defined as the relation between the social categories of women and men. The next relatum was division of labour, since this is where and how people and tasks are divided in working life. Division of labour was defined as differentiation on the one hand and as coordination on the other. However, these two dimensions were not enough to understand what generates the reproduction of gender segregation, since there is not only separation but also an uneven distribution of privileges and possibilities, and therefore power was brought into the display. Power was defined as an asymmetrical relation of 'power over' and 'power to'. As shown in the display – as three separate dyads and as a whole – all three relata interact with each other. Power in relation to gender generates gender power – in our society, this relation is often talked about as the gender order, a gender regime or a patriarchy. Power in relation to the division of labour generates stratification and unequal conditions; it ranks people and tasks into different positions and possibility structures. Gender in relation to division of labour generates a gendered division of labour in which women and men are working with different tasks in different spheres.

Besides the detailed display in Figure 3.5, in which the focus was to understand the different relations and relata as such, Ann Bergman also developed a simplified display, as shown in Figure 3.6. Here, the purpose was to emphasize the importance of not reducing gender segregation to one or two of the three necessary structures, but to see it as an interaction – a triad. Her next step in the theorizing process was to identify a number of mechanisms that were generated from the dynamic interplay of these structures – but that is another story and another display.

In Bergman's case, as in many others, displays tend to make fuzzy relations and relata look sharper than they are; therefore, displays depict relations and relata as more unproblematic than they might be. The clarifying virtue that is gained in prioritizing the 'I see!' dimension therefore makes theories or theoretical claims easier to criticize or praise. In Bergman's case, she discussed the displays' different relations

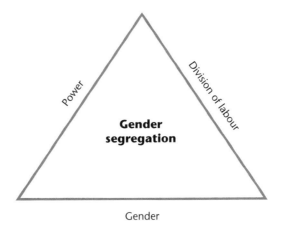

FIGURE 3.6 Simplified display and a synthetizing approach

and relata in depth in a textual format that also highlighted the contested concepts of gender and of power. Nevertheless, the invisible structures and extracted architecture linked together in the displays shown here was the foundation of her thesis and was valid all the way to the end.

Stepwise theorizing

When theorizing, the relations involved in a display will often have some bearing upon causality, or how relata are related to each other and what their causes and effects are. How to explain social or cultural patterns, events and activities in social science is often combined with a sense of uncertainty. How do we know that what we see, claim and explain with our theories is right? Well, we do not. Theories in social science are qualified guesses about how things work. However, to understand how things work – that is, to understand causality – is to understand social relations.

Jan Ch. Karlsson was curious to know what kind of organizations trade unions are. He therefore asked a number of common analytical questions (Danermark et al. 2002: 96–8). 'What do trade unions require for their existence?' 'Which relations are trade unions parts of?' 'Which kinds of relations are involved?' His first answer was that there has to be a counterpart in the form of employers or employer organizations (Figure 3.7).

He posited that for unions to exist, there have to be employer organizations. It seemed reasonable that there should be such an internal relation until it dawned on him that, historically, there were trade unions before there were employer organizations. Still, trade unions and employer organizations had to have *something* to do with each other. Could the question be reformulated? He asked this question: 'What does the connection between trade unions and employer organizations relate to?' His answer: 'Well, they are part of a relation between employers and employees in

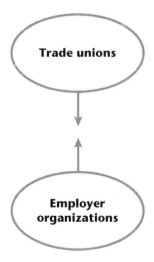

FIGURE 3.7 Trade unions and employer organizations

50 Tools for theorizing in social science

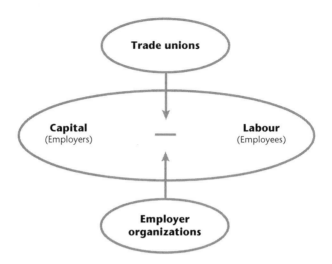

FIGURE 3.8 Unions, employer organizations, capital and labour

the labour market – or more abstractly, a relation between capital and labour.' With that thought, he extended the display to the shape in Figure 3.8.

The basic idea, which he recognized from several types of theories, was that the fundamental contradiction in the labour market is the one between capital and labour. Therefore, he thought, capital and labour organize in order to safeguard their respective interests. But what are those interests? Back to the questions. 'What do they require for their existence?' 'Can there be even more contradictions involved in the labour market?' When sketching different displays, he came up with the display shown in Figure 3.9.

The figure depicts a contradiction *within* labour that he had not included in any of the earlier displays. What did the contradiction concern? His answer became that the contradiction concerned the competition for jobs. Employees have to compete with each other for jobs, especially in tight labour markets. In an analogous way, employers have to compete with each other for labour power, especially when an economy is expanding.

His next problem was to compare the displays in Figures 3.8 and 3.9. How could he depict the contradictions in Figure 3.8 in relation to those in Figure 3.9? In other words, what were the relations between the contradictions *within* labour and capital, respectively, on the one hand, and the contradictions *between* labour and capital on the other hand? A clue was that he had already regarded the contradiction between the parties as fundamental. Could that still be the case? Back to analytical questions again: 'What must be the case for the contradiction within labour to exist?' The answer he found was that there has to be a contradiction between capital and labour – if not, there would be no grounds for the contradiction within labour. He also asked, 'what is required for the contradiction within capital to be at hand?' The answer turned out to be the same: a contradiction between capital and labour. It therefore seemed reasonable to put that contradiction in the middle and then to locate the others on each side (Figure 3.10).

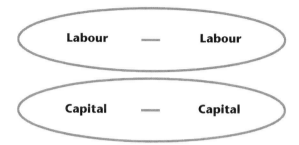

FIGURE 3.9 Contradiction within labour and capital, respectively

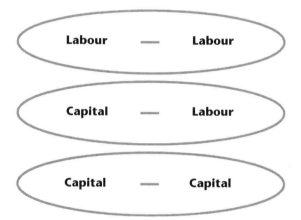

FIGURE 3.10 Contradiction within labour and capital, respectively, and the contradiction between labour and capital

He thus had a picture of the contradictions in the labour market, but he still had not answered the question he started out with in this phase of developing the analysis: 'Which interests are trade unions and employer organizations to look after?' In terms of displays, that meant that he had to locate trade unions and employer organizations in the display in Figure 3.10. For a start, it seemed apparent that in the upper part of the display, trade unions had their place somewhere between the contradiction within labour on the one hand, and between capital and labour on the other hand. But where? He experimented with different displays, such as the one shown in Figure 3.11.

There seemed to be a possible connection between these two types of contradictions, but what was it exactly? He made a corresponding display of the relation between the contradiction within capital and the contradiction between capital and labour. That was as far as he got until he considered these questions: 'In what way is the relation within labour and capital, respectively, related to the fundamental contradiction between labour and capital?' 'What is this type of organization doing there?' He started out with the contradiction within labour, creating the display in Figure 3.12.

52 Tools for theorizing in social science

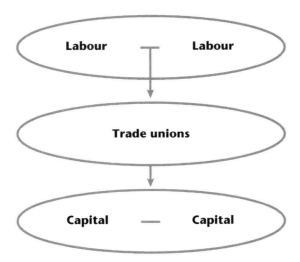

FIGURE 3.11 Trade unions placed between the contradiction within labour and the contradiction within capital

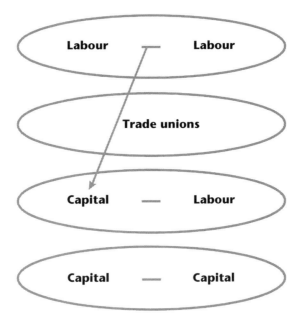

FIGURE 3.12 Trade unions as social weapons in relation to the contradiction between capital and labour

Trade unions possess a mechanism whereby they can reduce the contradiction within labour and thus gain strength in the fundamental contradiction to capital. In more concrete terms, trade unions are employee organizations in which the employees collectively define what conditions of work are acceptable. For example, members can

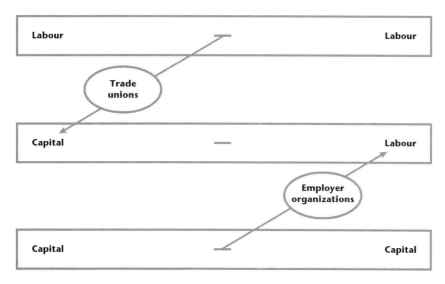

FIGURE 3.13 Contradictions and organizations on the labour market
Source: Danermark et al. (2003: 124).

agree not to accept a job in which the pay is lower than X. In this way, they can check internal competition for jobs by making it impossible for workers to underbid each other when it comes to pay. They thereby acquire a collective power to use against an employer that is interested in paying as little as possible for their labour power. Those kinds of agreements are mechanisms in wage labourers' part of the labour markets. In a parallel way, Karlsson finally constructed the display that provided the whole theoretical picture (Figure 3.13) – and that became the (hitherto) only published version of all the displays.

Employer organizations possess a mechanism to reduce the contradiction within capital and thereby gain strength in the fundamental contradiction to labour. In more concrete terms, employer organizations are organizations of companies in which employers collectively determine conditions for work. For example, employers can agree that none of them will pay more than X for a certain type of job. In this way, employer organizations try to check the internal competition for labour power by not overbidding each other when it comes to pay. Thereby, they acquire collective power that they can use against employees' interest in being paid as much as possible for their work. Those kinds of agreements are mechanisms in the employers' part of labour markets.

Summary

Playing about with displays helps us to understand the objects and processes involved. The main driver for constructing displays is curiosity, and important ingredients are creativity and playfulness. However, a display in itself is not a theory or an explanation. It always has to be accompanied by text, which is a necessity when theorizing. In this chapter, we have provided three examples of how displays can be used in the theorizing process. In the first example about different forms of learning, we showed how theorizing can be accomplished by extending existing theory into a different context or by adding one or more relata to it. In the second example of gender segregation, we demonstrated how in theorizing, displays can be made by mapping interaction between phenomena while simplifying them. In the last example of trade unions, we showed how a process of stepwise theorizing can be accompanied and driven by displays, which help the theorist to understand the essence of trade unions by defining what they do in relation to whom.

References

Argyris, Chris and Donald A. Schön (1974) *Theory in Practice. Increasing Professional Effectiveness.* San Francisco: Jossey-Bass.
Argyris, Chris and Donald A. Schön (1978) *Organizational Learning: A Theory of Action Perspective.* Reading: Addison Wesley.
Arthur, Jeffery B. and Lynda Aiman-Smith (2001) 'Gainsharing and Organizational Learning: An Analysis of Employee Suggestions over Time', *Academy of Management Journal*, 44(4): 737–54.
Bergman, Ann (2004) *Segregerad integrering. Mönster av könssegregering i arbetslivet.* Karlstad: Karlstad University Studies.
Bergman, Ann (2006) 'Segregated Integration', pp. 47–64 in Lena Gonäs and Jan Ch. Karlsson (eds), *Gender Segregation. Divisions of Work in Post-Industrial Welfare States.* Aldershot: Ashgate.
Bunge, Mario (1999) *The Sociology-Philosophy Connection.* New Brunswick: Transaction Publishers.
Danermark, Berth, Mats Ekström, Liselotte Jakobsen and Jan Ch. Karlsson (2002) *Explaining Society. Critical Realism in the Social Sciences.* London: Routledge.
Danermark, Berth, Mats Ekström, Liselotte Jakobsen and Jan Ch. Karlsson (2003) *Att förklara samhället.* Lund: Studentlitteratur.
Fiol, C. Marlene and Marjorie A. Lyles (1985) 'Organizational Learning', *Academy of Management Review*, 10(4): 803–13.
Kaplan, Abraham (1964) *The Conduct of Inquiry: Methodology for Behavioural Science.* San Francisco: Chandler.
Miner, Anne S. and Stephen J. Mezias (1996) 'Ugly Duckling No More: Pasts and Futures of Organizational Learning Research', *Organization Science*, 7(1): 88–99.
Senge, Peter M. (1990) *The Art and Practice of the Learning Organization.* New York: Doubleday.
Swieringa, Joop and Andre Wierdsma (1992) *Becoming a Learning Organization: Beyond the Learning Curve.* Reading: Addison Wesley.
Tosey, Paul, Max Visser and Mark N.K. Saunders (2011) 'The Origins and Conceptualizations of "Triple-loop" Learning: A Critical Review', *Management Learning*, 43(3): 291–307.

4
BASICS OF PROPERTY SPACES

Why do people have Global Positioning System (GPS) receivers in their cars or smartphones? Probably to know where they are or how to get where they want to go. This is achieved by a system of coordinates, based on latitudes in relation to the equator and longitudes in relation to the Greenwich meridian. These are properties, building a *property space* that makes it possible to orient, to answer the questions 'where am I?' and 'how do I get to where I want to go?' In an analogous way, we can build property spaces with other dimensions in social science. In similarity with the property space that is the basis of GPS, this is not only to find out where we are but also how to go further. Where we are means to keep track of concepts and typologies as building blocks of theories, while where to go means how to theorize. We start this chapter on the basics of property spaces by presenting the way in which they are built up, or what constitutes them. After pointing out that authors sometimes let the property space they build on stay hidden behind the text, we discuss three basic procedures for using property spaces in social science theoretical work: housekeeping, developing a terminology and elaborating on already existing theories.

One thing should, however, be clear from the outset: forming property spaces does not guarantee theoretical fruitfulness and success. As Kenneth D. Bailey explains, 'a classification is no better than the dimensions or variables on which it is based. If you follow the rules of classification perfectly but classify on trivial dimensions, you will produce a trivial classification' (1994: 2). We should be aware that many of the property spaces we construct when theorizing in the research process will end up in the waste-paper basket – the real one or the virtual. Conversely, some of them will turn out to be great tools in the generation of social theory. Compared to displays, property spaces have a more definite form, making them tools for systematically relating concepts to each other. It is in this way they are more bound than displays, which also means that they are tools for other tasks than that of displays.

Constructing a property space

The basic form of a property space can be found in Table 4.1 (the following terminology is close to the one suggested by Collier et al. 2008). First, we should note the *title* of the table, 'Parts of a property space'. The title is always important as it tells what the subject of the property space is; it is part of the property space. Further, there are two *dimensions*, X and Y, with two *properties* of each, A and B. We could have termed the dimensions 'variables' and the properties 'values', but as those words are so strongly associated with quantitative studies and seldom used in connection with qualitative investigations (but see Miles and Huberman 1994), we prefer the more neutral 'dimension' and 'property' – and, of course, we thereby also keep the connection to the name of the tool, property space. We thus want to emphasize that the analytical techniques we discuss are applicable independently of this methodological divide.

Later in this chapter we are going to come across two property spaces in which the dimensions are the same, but the outcomes or types are quite different (Tables 4.7 and 4.8) because their respective subject, expressed in the title, is not the same. (We have not been able to find or think of an example of property spaces in which the types are the same although the dimensions are different. Such cases should also be logically impossible.) This, again, indicates the importance of always keeping in mind the title of the property space. The title is as much a part of the property space as are dimensions, their properties and the types. It defines the empirical or theoretical field that the property space covers.

We call that part of a property space taken up by dimensions and properties its *frame* (shadowed) and the results of combining them its *matrix* (not shadowed). The frame is made up of a row dimension (X) and its properties, and a column dimension (Y) and its properties.

Of course, there can be more complex property spaces with more dimensions and more properties, but here we keep it simple to establish the terminology of property spaces we are going to use in the rest of the book. The matrix is made up of combinations of properties A and B of dimension X with properties A and B of dimension Y. The combinations of the matrix are the logical *types* that result from the frame – each type is logically distinct from the other types. There is therefore a logical relation between a property space and a typology in that the matrix makes up a typology – an 'organized system of types' (Collier et al. 2008: 152).

TABLE 4.1 Parts of a property space

| | | Dimension Y ||
		Property A	Property B
Dimension X	Property A	Type 1	Type 2
	Property B	Type 3	Type 4

Basics of property spaces   57

In Table 4.1 the combinations of the frame result in four types – 1 to 4. Each type is thereby unique:

- Type 1. A combination of property A of both dimensions
- Type 2. A combination of property A of dimension X and property B of dimension Y
- Type 3. A combination of property B of dimension X and property A of dimension Y
- Type 4. A combination of property B of both dimensions

Because of the four resulting types, this kind of property space is often called a *fourfold table* – and the fourfold table is the basic form of systematically relating concepts to each other through property spaces. This basic form can, however, be elaborated in many ways, which we will demonstrate in the following. We continue this chapter by presenting the *basics* of using property spaces as tools for creatively thinking theoretically. Then we go into techniques for handling concepts and theorizing by *reducing* the number of types in a property space (Chapter 5). The expression 'theorizing by reducing conceptual types' might seem a contradiction in terms, but in the practical use of property spaces it is not. Subsequently, we take up ways of *expanding* the number of types with the same aim: generating social theory (Chapter 6). In Chapter 9, we relate these two ways of using the tool of property spaces to each other and put them into the wider context of theorizing and writing social science.

Hidden property spaces

We mentioned earlier that many conceptual or theoretical argumentations are built on a property space, which the author does not show explicitly. Constructing the property space has been part of the conceptual development of the research process, but is not made part of reporting the results. It is therefore very practical to learn to recognize such hidden property spaces as it often helps you to understand the argumentation of a specific theory. Let us look at an example. The Australian social scientists, Richard Hall and Diane van den Broek (2012), studied the Sydney retail fashion market through a survey to store owners. They are curious about in which way this market is segmented by mapping variations in types of customers to which different stores turn. They explain how they do this:

> [W]e use the items relating to 'cost-conscious' and 'style-conscious' customers to construct three measures to represent three distinct segments within the retail fashion market. First, we define a *Boutique Style market* as constituted by stores whose customers are typically style-conscious (scoring 4 or 5 on the relevant Likert scale) but not very cost-conscious (scoring 1 to 3 on the relevant Likert scale). Second, we define a *Mass Style market* as made up of stores with customers who are both style- and cost-conscious (scoring 4 or 5 on both scales), the 'mass

market' notion implying some concern with 'value' or 'cost-consciousness'. Third we identify a *Value Fashion market* where customers are typically cost-conscious (scoring 4 or 5) but not very style-conscious (scoring 1 to 3).

(Hall and van den Broek 2012: 94)

Let us first try to sort out what is what in terms of a property space. Hall and van den Broek say that they distinguish between two types of customers, cost-conscious and style-conscious. Then they define three kinds of segment of this market, boutique style, mass style and value fashion, constituted by different combinations of types of customers. This means that the two types of customer make up the dimensions, but the authors have not explicitly told us what their properties are. Still, we know three types, namely the different kinds of market. What could the properties of the dimensions be in order to define these market types? Let us look at the definitions:

– Boutique style market: style-conscious, but not cost-conscious customers
– Mass style market: both style- and cost-conscious customers
– Value fashion market: cost-conscious, but not style-conscious customers

We can now see that the logic behind the definitions is whether a type of customer is present or not. It is not only the presence of something that is important here, but also the absence of that something. In the boutique style market, there are style-conscious customers, but not cost-conscious ones; in the value fashion market, it is the other way around; and in the mass style market, there are both style- and cost-conscious customers. The dimensions are, then, the types of customer (cost-conscious and style-conscious, respectively), which both have the properties of being present or absent, or just yes and no. Putting them together, we get the property space shown in Table 4.2.

The type of neither cost-conscious nor style-conscious customers is not mentioned in Hall and van den Broek's definitions. The reason is probably that this type is of less theoretical and empirical interest as it is not part of the market they study. In their analytical discussions it is therefore simply termed 'other'. The procedure that we describe concerning cost-conscious and style-conscious customers and their properties can be generalized: whenever you have two dimensions, you can combine them into a fourfold table by giving each one properties such as 'existing – non-existing', 'present – absent' or simply 'yes – no'.

TABLE 4.2 Segmentation of a retail fashion market

		Cost-conscious customers	
		Yes	No
Style-conscious customers	Yes	Mass style market	Boutique style market
	No	Value fashion market	Other

Basics of property spaces   59

We take a second example from Andrew Sayer (1992: 130–8), who discusses the relation between scientific explanations and predictions. He is quite critical of the positivist idea that explanations can also serve as predictions, such as expressed by Hempel and Oppenheim: 'An explanation is not fully adequate unless its explanans, if taken account of in time, could have served as a basis for predicting the phenomenon under consideration' (1948: 138). In his reasoning, he discusses non-explanatory predictions and non-predictive explanations. These formulations should put us on the track of a property space. It seems that 'explanation' and 'prediction' are two dimensions and that one of their properties is 'no' (non-explanatory and non-predictive); the other property should then be 'yes'. Putting them together, we get the property space in Table 4.3.

Sayer discusses the three types: explanatory prediction, non-explanatory prediction and non-predictive explanation. The reason that he does not explicitly mention non-predictive non-explanation is probably that it is not really part of the debate about the relation between these two dimensions – although it has its place in social science, for example, in the form of descriptions.

The fourfold table, such as those shown in Tables 4.2 and 4.3, is the crucial form of the property space. In a fourfold table, there are only two dimensions and just two properties of each, creating merely four types. Every part of this can be made much more elaborate, but the basics are the same. Constructing a property space involves giving it a title indicating its subject, formulating dimensions and their properties (its frame), which are combined in a systematic way to create a matrix which logically specifies different types (a typology). This analytical organization is the essential practical use of them in social science theory construction and development. Perhaps someone would expect a twofold table, that is a table with only two types, to be more basic than a fourfold one. We are certain that it has happened in the history of the social sciences that twofold tables have helped in theorizing. On the other hand, we only need to construct a couple of examples (Table 4.4) to see that something is *wanting* in such tables. In the first one, there are only dimensions, no properties. Apart from supporting the idea that the dimensions age, class and gender can be combined, its potential for theorizing is not really used until we put in properties of the dimensions. In the second example, only age has properties and it is easy to see that what is needed to make the table theoretically useful is adding properties of gender. Twofold tables can, at the most, be seen as steps towards fourfold or bigger tables.

TABLE 4.3 Prediction and explanation in the social sciences

		Explanation	
		Yes	No
Prediction	Yes	Explanatory prediction	Non-explanatory prediction
	No	Non-predictive explanation	Non-predictive non-explanation

Source: Danermark et al. (2003: 310, Figure 8.1).

TABLE 4.4 Two examples of twofold tables

	Class	Gender
Age		

	Age	
	Young	Old
Gender		

In the rest of this chapter, we discuss three analytically consecutive procedures as the grounds in applying property spaces to help your curiosity and theoretical thinking along. 'Analytically consecutive', because in real life social science, the procedures can appear in any order, including mixed ones. The first procedure is housekeeping of the frame, which here simply means keeping track of the dimensions and properties of your theoretical reasoning about your research objects – be it quantitative variables and their values or qualitative codes and their indicators. The second concerns what you do with the types when you have combined the dimensions and their properties. The ideal, which cannot always be reached immediately, is to put labels on the types – another word for such labels is 'terms'. The third is developing some part of an existing theory on the basis of the new terms. This is not such a modest task as it might seem, in fact that is the way a lot of new knowledge is produced in social science. Theorizing is seldom about producing an entirely new theory; it usually concerns further development of an already existing theory, including one that you have formulated yourself in your present research process – for example, in the form of displays of relations between concepts.

Housekeeping

You sit at your desk, hands on the keyboard, eyes on the screen, concentrated on your theoretical ideas – and suddenly you find yourself staring out of the window, thinking about your weekend plans. It happens to us all, and at those times it is difficult to imagine that at other times you will be indulged in ordering your thoughts systematically. In this you can, however, employ the help of property spaces – this is their first task.

We do not want to portray constructing property spaces as the only – or even necessarily the best – way of handling theoretical ideas. It is, however, a powerful way of doing it logically and systematically – as Bailey says:

> [A] well-constructed typology can be very effective in bringing order out of chaos. It can transform the complexity of apparently eclectic congeries of diverse cases into well-ordered sets of a few important dimensions. A sound

typology forms a solid foundation for both theorizing and empirical research. Perhaps no other tool has such power to simplify life for the social scientist.

(Bailey 1994: 33)

Or just, 'the fourfold table with types as entries in the cells is a standard tool of sociological theorizing' (Stinchcombe 1968: 46). Mills elaborates a bit more:

> Good types require that the criteria of classification be explicit and systematic. To make them so you must develop the habit of cross-classification. The technique of cross-classifying is not of course limited to quantitative materials; as a matter of fact it is the best way to imagine and to get hold of *new* types as well as to criticize and clarify old ones. Charts, tables, and diagrams of a qualitative sort are not only ways to display work already done; they are very often genuine tools of production. They clarify the 'dimensions' of the types, which they also help you to imagine and build. As a matter of fact, in the past fifteen years, I do not believe I have written more than a dozen pages first-draft without some little cross-classification – although, of course, I do not always or even usually display such diagrams. Most of them flop, in which case you have still learned something. When they work, they help you think more clearly and write more explicitly.
>
> *(Mills 1977 [1959]: 21)*

Finally, in a somewhat more ironic vein, Rueschmeyer says:

> When we explore a new set of issues, it is often useful to have devices for ordering ideas. Resorting to a simple two-by-two classification of conditions or outcomes is so common that some wits have claimed that social scientists respond to any serious problem by making the sign of the cross.
>
> *(Rueschmeyer 2009: 296)*

In logic, there are two demands that a classification has to live up to and if it does not it is regarded as fuzzy, which is a big sin in ordinary logics. First, it has to be *exhaustive*. This means that everything that is to be classified must be part of one class or another. Nothing is to be left out. (In the following examples, we elaborate on Lazarsfeld and Barton 1965 [1951]: 158–9.) Let us say that we want to make a typology of sources of influence on people's decisions on which political party to vote for. We construct this typology: 'family', 'friends', 'fellow workers' and 'neighbours'. Have we missed any possible sources? One rather obvious source is politicians themselves and another what we hear perfect strangers talking about. It is a classification that cannot live up to the demand for exhaustiveness. Second, the classification has to be *mutually excluding*. Nothing is to be included in more than one class or type. There are two ways in which the researcher can break this rule. One is to mix levels of analysis. An example is a typology of sources of information containing 'Internet', 'Facebook', 'newspapers' and 'television'. Obviously, Facebook is a subclass of the Internet and therefore does not belong to this typology. Either we have to stick to Internet as a category and exclude Facebook, or create subcategories of Internet, such as Facebook, Twitter, Wikipedia and so on. The other mistake is to mix different aspects of what is to be classified in the same classification. Consider this typology of output from a radio station: 'musical programmes', 'dramatic programmes', 'children's programmes' and 'recorded programmes'. Children's programmes can be musical as well as dramatic and they can be recorded or sent live. Musical programmes can also be recorded in advance or sent live. And so on. Here it is necessary to sort out all dimensions that are involved and build the classification on this complete set of aspects. Property spaces help us to live up to the rules of exhaustiveness and mutual exclusion. In ordinary – or Aristotelian – logic fuzziness is not acceptable, but generating and developing social theory has more aspects to it than this kind of logic. There is even a fully worked-out methodology of 'fuzzy sets' by Charles C. Ragin, in which he makes a point of analyses in which there are degrees of being a member or not being a member of a type. Still, property spaces are helpful as parts of this method too (Ragin 2000: Ch. 3; for further examples, see Basurto and Speer 2012; Greckhamer et al. 2008).

Let us start this section about housekeeping of concepts with the help of property spaces with an example. Imagine that we are studying attitudes to work, whereby we have found that there are two different kinds of attitudes: (i) instrumental, which means that the only reason to work is the pay it provides; (ii) committed, meaning that there are reasons in work itself to work. Further, we have found that there are a number of mechanisms that influence whether employees harbour an instrumental or committed attitude to their work: whether the employee is young or old (age), blue or white collar worker (position), man or woman (gender) and has a good or bad work environment. In the terms of quantitative studies, they are all independent variables and the attitude to work is dependent (Eriksson et al. 2011). If we want to use property spaces to keep track of these variables or codes, we can build a series of fourfold tables (Table 4.5).

Each relation between dimensions is here constructed as a property space of its own. But mechanisms can combine to strengthen a certain empirical result or they can counteract each other and thereby produce a quite different result. We therefore might be curious about such combinations of mechanisms. For example, we could be interested in the way in which age and position is related to each other in producing attitudes to work. As we see in Table 4.6, this results in a somewhat more complicated property space than a fourfold table.

One of the mechanisms has to appear twice in the property space depicted in Table 4.6. It does not matter which one, and here we arbitrarily choose 'position'. Under the property 'young' of the dimension 'age', we put the dimension 'position' with its two properties 'blue collar' and 'white collar'; this is repeated under the other property 'old' of 'age'. As two mechanisms are now combined, the result is not a fourfold, but an eightfold table. We could have placed the dimensions in a different order, but still the same eight types would be the result.

In the way depicted in the table, we can systematically explore the types of all combinations of two dimensions: age and gender, age and work environment, gender

Basics of property spaces 63

TABLE 4.5 Mechanisms behind attitudes to work

| | | Age ||
		Young	Old
Attitude to work	Instrumental		
	Committed		

| | | Position ||
		Blue collar	White collar
Attitude to work	Instrumental		
	Committed		

| | | Gender ||
		Woman	Man
Attitude to work	Instrumental		
	Committed		

TABLE 4.6 Attitudes to work, age and position

		Age			
		Young		Old	
		Position		Position	
		Blue collar	White collar	Blue collar	White collar
Attitude to work	Instrumental				
	Committed				

and position, gender and work environment and so on. It is also possible to add another dimension and thereby combine three mechanisms. The layout can, however, easily become too complex for comfort – or, rather, clarity. If you still want to do that, there are ways of technically simplifying the property space to make it more readable. If we, for example, add gender to our former dimensions, we can construct the property space in the way shown in Table 4.7. What we have done here is exclude the titles of the dimensions, only keeping the properties in order to make the property spaces easier to read. But all sixteen logically possible types are represented in a clear way in the property space – and that is what is important when you want to keep track of dimensions, properties and types of combining them.

Now, if we compare Tables 4.5 and 4.7, we can notice a certain likeness in that both tables are constructed by separate property spaces. Each table is made up of a number of smaller tables. In the case of Table 4.5, we found that the separate tables could be put together in a single property space, shown in Table 4.6. Is this possible also for the separate property spaces in Table 4.7? The answer can be found in

64 Tools for theorizing in social science

TABLE 4.7 Attitudes to work, age, position and gender 1

	Young	
	Blue collar	
	Woman	Man
Instrumental		
Committed		

	Young	
	White collar	
	Woman	Man

	Old	
	Blue collar	
	Woman	Man
Instrumental		
Committed		

	Old	
	White collar	
	Woman	Man

TABLE 4.8 Attitudes to work, age, position and gender 2

	Young				Old			
	Blue collar		White collar		Blue collar		White collar	
	Woman	Man	Woman	Man	Woman	Man	Woman	Man
Instrumental								
Committed								

Table 4.8. In a parallel fashion with Table 4.6, Table 4.8 is a single property space. In this case, it combines three dimensions (age, position and gender, although they are not explicitly named), with two properties of each, resulting in sixteen types.

In this way, property spaces can be used as a tool in the housekeeping of research. It is necessary when building social theory to keep track of concepts in the form of dimensions and their properties, as well as ways of combining them. Next, we discuss what to do with these outcomes of the combinations.

Labelling the types: terms

In the matrix, each type – each cell or outcome – of the property space receives a specific content by representing a unique combination of properties of different dimensions. Thereby you have generated a *concept*, a building block of social theory. If you think through the *meaning* of the content of each type, you might come up with a word – a *term* – that expresses this meaning of the concept. This is not always an easy thing to do:

> Discovering a new phenomenon constitutes one of the most important tasks in social science, and finding the right word(s) to describe it, and in this way really capture it, often represents a frustrating task. But if this is not done, the

phenomenon can slip between one's fingers. It can similarly be hard to find a new name that fits the new phenomenon and provides it with a distinct identity.

(Swedberg 2012: 20)

The term should, then, capture the meaning of the concept. Although sometimes difficult, the rewards are great: 'Employing vivid names for the types enhances scholarly communication. More fundamentally, careful work with cell types pushes the researcher towards better conceptualization' (Collier et al. 2008: 167).

There are several sources that can be used for finding a term that expresses the 'distinct identity' of a concept in the property space. An obvious starting point is the words already used in the frame to formulate the properties of the dimensions (which we saw in Table 4.3 and which we will meet again in Table 4.13). Another is words that you find in the everyday language of people that are involved in the social processes that are the subject of your property space. In the tradition of Grounded Theory such words are called 'in vivo codes' (Glaser and Strauss 1967). A self-evident source is existing social theory, in which you may find that the same concept has already been given a term or that there are terms that you can modify or change in other ways (Collier et al. 2008: 159–60). Another important resource is fiction and poetry – often authors of novels and poems express concepts in extremely apt terms that you can borrow (Layder 1998: 106). The important thing is that there is no reason to censure any source of terms – anything goes as long as the term 'fits' and provides the phenomenon with a 'distinct identity'.

We start our discussion of labelling types with an illustration that we met in Chapter 1 when we discussed good examples of theorizing, namely Wright's analysis of social classes. It all started with a quantitative study of income inequality in which some of the researchers' data were organized in two variables, '(1) whether the individual was self-employed; and (2) whether the individual supervised the labour of others' (Wright 1985: 44). The variables can be regarded as dimensions in a property space:

X: Supervise the labour of others
Y: Self-employed

For each dimension, two properties can be formulated:

(A) The dimension is present
(B) The dimension is absent

Putting the presence or absence of the individual supervising the labour of others and being self-employed in relation to each other, the property space found in Table 4.9 can be constructed.

It is difficult to know in advance whether the content of the types of a property space is *fruitful* for classificatory or other theory generating purposes. One strong indicator is, however, whether you can find captivating, meaningful terms for them. In Wright's case, three of the outcomes fell nicely into the usual class categories (Table 4.10).

66 Tools for theorizing in social science

TABLE 4.9 Dimensions in Wright's initial typology of class structure in the development of the concept of contradictory class locations

		Self-employed	
		Yes	No
Supervise the labour of others	Yes		
	No		

Source: Wright (1985: 44).

TABLE 4.10 Wright's initial typology of class structure in the development of the concept of contradictory class relations

		Self-employed	
		Yes	No
Supervise the labour of others	Yes	Capitalists	Managers
	No	Petty bourgeoisie	Workers

Source: Wright (1985: 44, Table 2.1).

The self-employed individuals who supervise others (upper left hand cell) are capitalists, while those who are not self-employed and do not supervise others (lower right) are workers. Equally unproblematic form the point of view of traditional class analysis are those who are self-employed without supervising the labour of others (lower left) – they belong to the petty bourgeoisie. But what about those who are not self-employed but supervise others (upper right)? They are managers, but where are they to be placed in the class locations? It was this outcome of the typology that was first regarded as an 'ambiguous class character' but was later to become the 'contradictory class character' that triggered Wright's whole theorizing of new class schemes.

We continue discussing how to theorize in social science through the use of property spaces by presenting an example where the preconditions are a bit more complicated than in the former case (building on Jonsson 2007). Let us say that you are studying flexibility in working life. One of your findings after interviewing senior managers and ordinary employees is this:

– Both the work organization (represented by senior managers) and the workers want flexibility.
– Both the work organization and the workers want stability.

Among the theoretical codes which you can play about with are, then, *flexibility*, *stability* and *wanting* something. Further, there is a code which we have not mentioned yet, namely:

– *Variability*, which means that something changes or it does not.

TABLE 4.11 Wanted and not wanted change and no change

	Wanted	Not wanted
Change		
No change		

TABLE 4.12 Interrelations among the concepts of flexibility, stability, instability and inflexibility

	Wanted	Not wanted
Change	Flexibility	Instability
No change	Stability	Inflexibility

Source: Modified from Jonsson (2007: 34, Tables 3.1 and 3.2).

Flexibility and stability seem to somehow be connected to variability, the presence or absence of change. It is also already clear that both flexibility and stability are wanted by the organization as well as the workers. A reasonable question to ask is whether flexibility and stability can be types in a property space constituted by the dimensions 'variability' and 'wanted'. Two dimensions can always be combined by assigning the properties 'present' and 'not present', resulting in 'wanted' and 'not wanted' and 'change' and 'no change' as in Table 4.11.

To test the fruitfulness of this fourfold table, you seek types which you can label 'flexibility' and 'stability', respectively. Are there such types? Yes, there are (Table 4.12). The combination in the top left-hand cell of the matrix, meaning that something is wanted and that that something is changing indicates a situation of flexibility. The type in the bottom left-hand cell, in which no change is wanted and no change is at hand, clearly indicates stability. So far, so good. You have now constructed a property space with dimensions that came from the analysis of your interviews. The same goes for the two types you have now termed flexibility and stability. That leaves two empty cells, the ones to the right. Led by the terms you now have and their meanings, you soon find a suggestion: change that someone does *not* want can be termed 'instability', and the double negation of no change that is not wanted means 'inflexibility'.

The terminology you have generated to analyse questions about flexibility in working life looks, according to the property space you have just constructed, like this:

– Flexibility is wanted change
– Stability is wanted non-change
– Instability is unwanted change
– Inflexibility is unwanted non-change

Perhaps you can later find a more positively formulated term for 'non-change' that allows you to get away from the clumsy expressions it easily leads to. The most important thing is, though, that the whole exercise resulted in the evaluation that you most likely have constructed a theoretically fruitful property space as you have been able to formulate meaningful terms for the types.

In constructing the property space depicted in Table 4.12, a new principle for theorizing is illustrated. Earlier, we combined dimensions and their properties – the frame – to systematically produce types in the matrix. Now, though, we have gone the other way around. We took our point of departure in certain types (flexibility and stability) seeking dimensions of the frame, finding variability and wanting something. Thereafter, we constructed the frame, which resulted in two new types, instability and inflexibility. It is, then, important to notice that it is not only possible to go from frame to matrix, but also from matrix to frame (and in both cases back again) when theorizing.

When you relate this typology to work organizations and employees, it perhaps shows its fruitfulness again by functioning as a tool for formulating new suggestions. For example, these hypotheses (Jonsson 2007; Karlsson 2007):

H_1: Flexibility for the work organization means instability for the employees
H_2: Flexibility for the employees means instability for the work organization
H_3: Stability for the work organization means inflexibility for the employees
H_4: Stability for the employees means inflexibility for the work organization

Into the field again! New interviews, new observations, new data. Perhaps new displays and property spaces.

Developing existing terminology

The two basic ways of using property spaces as tools when theorizing what we have discussed so far are housekeeping and allotting terms to types and frames. The third way is to develop an existing terminology, whether it is your own or somebody else's. You take a set of concepts from your evolving theory or from the literature as your point of departure. Then you start playing about with the concepts to see if they can be constructed in the form of one or more property spaces. If that is possible, a logical gap is sometimes revealed – a gap that you can try to fill in by supplementing the terminology. You can, in other words, generate new concepts.

Our first example comes from an enormously influential study, Albert O. Hirschman's (1970) *Exit, Voice, and Loyalty*. The theory is a bit more complicated than we take into account now, but that is just to make some points. According to Hirschman, there are two possible ways of action for discontented employees: they can exit the organization or voice their displeasure. In the first case, they simply quit in order to seek better employment; in the second case, they stay and try to correct what is wrong at the workplace. Can you develop this dichotomy into a property space? You can try these steps, which probably

TABLE 4.13 Exit and voice

		Voice	
		Yes (protest)	No (silence)
Exit	Yes (leaving)	Protesting and leaving	Silently leaving
	No (staying)	Protesting and staying	Silently staying

are well-known by now (for a somewhat different solution, see Collier et al. 2008: 157):

- Regard the concepts of the dichotomy as dimensions, which can be, or not be, present: Exit: yes – no; voice: yes – no
- Construct a property space (Table 4.13)

First, you give the properties alternative names in order to make the terms a bit livelier. Exiting becomes 'leaving' and not exiting becomes 'staying'; giving voice becomes 'protest' and not giving voice becomes 'silence'. It turns out that the property space you have constructed could be a fruitful one. It is interesting for most social scientists to fill in gaps, but we must be aware that not all gaps are interesting to fill in: 'To my knowledge, no one has studied leaders' sock preferences, but it isn't clear why anyone should' (Pratt 2009: 858). This one seems to be interesting, though, as you have found four distinct types, and you have been able to attach terms to them: 'protesting and leaving', 'silently leaving', 'protesting and staying' and 'silently staying'. The next step is, of course, to go back to your data and perhaps even back into the field to search for empirical instances of each type.

Our second example is a bit more complicated in a way – and in another way it is not. It is more complicated in that there are three concepts at the outset, which makes impossible our usual strategy of creating two dimensions and attaching properties to them, thereby constructing a fourfold table. It is less complicated in that there are clues in the theory itself for labelling the type that makes up a gap. Further, in the same way as when discussing Hirschman's theory, we simplify by leaving out some aspects. The theory is presented by Alvin Gouldner (1954) in the classic book *Patterns of Industrial Bureaucracy*. (We take the example from Edwards and Wajcman 2005: 101–2.) Gouldner found three types of rules in operation at the workplace he studied:

- Representative rules, which are accepted by both management and workers; examples are rules regarding safety.
- Punishment-centred rules, such as when management sanctions employee absenteeism.
- Mock rules, which nobody really bothers about; an example is a no smoking-rule that – at that time – was totally neglected by both management and workers.

70 Tools for theorizing in social science

The classification is built on a threefold logic that we will meet in a later example of expansion of a property space through adding properties on a dimension. This logic makes distinctions between 'full, some or none', in Gouldner's version 'both, one, or neither'. He applies this logic to the question of which party – management or workers – values a certain rule: (i) rules valued by both parties (representative); (ii) rules valued by one party (punishment-centred); and (iii) rules that no party values (mock). Can it be developed into a property space? Let us try to find two dimensions that we can start with according to our former strategy. One suggestion is to pick up on valuing – to 'value' could be regarded as a dimension with the properties 'high' and 'low'. Another candidate is, of course, the parties involved – 'management' and 'workers'. That would result in the property space found in Table 4.14.

We find places for all types of rules, but this exercise has not brought the theory forward. In fact, it seems to have made it more imprecise, as this property space does not discriminate between all the terms: the types are not mutually excluding, as both representative and mock rules can be found in more than one type. Further, it is not exhaustive, as one type contains both representative and punishment-centred rules. Table 4.14 turns out to be a property space for the waste-paper basket. We must try another way than making 'management' and 'workers' properties of the dimension 'parties', and 'high' and 'low' properties of a dimension that only concerns 'values'. We have to play about some more with the concepts of Gouldner's theory. An alternative way is to construct two other dimensions, namely 'value to workers' and 'value to management' with the properties 'high' and 'low' on both (Table 4.15).

This is more promising and we can even regard the results in Table 4.14 as a *productive mistake* on the way to constructing Table 4.15. We can now easily find

TABLE 4.14 Parties and value of rules

		Value	
		High	*Low*
Parties	Management	Representative Punishment-centred	Mock
	Workers	Representative	Mock

TABLE 4.15 Types of workplace rules 1

		Value of rules to management	
		High	*Low*
Value of rules to workers	High	Representative	
	Low	Punishment-centred	Mock

Source: Modified from Edwards and Wajcman (2005: 101, Table 5.1).

TABLE 4.16 Types of workplace rules 2

		Value of rules to management	
		High	Low
Value of rules to workers	High	Representative	Indulgency pattern
	Low	Punishment-centred	Mock

Source: Edwards and Wajcman (2005: 101, Table 5.1).

types suitable for all three types of rule, fitting in with Gouldner's threefold logic: representative rules are highly valued by both workers and management, punishment-centred rules are valued highly by management and low by workers and mock rules are given a low valuation by both parties. This property space also uncovers a gap in the theory, located in the top right-hand cell. What could the combination of low value to management and high value to workers mean? The answer can, in fact, be found in another part of Gouldner's theory, in which he analyses what he calls an 'indulgency pattern'. This is a pattern in which workers have collectively developed rules for their own conduct, which they value highly – rules that management tolerates or has to tolerate. Gouldner gives an example:

> [W]orkers defined their role as incurring 'technical' obligations. Since they conceived of themselves as being in the plant, as one remarked, 'to do a job', fewer tensions arose about their production responsibilities. Their obligations to 'superiors' were, however, thought of as auxiliary, as legitimate only insofar as necessary to do a particular job.
>
> *(Gouldner 1954: 48)*

If we regard the indulgency pattern as a type of highly valued rules by workers and lowly valued by management, the property space is complete (Table 4.16).

With these experiments with different dimensions and properties, we have identified a gap in an influential theory and succeeded in filling it by playing about with different property spaces.

Summary

Compared to displays, property spaces have a more bound form in that they logically and systematically depict conceptual relations. In this first chapter on property spaces as tools for theorizing, we have presented the basics of how to construct them and three ways of using them. In the first case, we take our point of departure in what is undoubtedly the most used form of property spaces, the fourfold table. The title of the table is important as it stakes out the field – be it empirical, theoretical or both – that is covered by the property space. The table itself is made up of two parts, the frame and the matrix. In the frame, we find the dimensions involved and the properties belonging to each dimension. The matrix consists of the outcomes or cells of the combination of the properties of the dimensions – they are the types of the typology.

One basic reason for constructing property spaces when you work with social theory is housekeeping of the ideas and concepts you are playing about with. It makes your life easier. We showed a number of ways in which the frame can be built up in order to make the matrix perform the task of ordering your concepts and check that the typology lives up to the demands of being exhaustive and mutually excluding. The second basic reason is to get input to a terminology. When you consider the meaning of each outcome, each type in the matrix, you can find inspiration in words capturing this meaning. Each type is a concept, but you need terms for them to make it easier to think and communicate about them. Finally, property spaces can be used as tools in developing existing social theory. This can be theories found in the literature, but it can also be concepts or a preliminary theory you have generated at the present stage of your research process. You try out different ways of combining the concepts in frames and matrices, seeking new theoretical possibilities. Almost certainly, many of the property spaces resulting from those experiments will end up in the wastepaper basket, but some of them will lead you to new insights in your theorizing.

Now we know how to construct the basic form of property spaces and how to use them as tools for the housekeeping of concepts, labelling the types with terms and elaborating existing theory. We are thereby equipped to go on to the first kind of operation through which property spaces are further helpful in theorizing – reduction of their content.

References

Bailey, Kenneth D. (1994) *Typologies and Taxonomies. An Introduction to Classification Techniques*. London: Sage.

Basurto, Xavier and Johanna Speer (2012) 'Structuring Calibration of Qualitative Data as Sets for Qualitative Comparative Analysis (QCA)', *Field Methods*, 24(2): 155–74.

Collier, David, Jody LaPorte and Jason Seawright (2008) 'Typologies: Forming Concepts and Creating Categorical Variables', pp. 152–73 in Janet M. Box-Steffensmeier, Henry E. Brady and David Collier (eds), *The Oxford Handbook of Political Methodology*. Oxford: Oxford University Press.

Danermark, Berth, Mats Ekström, Liselotte Jakobsen and Jan Ch. Karlsson (2003) *Att förklara samhället*. Lund: Studentlitteratur.

Edwards, Paul and Judy Wajcman (2005) *The Politics of Working Life*. Oxford: Oxford University Press.

Eriksson, Birgitta, Jan Ch. Karlsson and Tuula Bergqvist (2011) 'The Development of Attitudes to Work in Sweden', pp. 126–38 in Bengt Furåker, Kristina Håkansson and Jan Ch. Karlsson (eds), *Commitment to Work and Job Satisfaction. Studies of Work Orientations*. London: Routledge.

Glaser, Barney G. and Anselm Strauss (1967) *Discovery of Grounded Theory*. Chicago: Aldine.

Gouldner, Alvin W. (1954) *Patterns of Industrial Bureaucracy*. New York: Free Press.

Greckhamer, Thomas, Vilmos F. Misangyi, Heather Elms and Rodney Lacey (2008) 'Using Qualitative Comparative Analysis in Strategic Management Research', *Organizational Research Methods*, 11(4): 695–726.

Hall, Richard and Diane van den Broek (2012) 'Aestheticising Retail Workers: Orientations of Aesthetic Labour in Australian Fashion Retail', *Economic and Industrial Democracy*, 33(1): 85–102.
Hempel, Carl G. and Paul Oppenheim (1948) 'The Logic of Explanation', *Philosophy of Science*, 15(2): 135–75.
Hirschman, Albert O. (1970) *Exit, Voice, and Loyalty. Responses to Decline in Firms, Organizations, and States*. Cambridge: Harvard University Press.
Jonsson, Dan (2007) 'Flexibility, Stability and Related Concepts', pp. 30–41 in Bengt Furåker, Kristina Håkansson and Jan Ch. Karlsson (eds), *Flexibility and Stability in Working Life*. Basingstoke: Palgrave Macmillan.
Karlsson, Jan Ch. (2007) 'For Whom Is Flexibility Good and Bad? An Overview', pp. 18–29 in Bengt Furåker, Kristina Håkansson and Jan Ch. Karlsson (eds), *Flexibility and Stability in Working Life*. Basingstoke: Palgrave Macmillan.
Layder, Derek (1998) *Sociological Practice. Linking Theory and Social Research*. London: Sage.
Lazarsfeld, Paul F. and Allen H. Barton (1965 [1951]) 'Qualitative Measurement in the Social Sciences: Classification, Typologies, and Indices', pp. 155–92 in Daniel Learner and Harold D. Lasswell (eds), *The Policy Sciences*. Stanford: Stanford University Press.
Miles, Matthew B. and A. Michael Huberman (1994) *Qualitative Data Analysis*. Thousand Oaks: Sage.
Mills, C. Wright (1977 [1959]) *The Sociological Imagination*. Oxford: Oxford University Press.
Pratt, Michael G. (2009) 'For the Lack of a Boilerplate: Tips on Writing up (and Reviewing) Qualitative Research', *Academy of Management Journal*, 52(5): 856–62.
Ragin, Charles C. (2000) *Fuzzy-Set Social Science*. Chicago: Chicago University Press.
Rueschmeyer, Dietrich (2009) *Usable Theory. Analytical Tools for Social and Political Research*. Princeton: Princeton University Press.
Sayer, Andrew (1992) *Method in Social Science. A Realist Approach*. London: Routledge.
Stinchcombe, Arthur (1968) *Constructing Social Theories*. Chicago: University of Chicago Press.
Swedberg, Richard (2012) 'Theorizing in Sociology and Social Science: Turning to the Context of Discovery', *Theory and Society*, 41(1): 1–40.
Wright, Erik Olin (1985) *Classes*. London: Verso.

5
REDUCTION OF PROPERTY SPACES IN THEORIZING

In the former chapter, we were interested in how to construct property spaces. Now we will look at ways of refining them when you have them in front of you, when they are already constructed. Property spaces are helpful tools for theorizing – not just when you combine dimensions and their properties in building them or seeking a frame from types. There are many further uses of them for theoretical purposes. These uses can be classified in two types: reduction and expansion of a property space, respectively. In this chapter, we take up reduction, in the next, expansion. In both cases there are theoretical costs involved in the operations and we discuss these risks in each case.

When reducing a property space, you merge two or more types into one single type. We have already seen that a property space can easily become very complex, which makes reduction necessary if it is to continue to function as a tool for theorizing – you want to 'reduce complexity or achieve parsimony' (Bailey 1994: 12). You simply need to get down to a manageable number of types. This reduction cannot, of course, be made in an arbitrary or capricious way; some degree of systematics has to be involved. In this chapter, we discuss a number of fairly organized, although partly overlapping, ways of reducing property spaces. One is to decrease the number of dimensions or properties (rescaling) and another is to create an index and then merge all types with the same value (indexing). Further, you can cut out types that are logically contradictory (logic reduction), those that are empirically empty (empirical reduction) or outside the theoretical area in which you are working (theoretical reduction). Finally, you can disregard those types that you find uninteresting for answering your research questions (pragmatic reduction). We will discuss all these ways of reducing property spaces, as well as the risks each of them involves when it comes to theorizing. In practice, they can, of course, intersect, but we think it is clarifying to present them in this 'pure' form.

Rescaling

When you diminish the number of dimensions of a property space or curtail their properties, you rescale it. Let us go straight into an example that is linked up with one you know from the former chapter: attitudes to work. More precisely, you are studying people's commitment to their work. So far, your results indicate that the degree of commitment varies with two dimensions: age, simply divided into young and old, and position on the labour market, such as blue collar worker, white collar worker and small firm owner. Further, you classify commitment in three degrees of intensity. The point of departure is, then, these dimensions and properties:

– Commitment to work: high, middle, low
– Position on the labour market: blue collar worker, white collar worker, small business owner

You construct a property space, and as there are two dimensions with three properties on each in the frame, there will be nine types in the matrix (Table 5.1).

What interests you most theoretically are, however, two things. One is to compare people with high commitment to work with those with lower commitment; the other is to contrast employees, whether blue or white collar workers, with small business owners. Therefore, you merge the properties 'Blue collar worker' and 'White collar worker' on the dimension 'Position on the labour market' to the single property 'Employee'; thereby, you create a dichotomy, where the other property is 'Small business owner'. Likewise, you merge the properties 'Middle' and 'Low' on the dimension 'Commitment to work' to the property 'Low', which means that you are left with a dichotomy on the dimension 'Commitment to work' as well: 'High' and 'Low' (Table 5.2).

Through this reduction of the property space in Table 5.1 to a fourfold table, you can, first, differentiate those whose commitment to work is high from those with a lower degree of dedication, and second, employees from small business owners. In this example, the dimensions 'Commitment to work' and 'Position on the labour market' are left intact; what you reduce is the number of properties on both dimensions. A property space can also be reduced by merging dimensions, of which

TABLE 5.1 Commitment to work and position on the labour market

		Position on the labour market		
		Blue collar worker	White collar worker	Small business owner
Commitment to work	High			
	Middle			
	Low			

TABLE 5.2 High and low commitment to work, and employee and small business owner

| | | Position on the labour market ||
		Employee	Small business owner
Commitment to work	High		
	Low		

we will encounter an example in the next chapter (see the relation between Tables 6.5 and 6.6).

We must, however, be aware of a risk that is associated with this type of operation. Some of the types of the property space become 'more inclusive', Elman (2005: 302) points out, 'hence potentially grouping cases which may not fit together'. In the worst case, this might lead to bad or 'chaotic' abstractions and conceptions rather than good and rational ones (Sayer 1992):

> A rational abstraction is one which isolates a significant element of the world which has some unity and autonomous force, such as a structure. A bad abstraction arbitrarily divides the indivisible and/or lumps together the unrelated and the inessential, thereby 'carving up' the object of study with little or no regard for its structure and form.
>
> *(Sayer 1992: 138)*

In the case of Tables 5.1 and 5.2 we have, however, good theoretical reasons to make the reduction in this way (Karlsson 2004). Both blue and white collar workers belong to the same work form, namely wage labour; both are employed by someone else. Small business owners, on the other hand, are not employed by anyone at all – they are self-employed.

Indexing

A quite different way of reducing the types of a property space is through constructing an index. This is – in contrast to the other techniques – a quantitative type of reduction. Barton describes it by saying that one can 'give each category [in our terms, property] on each dimension a certain weight, and add these together to get index scores for each cell' (1965: 46). You assign a numerical value to each property and calculate a simple additive index for each type, after which all types with the same index score can be merged. Let us look at an example.

You are curious about the quality of text and melody of songs. You regard both as dimensions with the properties good, middle and bad. Further, you give the properties different numerical values, for example like this:

- Good = 2
- Middle = 1
- Bad = 0

The first step is to put those values into the property space. The next step is to calculate the index by adding the weights in each type, represented by the numbers in the cells. The result can be found in Table 5.3. You can now compare the cells with each other, looking for types that have received the same indexed value. Two types have a value that no other cell has: top left-hand and bottom right-hand. All other types share their value with at least one other cell, shown by shadowing. In this way, you reduce the nine types to five, namely the indexed values 4, 3, 2, 1 and 0.

The risk involved in indexing as a form of reduction of property spaces is that the quantitative values can hide important qualitative differences between types. For example, the value 3 can be a result of 2+1 and of 1+2; 2 of 2+0, 1+1 and 0+2; and 1 of 1+0 and 0+1; all these combinations are not the same in qualitative terms. Reduction through indices is therefore a very gross measure and the risk of chaotic concepts is great:

> Indexing presents more complex difficulties than its seeming simplicity would suggest. What is the appropriate weight for the high-mid-low rank on each attribute? Do low ranks offset high ranks on other attributes? Are all the attributes equal, or should some be weighed more heavily? Perhaps most importantly, indexing presupposes that equal scores are equivalent. . . . Indexing is an admittedly blunt and arbitrary tool, and the results necessarily rest on a host of predicate choices and assumptions.
>
> *(Elman 2005: 305)*

Conversely, these are risks when using indexing as a quantitative measure, but it can give input to qualitatively forming new concepts which can be further tested.

Indexing must be distinguished from adding other types of numerical values of the cells of a property space. An example can be found in Table 5.4 concerning how often per week people in different income classes in USA visit casinos. The researchers have grouped together some cells according to their theoretical interests. Those that concern them most are the extremely frequent casino visitors (groups 5, 6 and 7), which can be found in the extreme right-hand column. We will not go into the study itself, only note two things: (i) this is a different way of handling numerical values in a property space from indexing; and (ii) types can be clustered according to your theoretical concerns.

TABLE 5.3 Numerical values and indices of text and melody of songs

		Melody		
		Good (2)	*Middle (1)*	*Bad (0)*
Text	Good (2)	4	3	2
	Middle (1)	3	2	1
	Bad (0)	2	1	0

78 Tools for theorizing in social science

TABLE 5.4 Casino visits per week and income classes

Casino visits / income	0 times	1–4 times	5–7 times	8–12 times	12–24 times	25+ times
Extremely low	Group 1 15.4%					Group 5 0.2%
Low		Group 2 44.7%		Group 4 32.2%		Group 6 0.9%
Moderate						
High						
Very high						
Extremely high	Group 3 6.5%					Group 7 0.1%

Source: Perfetto and Woodside (2009: 302, Figure 1).

Logic reduction

Property spaces are systematic and logical devices, but that does not mean that all types of all property spaces are logically consistent. Sometimes, we may find that there is 'a connection between two or more of the typology's dimensions such that some combinations are logically impossible or highly improbable' (Elman 2005: 305). In those cases, we can reduce the property space by simply disregarding those types.

When analysing different forms of work through history, two of the most important theoretical concepts are 'means of production' and 'labour power'. By means of production, it is usually meant the things a worker uses when producing something, for example, tools, machines and work material. Labour power is people's capacity to work – or with a classic definition, 'the aggregate of those mental and physical capabilities existing in a human being, which he exercises whenever he produces a use-value of any description' (Marx 1998: 242). The analytical question has often concerned who controls the means of production and the worker's or the immediate producer's labour power – the workers themselves or someone else. Towards this background you can differentiate between two dimensions:

– Whether the immediate producers control the means of production they use
– Whether the immediate producers control their own labour power

You give both dimensions the properties 'yes' and 'no', whereby you can create the property space in Table 5.5. This is a simplified version of a more intricate discussion we will take up in the next chapter in connection with Tables 6.3 and 6.4, which starts with the same table (then called 6.3).

If the immediate producers control both the means of production and their labour power, for example, when, where, how and with what they are going to work, they are independent producers. In our type of society, they are often called small business owners or self-employed. When the immediate producers still control their labour

TABLE 5.5 The immediate producers and control of means of production and labour power

		The immediate producers control the means of production they use	
		Yes	No
The immediate producers control their own labour power	Yes	Independent producer	Wage labourer
	No	—	Slave

power, but not the means of production, they are wage labourers (or with another term, employees). They are free to offer their labour power on the labour market to anyone who can pay for it, but the things they use in work belong to the employer. If the immediate producers have no control of neither the means of production nor their own labour power, they are slaves. Instead of a labour market where labour power is the commodity, there is a slave market where human beings themselves are bought and sold in order to get at their labour power.

One type remains and it is marked with a dash to indicate that it is logically contradictory. A precondition for the immediate producers to control the means of production is that they also control their own labour power. If they cannot decide when, where and how they are going to work or who they are to work for, they cannot control the means of production – that is a logical impossibility. It is worth noting that this is not an autonomous logic independent of context; on the contrary, it is dependent on the underlying theory we are connecting to in the property space that includes specific meanings of the concepts it builds on in the frame. Further, it is of importance not to leave this type out of your argumentation. Absences can be as significant as presences when it comes to theorizing. We will soon come to a specific theoretical conclusion of this absence.

Logic reduction involves less risk than the other types of reduction we discuss – something that Elman (2005: 320) also points out. The reason is that it is so strongly tied to the underlying or developing theory that is involved. Therefore, perhaps the greatest risk is that logical inconsistencies tend to confirm the theory, hampering your creativity in developing it further.

Empirical reduction

A property space can be reduced according to logical criteria, but also with reference to empirical patterns. One way of doing that is to disregard some types because there are empirical reasons to assume that they are empty. But another way is to elaborate on the empirically missing types in order to see if they have anything in common. In this way, absences can provide bases for theorizing.

Starting with the first way of empirical reduction, our example comes from Amitai Etzioni's (1975) influential theory about the nature of different types of organizations. He makes a distinction between two levels of members of an organization, the representatives who are higher in rank in the internal hierarchy, and the lower participants who, of course, are inferior in rank. He then differentiates between three types of power that the representatives can exercise (1975: 4–8), and three kinds of involvement in the organization among the lower participants (1975: 8–11).

The first type of power is *coercive*; it means that the lower participants are, or are threatened to be, physically punished in some way, for example denied satisfaction of needs such as food or sex, locked up, tortured or killed. The second type is *remunerative*: control of material resources leads to the distribution of rewards such as salaries and wages, services and commodities. The last one is *normative* power – this involves access to symbolic rewards, including social esteem and prestige. Further, there are, according to Etzioni, three ways in which the lower participants can orient themselves in relation to the organization. These types of involvement are: *alienation*, which means an intensely negative orientation; *calculative*, which is a neutral form of involvement; and *moral*, meaning a positive orientation of high intensity. What Etzioni provides us with is, in our terms, two dimensions (type of power and type of involvement) and three properties on each (coercive, remunerative and normative; and alienative, calculative and moral, respectively). Etzioni constructs a property space of this terminological set-up (Table 5.6).

Three types of the matrix make up different kinds of organizations. The combination of representatives' coercive power and lower participants' alienative involvement results in a coercive organization, such as a prison. Remunerative power and calculative involvement make up a utilitarian organization, with a capitalist company as an example. Normative power and moral involvement, finally, form a normative organization of which a church is an example.

What does Etzioni do with the six empty cells? He does not regard them as conceptual gaps to be filled-in; rather, he reduces the property space to the three types coercive, utilitarian and normative organization, presenting the following argumentation. First, these three types are empirically more common than the other six types. Second, the reason for this is that they are congruent in the relation between the form of power and the type of involvement. Coercive power does not, for

TABLE 5.6 Types of power and types of involvement in organizations

		Lower participants' type of involvement		
		Alienative	*Calculative*	*Moral*
Representatives' type of power	Coercive	Coercive organization (prison)		
	Remunerative		Utilitarian organization (company)	
	Normative			Normative organization (church)

Source: Modified from Etzioni (1975: 12, Table).

example, fit very well with calculative or moral involvement, and the same goes for remunerative power and alienative or moral involvement, or normative power with alienative or calculative involvement. Third, organizations therefore tend to move from incongruence (the empty cells) to congruence. And, fourth, congruent organizations tend to counteract mechanisms that threaten congruence. In this way, Etzioni reduces the property space on empirical grounds – and a theoretical explanation for the empirical pattern – to three instead of nine types.

The second example of empirical reduction does not take its point of departure in the presence of empirically existing outcomes, but in the absence of such outcomes. Undeniably, Etzioni also did this and it was an important part of his argumentation for the presence of the types he presented, but in this case, we are only looking at the absent ones to theorize. The example comes from Ragin's reasoning on limited diversity in cases as configurations (Ragin 2000: Ch. 3), in which he does not formally use a property space, but it is easy to construct one (Table 5.7) from his set theory table.

In this fictitious example from a social science department at a large state university in the United States, there are four dichotomous dimensions. Rank (untenured and tenured), pay (below and above average relative to years in seniority), gender (male and female) and ethnicity (European American and minority). Of the sixteen outcomes, the eight ones of which there are no empirical instances (shadowed) are of interest in this example. These are, then, the absent ones. In order to theorize, we can study not only the outcomes for which we have found present empirical instances, but also those absent in this regard. Do they have anything in common?

If we start looking at the 'male-minority' outcomes, we find that both absent types are tenured. We can therefore form the concept 'male-minority-tenured' as a first suggestion, covering the outcomes (3) and (4). We also find that female untenured with pay above average and of both ethnicities are absent, which leads to the concept 'female-above' outcomes (10), (12), (14) and (16). Going on like this, we will eventually find that there are two concepts that together cover all of the absent outcomes. On the one hand, there is the combination 'female-above', and on the other, 'minority-tenured', covering the absent outcomes (10), (12), (14),

TABLE 5.7 Rank, pay, gender and ethnicity among members of a social science department at a large US state university (fictitious)

				Gender			
				Male		Female	
				Ethnicity		Ethnicity	
				Minority	European	Minority	European
Rank	Untenured	Pay	Below	(1) Yes	(5) Yes	(9) Yes	(13) Yes
			Above	(2) Yes	(6) Yes	(10) No	(14) No
	Tenured	Pay	Below	(3) No	(7) Yes	(11) No	(15) Yes
			Above	(4) No	(8) Yes	(12) No	(16) No

Source: Built on Ragin (2000: 83, Table 3.3).

(16) and (3), (4), (11) and (12), respectively. These concepts can, Ragin points out, in their turn, lead to formulating hypotheses to test in further research:

> [B]ecause . . . there are no minority members who are tenured, it is possible to deduce that (1) if a member is minority, he or she is also not tenured, and (2) if a member is tenured, he or she is not a member of a minority. These two deductions can be made because minority members are a subset of untenured faculty, and tenured faculty are a subset of nonminority members. . . . Similarly, [because] there are no female members with above-average pay, it is possible to deduce that (1) if a member is female, her pay is below average, and (2) if a member's pay is above average, the member is not female. In other words, females are a subset of members with below-average pay, and members with above-average pay are a subset of male members.
>
> *(Ragin 2000: 85)*

As is exemplified here, reduction by analysis of missing or absent empirical outcomes can be very productive when it comes to developing concepts, hypotheses and social theory.

At the same time, we should be aware that there are at least two risks involved in empirical reductions. First, a basic one is that, in principle, it is very difficult, if not impossible, to claim with any certainty that there are no empirical examples of a specific type. Scientific knowledge is fallible – it is not exhaustive and with hindsight it often turns out to have been wrong. Claims of empirical existence and non-existence of specific cases are always provisional. We should also note that Etzioni carefully works out theoretical motivations for regarding certain types as empirically empty. Second, one of the most important thought procedures in social science is counterfactual thinking:

> We ask questions like: How would this be if not . . . ? Could one imagine X without . . .? Could one imagine X including this, without X then becoming something different? In counterfactual thinking we use stored experience and knowledge of social reality, as well as our ability to abstract and think what is not, but what might be.
>
> *(Danermark et al. 2002: 101)*

Empirical reductions might hamper counterfactual thinking by reducing the creativity of pondering cases that seem strange, but they can help in theorizing.

Theoretical reduction

Behind Etzioni's empirical reduction in Table 5.6, there is also a theoretical argumentation about the effects of congruence and incongruence on type of power and type of involvement. Theoretical considerations can also in themselves lead to reductions of property spaces. In these cases, the reason is that some types belong to conceptual areas that are *outside* the theory that the reasoning covers (in the case of Etzioni's model, the incongruent types are part of his theory). Here is an example of theoretical reduction.

Under what conditions is social compromise between employers and employees possible at capitalist workplaces? This is a question of great interest to many people. The following is about the beginning of one answer, building on constructing property spaces (later we return to this example, whereby more of the answer is given). The researchers (Edwards and Bélanger 2008; Edwards et al. 2006) go to a more abstract level than relations between employers and employees in order to build a theoretical framework, which can explain compromise at workplaces. The concepts at this structural level are 'capital' and 'labour' in a 'capitalist system', whereby, the 'focus is structures and processes, not people' (Edwards et al. 2006: 129). In constructing their framework, the authors make clear that they do not put conflict and co-operation against each other as opposing dimensions. Instead, they regard those phenomena as always being present: they are two sides of the same coin. There are specific *concerns* of capital and labour respectively, which influence conflict and co-operation. One of them is *control concerns*, 'covering rights and power in day-to-day relations: how far the managerial right to hire and fire is limited, who determines workloads and work allocation, and so on' (Bélanger and Edwards 2007: 715–16). The other is more long-term *developmental concerns*:

> [These] relate to potentially shared objectives, in spite of the structural division between capital and labour. Matters such as investment in technology, training or innovative work practices may represent costs for both sides but they may also foster the viability of a given production unit and the continuity of 'good jobs' over a longer period of time.
>
> *(Bélanger and Edwards 2007: 716)*

Usually, though, the same developmental concern is regarded from quite different perspectives by capital and labour. For example, for capital it can be efficiency and profit, while for labour it can be good working conditions and secure jobs.

In this chain of argument, we can note that there are two concerns – control and developmental – which capital and labour can pursue to different degrees. Each concern can therefore be regarded as a dimension, and each dimension can be given the properties high and low. Using this frame, the authors start by constructing a fourfold table for labour's concerns (Table 5.8) and another for capital's concerns (Table 5.9). The frame is, then, the same in both property spaces, but the types are different because the first deals with labour's concerns and the second with capital's concerns. The title of the table is, again, extremely important as it defines the field covered by the respective property space.

Where labour has a relatively high level of control and its developmental concerns in relation to capital are fulfilled to a high degree, there is economic and industrial democracy at the workplace. If the control is high but developmental concerns low, the results are battles at the shop-floor to reach these concerns. In cases where labour's control is low, but developmental concerns are still largely fulfilled, questions belonging to long term interests are attended to rather than shop-floor problems – for which the term is corporatism. Finally, when both of labour's concerns are reached to a low degree, labour is powerless in the workplace. The picture is to some extent the same when it comes to capital's concerns, but mostly it differs (Table 5.9). As long as capital has a high degree of control, the types are about the same as in the former property space, although when the value is high, also concerning the developmental concerns, the interest is productivity rather than democracy. In the case of high developmental concerns and low control, capital is prepared to delegate some decisions to labour. Finally, when both of capital's concerns are low, the system falls apart; capitalism cannot function in the long run if capital does not reap profit.

This feature appears even clearer if labour's and capital's concerns are regarded in relation to each other. This relation applies to the developmental concerns in Table 5.10. Note that what was part of the title in Tables 5.8 and 5.9 – capital and labour, respectively – is now parts of the property space itself, as these dimensions are to be related to each other. The title tells which subject is the phenomenon to be compared, what the property space covers. When labour's developmental concerns are fulfilled to a high degree and capital's to a low degree, the result is worker's control. This, Edwards et al. (2006) point out, is a situation 'in which labour has been able to develop its long-term developmental interests without capital.... Workers' control states refer to *non- or post-capitalist* conditions' (2006: 132, our emphasis). This type is shadowed, because it is positioned *outside* the area that is covered by the theoretical interest of the authors, which is capital, labour and capitalism. The

TABLE 5.8 Labour's concerns

		\multicolumn{2}{c	}{*Level of fulfilment of developmental concerns*}
		High	Low
Level of fulfilment of control concerns	High	Economic and industrial democracy	Shop-floor battles
	Low	Corporatism	Powerlessness

Source: Modified from Edwards et al. (2006: 130, Figure 1).

TABLE 5.9 Capital's concerns

		\multicolumn{2}{c	}{*Level of fulfilment of developmental concerns*}
		High	Low
Level of fulfilment of control concerns	High	Productivity coalition	Shop-floor battles
	Low	Delegation of powers	System failure

Source: Modified from Edwards et al. (2006: 131, Figure 2).

TABLE 5.10 Developmental concerns

		\multicolumn{2}{c}{*Labour*}
		High	*Low*
Capital	High	Mutual gains enterprise	Economic development, labour marginalized
	Low	Worker's control	Struggles for control

Source: Edwards et al. (2006: 132, Figure 3).

boundaries of the theory are the boundaries of capitalism – and cases in which workers are in control lie outside those confines. The matrix of the property space is therefore reduced on theoretical grounds to the other three types: a mutual gains enterprise, economic development with marginalized labour and struggles for control over the labour process, which are all situated within the theory of capitalism. Note that this absence has an important theoretical function in that it defines a boundary for the theory. Let us repeat: reduction cannot only simplify things for the researcher by diminishing the complexity of a property space – it can also make a theory more precise by defining (parts of) its border. We return to this question and this fourfold table in the next chapter, in which we discuss expansion of property spaces.

There is a risk involved in this procedure in that what is left out can be regarded as uninteresting in the continued theorizing – perhaps even forgotten. Theoretical reduction produces a well-defined absence, which can later become fruitful for understanding entities and mechanisms within the confines of the theory you are developing. In fact, the absence of worker control has important things to say about capitalism.

Pragmatic reduction

It is not always the case that researchers give elaborate logical, empirical or theoretical reasons for reducing property spaces. Sometimes when your research question or current phase of theorizing leaves a number of outcomes empty, you can pragmatically disregard them.

In this example, the research question is how professional jazz musicians get their repertoires. The working repertoires of jazz groups are classified according to four characteristics (Faulkner and Becker 2009: 170–2): (i) size: number of tunes they play; (ii) diversity: variety of tunes to play; (iii) capaciousness: amount of possibilities for improvisation among the players; and (iv) variability: of set and performance at different gigs. Each characteristic is divided into two values, high (H) and low (L), resulting in a property space with 16 types. Faulkner and Becker choose to present the logical possibilities not as a property space, but as a logical list or display (Table 5.11). They discuss, however, only four of them with this motivation: 'Here are some of these possibilities as they appear in real life, embodied in some of the groups we

TABLE 5.11 Logical possibilities of professional jazz groups' repertoire

Type	Size	Diversity	Capaciousness	Variability
1	H	H	H	H
2	H	L	H	H
3	H	L	L	H
4	H	L	H	L
5	H	L	L	L
6	L	L	L	L
etc.				

Source: Faulkner and Becker (2009: 171, Table).

TABLE 5.12 Types of working repertoires of professional jazz groups

			Size			
			High		Low	
			Diversity			
			High	Low	High	Low
Capacious	High	Variability	High	Laine			
			Low				Tristano
	Low		High	MacLeod	Pinardi		
			Low				

Source: Based on Table 5.11.

have been using as examples throughout (and whose names we have somewhat whimsically used for the types)' (Faulkner and Becker 2009: 171). This is a pragmatic reduction of the total property space that their dimensions result in into the four types they theoretically and empirically find being the most fruitful ones for their analysis of how musicians get their repertoires (Table 5.12).

The terms are taken from the names of band-leaders, whose styles represent the different types:

- Laine: 'Many tunes, lots of improvising on the chord changes, continual novelty and, once introduced the tunes will probably be repeated now and then over the life of the group.' (HHHH)
- Tristano: 'A very few tunes . . . low turnover in tunes introduced . . . the players improvise as long as they like, as many as eight or ten choruses . . . low turnover in tunes selected.' (LLHL)
- Pinardi: 'The leader continually introduces new tunes, in a variety of styles, into the group's repertoire, and then makes a constantly changing selection from this variety. . . . The players take two or, at the most, three choruses on a tune. The set list varies greatly, from night to night, with the constant introduction of new material.' (HLLH)

- MacLeod: 'A leader intent on pleasing the clients who have hired him for their party organizes a great variety of songs to fill an entire evening.' (HHLH)

(Faulkner and Becker 2009: 171–2)

All types in the matrix could, in principle, be empirically possible and theoretically interesting, but the authors choose to comment only on the types they find the most theoretically relevant and empirically salient. Pragmatically, they disregard all other types. The flipside of this is that 'the typology is likely to be limited to the immediate research purpose at hand' (Elman 2005: 320–1). At the same time, Faulkner and Becker – or other researchers – could at a later stage try to fill in now empty types by further studies of how jazz musicians get their repertoire.

Summary

One way of using an existing property space – one you have constructed yourself or someone else's – to develop new concepts and theoretical ideas is to try to reduce or simplify it. This means that you play about with possibilities to merge two types into one, or perhaps three or four into one. We suggest a number of ways of doing this. Rescaling is one of them, meaning that you search arguments for two or more types being the same type or parts of a higher order type. This is done by assimilating properties of a dimension, as when we let the types 'blue collar worker' and 'white collar worker' become merged in the higher order concept 'employee'. The effect of diminishing the number of properties in the frame of a property space is, of course, that there are also fewer types in the matrix.

Indexing is a second possibility. You assign each property of each dimension a number, thereby creating a scale. You then construct indices by adding the values of each type and can then compare the indices of them. Third, you can try to reduce a property space by scrutinizing the logical plausibility of the types. Maybe some of them are logically impossible. This kind of reduction can be very clarifying also when it comes to the boundaries of the theory you are working on.

Fourth, reductions can also be the result of considering empirical patterns. Etzioni's typology of organizations is one example. According to the dimensions and their properties, there are nine possible types of organizations, but Etzioni reduces them to three. His argumentation for this starts with the empirical claim that they are the most common types and he also puts forward theoretical reasons why that is so. Another kind of empirical reduction is to study the empirically absent outcomes, that is, the types that cannot be found empirically. This process can also lead to new concepts being formulated.

A fifth way is theoretical reduction. You think through the types of a property space with the boundaries of your or someone else's theory in mind: do they all belong to the theory or are there types that lie outside the field that the theory covers? Our example was a typology of the possibilities of social compromise between capital and labour at workplaces. One of the types pointed out conditions in which workers are in control. Such conditions are clearly not part of capitalism and are therefore positioned outside the boundaries of the theory. Finally, there is pragmatic reduction, so called because the researchers simply choose to disregard possible types they are not interested in at present.

There is an opposite process to reducing property spaces, although the aim is the same: to theorize. This process is to expand them.

References

Bailey, Kenneth D. (1994) *Typologies and Taxonomies. An Introduction to Classification Techniques*. London: Sage.

Barton, Allen H. (1965) 'The Concept of Property-Space in Social Research', pp. 30–53 in Paul F. Lazarsfeld and Morris Rosenberg (eds), *The Language of Social Research*. New York: Free Press.

Bélanger, Jacques and Paul Edwards (2007) 'The Conditions Promoting Compromise in the Workplace', *British Journal of Industrial Relations*, 45(4): 713–34.

Danermark, Berth, Mats Ekström, Liselotte Jakobsen and Jan Ch. Karlsson (2002) *Explaining Society. Critical Realism in the Social Sciences*. London: Routledge.

Edwards, Paul and Jacques Bélanger (2008) 'Generalizing from Workplace Ethnographies. From Induction to Theory', *Journal of Contemporary Ethnography*, 37(3): 291–313.

Edwards, Paul, Jacques Bélanger and Martyn Wright (2006) 'The Bases of Compromise in the Workplace: A Theoretical Framework', *British Journal of Industrial Relations*, 44(1): 125–45.

Elman, Colin (2005) 'Explanatory Typologies in Qualitative Studies of International Politics', *International Organization*, 59(2): 293–326.

Etzioni, Amitai (1975) *A Comparative Analysis of Complex Organizations. On Power, Involvement, and Their Correlates*. New York: Free Press.

Faulkner, Robert R. and Howard S. Becker (2009) *'Do You Know . . . ?' The Jazz Repertoire in Action*. Chicago: University of Chicago Press.

Karlsson, Jan Ch. (2004) 'The Ontology of Work. Social Relations and Doing in the Sphere of Necessity', pp. 90–112 in Steve Fleetwood and Stephen Ackroyd (eds), *Critical Realist Applications in Organisation and Management Studies*. London: Routledge.

Marx, Karl (1998) *Capital. Volume I*. London: ElecBook.

Perfetto, Ralph and Arch G. Woodside (2009) 'Extremely Frequent Behavior in Consumer Research: Theory and Empirical Evidence for Chronic Casino Gambling', *Journal of Gambling Studies*, 25(2): 297–316.

Ragin, Charles C. (2000) *Fuzzy-Set Social Science*. Chicago: Chicago University Press.

Sayer, Andrew (1992) *Method in Social Science. A Realist Approach*. London: Routledge.

6

EXPANSION OF PROPERTY SPACES IN THEORIZING

Expansion of property spaces makes is possible to 'discover missed combinations and suppressed assumptions, and to identify important cases' (Elman 2005: 294). One way of doing this is to take the existing dimensions in the frame of the property space as a point of departure, and try to identify more properties for one or more of them, thereby expanding the matrix. Another way is to search for more dimensions and thus going into the field that the property space covers in more detail. In cases in which we are playing about with two or more property spaces, we can test the possibility of combining them into a single one, thereby expanding each one of them. In social science, we are usually studying phenomena that change; to take this into account, we need ways of expressing processes, and in connection with property spaces, this is often done by inserting arrows, symbolising directions of changes. A final possibility of expanding property spaces is to transform dimensions or properties into scales, measuring degrees of intensity, range, scope and so on. We will discuss examples of all these ways of expanding property spaces in order to theorize as well as theoretical risks connected to them, but we will start by going back to the classics of property space construction.

Substruction

In the early analyses of property spaces (Barton 1965; Lazarsfeld 1937; Lazarsfeld and Barton 1965 [1951]) the opposite operation to reduction is called *substruction*. The term comes from this idea: most or all typologies presented by social scientists are incomplete. Usually without the researcher being aware of it, the typology is a reduction of a more comprehensive property space to which it can be substructed. Thereby the typology is expanded. This is an important step in theorizing, because by thinking in this way a researcher 'would see whether he has overlooked certain cases; he could make sure that some of his types are not overlapping; and he would probably make the classification more useful for actual empirical research' (Lazarsfeld 1937: 133). To do this, you work backwards, as it were, from the typology to the property space from which it was reduced.

To exemplify this procedure, we will follow the most common illustration they use (Barton 1965: 52–3; Lazarsfeld 1937: 133–6; Lazarsfeld and Barton 1965 [1951]: 177–9), namely substruction of Erich Fromm's analysis of authority structures in the family. Fromm's study was built on questionnaires to parents and children in which – if we simplify a bit – the parents were asked if they used corporal punishment and if they interfered with children's spare time activities, while the children were asked if there often were conflicts with their parents and if they had confidence in them. Fromm constructed a typology of authoritarian relations between parent and child as a theoretical guide for the research, containing four situations: (i) Parents' complete authority; (ii) parents' simple authority; (iii) parents' lack of authority; and (iv) children's rebellion.

In Lazarsfeld and Baron's combination of reduction and substruction of this typology, they started with relating the two questions to parents to each other and the two questions to children to each other (Table 6.1). Each results in a fourfold typology, in which one outcome is dropped as contradictory. When parents both punish children corporally and interfere with their children's leisure activities, their intensity of authority is strong, but when the opposite is at hand in both cases the authority is weak. Corporal punishment without interference is not a probable combination. The last one can therefore be positioned somewhere between strong and weak intensity of authority.

Among children, absence of conflicts with and presence of confidence in parents indicate strong acceptance of parents' authority, while the inverse type is weak. The combination of conflict and confidence can be dropped as improbable. Finally, no conflicts and no confidence comes somewhere between strong and weak acceptance of parents' authority. Thereby, Lazarsfeld and Barton say, 'two separate reductions have been carried through: The two-dimensional space constituted of corporal

TABLE 6.1 Intensity of (a) parent's exercise of authority and (b) children's acceptance of authority

(a)

		Parent's corporal punishment	
		Yes	No
Parent's interference	Yes	Strong	Medium
	No	—	Weak

(b)

		Children's experience of conflicts	
		Yes	No
Children's confidence in parents	Yes	—	Strong
	No	Weak	Medium

TABLE 6.2 Types of authority structures in families

		Children's acceptance of authority		
		High	*Medium*	*Low*
Parent's exercise of authority	Strong	1	2	3
	Moderate	4	5	6
	Weak	<u>7</u>	8	<u>9</u>

Source: Modified from Barton (1965: 52, Table 11).

punishment and interference has been reduced to the serial "exercise of authority". In the same way, conflict and confidence were reduced to "acceptance of authority'" (1965 [1951]: 178). In both cases, the types are strong, medium and weak.

In the next step, Fromm's original typology of parents' complete authority, their simple authority, their lack of authority and children's rebellion, can be substructed through the property space that results if we relate parent's exercise of authority and children's acceptance of parental authority to each other (Table 6.2). Relating this to Fromm's typology, we find that complete authority is covered by outcomes 1 and 2 in the matrix; simple authority is represented by outcomes 4 and 5. Lack of authority can be found in combination 8; and rebellion, finally, in 3 and 6. The underlined outcomes 7 and 9 are not covered in Fromm's typology. This substruction could have given him impetus for new empirical studies of, for example, cases in which children want an authority that they do not have.

Substruction – often in combination with reduction – is, then, a form of expanding a property space. It carries the risk of producing too many types to keep up theoretical precision, while reduction involves the opposite risk of resulting in too few types to inspire theorizing. That is why movements between these two types of operation are preferable. Lazarsfeld and Barton thought that substruction was the only way of expanding a property space, and so does Elman (2005). We have, however, found also other ways of doing this, to which we now turn. Some of them can, though, be regarded as different operations of substruction.

More properties of existing dimensions

One way of reducing property spaces that we showed in the former chapter was to diminish the number of properties; the opposite is, of course, to expand a property space by putting in more properties of one or more of the dimensions you are playing about with. Our example of this procedure deals with theoretical typologies of the most important forms of work in the history of human beings (Karlsson 2004: 103–6; Karlsson 2013 [1986]: Ch. 4). In the literature, there is what can be called a conventional typology of three work forms: 'The free, contractual wage-earner, the serf and the slave. Everyone must somehow be fitted into one of these categories' (Finley 1981: 142). Sometimes, a fourth work form, independent producer, is added. The theoretical basis of this typology is, however, unclear. A common suggestion is

92 Tools for theorizing in social science

that work forms can be distinguished through the dimensions of the ownership of – meaning effective control over – the means of production and the immediate producer's own labour power (as we discussed in the former chapter in connection with logic reduction). Let us construct a property space with these dimensions and the properties whether they are present or not (Table 6.3; cf. Table 5.5).

The result seems to be that we become even more confused than before. Here, the independent producer gets a place, as does the wage labourer and the slave. Independent producers own both their labour power and the means of production. Wage labourers too control their labour power, but they do not own the machines or other equipment they use; slaves do not own anything at all. Finally, one cell is marked with a dash, indicating that it is logically contradictory and probably empirically empty. If the immediate producers do not control how to use their own labour power, it is not possible to control the means of production used in work. Further, we cannot find a place for one of the work forms of the conventional typology in this property space, namely serfdom.

A solution to the problem can be found in a chain of reasoning presented by Gerald Cohen (1978: 67–9). He expands Table 6.3 by adding the properties to make it a three-part division: 'all', 'some' and 'none', although he does not present the result as a property space, but as an ordinary table (Table 6.4). In a later table (Cohen 1978: 66, Table 2), he also complements this with combinations that are not shown here. We think that the relations become clearer if we construct a property space that includes all possible types of this expansion by changing the properties 'yes'

TABLE 6.3 Historical work forms based on the immediate producer's ownership of means of production and labour power

		Ownership of means of production	
		Yes	No
Ownership of labour power	Yes	Independent producer	Wage labourer
	No	–	Slave

TABLE 6.4 Historical work forms based on the immediate producer's ownership of means of production and labour power according to Cohen

		His labour power	The means of production he uses
Slave		None	None
Serf	owns	Some	Some
Proletarian		All	None
Independent producer		All	All

Source: Cohen (1978: 65, Table 1).

Expansion of property spaces in theorizing 93

TABLE 6.5 The immediate producer's ownership of means of production and labour power

		Ownership of means of production		
		None	*Some*	*Full*
Ownership of labour power	None	Slave	←X	–
	Some	↱	Serf	–
	Full	Wage labourer	↔	Independent producer

Source: Modified from Karlsson (2013 [1986]: 63, Figure 1).

and 'no' to the threefold 'none', 'some' and 'all' (Table 6.5). The slaves own neither their own labour power nor the means of production; in fact, the slave is instead the property of the slave master, who owns both the slave's labour power and the means of production used in work. The serfs control some of the means of production and some of their own labour power. They work for the feudal lord with the lord's equipment on the lord's land certain days of the week; other days of the week they can use their own means of production to cultivate the patches of land they have the use of for their own survival. The wage labourers – or with Cohen's term, the proletarians – do not own any means of production at all, but they have command over their own labour power, meaning that they can rent it out to any capitalist or another employer. The independent producers, finally, own both the labour power and the means of production, and therefore, have no relation to a master, lord or capitalist, only to customers.

In this way of extending Table 6.3, it is possible to include all four historical work forms of the conventional typology in a single theoretical frame. Two of these work forms are usually labelled 'free' work forms, namely wage labour and independent producer, and it is now possible to clearly see what they have in common: both producers control their own labour power in full.

The construction of this property space also leaves a number of types that are not labelled by terms. Cohen (1978: 66–9) discusses them in ways that we give different symbols in the table. In the same way as in Table 6.3, '–' stands for a type that is logically contradictory and probably empirically empty. The symbol '←X' means that the type is logically possible, but it cannot be empirically distinguished from the slave; '↱' denotes a transitional form from serf to wage labourer, while '↔' symbolizes a transitional form between wage labourer and independent producer. This is an example of how the operations of expansion and reduction of property spaces can be combined. One consequence of the expansion in Table 5.5 as compared to Table 6.3 is that two types become logically contradictory and thereby can be left out of the property space. This expansion is, then, at the same time a reduction and a substruction.

There are, however, a number of transitional forms that Cohen does not mention. Look, for example, at the '↱' cell, the transition from serf to wage labourer. The following transitions are also possible: from serf to slave, from slave to wage labourer, from slave to serf, from wage labourer to slave and from wage labourer to serf.

Probably all of them are represented in the history of work forms, although one might vindicate Cohen omitting them through claiming that the one he does mention is the empirically most common and/or theoretically most important. This indicates that maybe even this expanded property space ought to be further expanded. Perhaps there is an even bigger property space to which this typology can be substructed.

At the same time, this indicates the risk that you may end up in a process of infinite regress to ever growing property spaces. Perhaps it is always possible to find a more comprehensive typology, finally becoming so big that it stops working as a tool for theorizing – which means that you have to turn back to reduction of property spaces again.

More dimensions

So far, we have expanded a property space by adding properties to dimensions, from yes and no to all, some and none. Another way is, of course, to instead add more dimensions. Cohen (1978: 65n) makes a short suggestion for extending the typology that we have elaborated in Table 6.5. He says that 'means of production' can be split in two dimensions, namely 'instruments of production' and 'raw materials'. We take the former to mean the tools and implements used in work, and the latter what is worked on. The result of this expansion of the property space is shown in Table 6.6. In this property space, it is perhaps even clearer than in Table 6.5 that ownership of labour power is a key theoretical dimension of work forms. Where there is a lack of control over your own labour power, either some combinations are logically and/or empirically impossible or the work forms in question are unfree. There are twenty-seven types in the property space, and ten of them are self-contradictory: you cannot fully own instruments of production or raw materials without fully owning your labour power. These cases (the underlined cells 3, 6 to 9, 12 and 15 to 18) are probably also empirically empty. The other cases where the immediate producers do not control their labour power at all (cells 1, 2, 4 and 5) imply slavery. As long as the immediate producers do not own at least some of their labour power, the work form is slavery, independent of if it is instruments of production or raw materials that are partly owned.

When it comes to immediate producers who partly own their labour power, we restrict ourselves to noting that the distinction between instruments of production

TABLE 6.6 The immediate producer's ownership of instruments of production, raw materials and labour power

Instruments of production		None			Some			Full		
Raw materials		None	Some	Full	None	Some	Full	None	Some	Full
Labour power	None	1	2	<u>3</u>	4	5	<u>6</u>	<u>7</u>	<u>8</u>	<u>9</u>
	Some	10	11	<u>12</u>	13	14	<u>15</u>	<u>16</u>	<u>17</u>	<u>18</u>
	Full	19	20	21	22	23	24	25	26	27

Source: Karlsson (2013 [1986]: 65, Figure 2).

and raw materials stands out as especially important. The ownership of land is, for example, basic for the peasantry, giving the farmer a considerably stronger position than the ownership of instruments of production does. Finally, there are the cases in which the immediate producers fully own their labour power. The wage labourers, who control nothing else, can be found in cell 19; the independent producers, who have full ownership on all dimensions, in cell 27.

Apart from the relations we have mentioned, we cannot see that this more complicated property space makes the typology of Table 6.5 much more nuanced, although it might guide historical empirical research in looking for not yet observed work forms. Let us also remind you that when we in Chapter 5 discussed reduction of property spaces, we presented an example of doing this through merging properties of dimensions (Tables 5.1 and 5.2). Instead, we have an example of merging dimensions in that Table 6.5 can be regarded as a successful reduction of Table 6.6.

We want, however, to finish this section on a more positive note on the possibility of using expansion of property spaces in order to theorize. Let us therefore return to a theme from both Chapters 4 and 5, namely, attitudes to work among different groups on the labour market. This time we do not only analyse attitudes to work, but expand this dimension into two forms: absolute and relative attitudes, respectively as depicted in Table 6.7.

All attitudes have an object: they are directed towards something. Earlier, for example in Tables 5.1 and 5.2, the object was simply work. Now, however, we look on the one hand at work in itself, work without comparison with anything else. This is the absolute attitude to work. The relative attitude to work is, on the other hand, when work is compared to other things in life, for example, family and leisure activities. In the first case, one can, for example, ask people to agree or disagree (on some scale) with this statement: 'This job is just like any other – one does one's job and the only thing that matters is the salary.' In the second case, a fairly common measure is to ask respondents the following:

[C]hoose and rank the three most important factors in life from the following: being healthy, spending time with family and friends, having an interesting job,

TABLE 6.7 Absolute and relative attitude to work and position on the labour market

		Position on the labour market		
		Blue collar worker	White collar worker	Small business owner
Absolute attitude to work	Positive			
	Neutral			
	Negative			
Relative attitude to work	Positive			
	Neutral			
	Negative			

making money, pursuing meaningful leisure activities, having a good place to live, being able to make an active contribution to society and being able to enjoy good food and drink.

(Eriksson et al. 2011: 129)

In this way, more nuanced and much more theoretically fruitful analyses of people's attitudes can be achieved.

Expanding property spaces by adding more dimensions still carries the risk of you ending up in what can be called a *rage of classification*, in which you drown in a matrix of very complicated types for which it is extremely difficult to find terms. In this case too, it might be wise to return to the process of reduction.

Combining property spaces

When discussing theoretical reduction of property spaces in the former chapter, we took an example from a number of fourfold tables structuring capital's and labour's concerns in an analysis of bases of compromise in the workplace under capitalism. In the last of those property spaces (Table 5.10), there was one type that was shadowed, because it was positioned outside the theory of labour, capital and capitalism. This table was the result of combining parts of two other property spaces, depicting labour's and capital's concerns (Tables 5.8 and 5.9). Just a short remainder that one type of concern is control, which is centred on power between the two parties. To what extent does capital control labour and labour control capital? The other is developmental concerns, which are things that capital and labour might agree upon; even acknowledging the conflict between the two sides, they can negotiate compromises that both regard as advantageous.

Tables 5.8 and 5.9 can now be expanded by simply combining them without adding further dimensions or properties; thereby capital's control and developmental concerns can be related to labour's control and developmental concerns (Table 6.8). Note that the cells containing high and low control under labour's developmental concerns are the same as the cells in Table 5.8, and the corresponding cells under capital's developmental concerns equals the types in Table 5.9. Each type in those two fourfold tables has, then, now been expanded to four cells. That goes, at the same time, also for the shadowed cell in Table 5.10, which has been expanded to four types. As this is a theory about capitalism, cases in which labour's control is high and that of capital low are situated outside the theory: they are simply not cases of capitalism.

We will not go into the empirical examples of the types provided by the authors, only mention the basic results concerning under which circumstances one can expect compromises being established between capital and labour. There are three blocks in this model and the conditions differ between them. In block one, the conditions are favourable for social compromises, as the developmental concerns have high values for both capital and labour. Block two means asymmetric relations in that capital's control is high, while labour's control is low. In such situations, capital does not have

TABLE 6.8 Combination of capital's and labour's concerns

				\multicolumn{4}{c}{*Labour: developmental*}
				\multicolumn{2}{c}{*High*}	\multicolumn{2}{c}{*Low*}
				\multicolumn{2}{c}{Control}	\multicolumn{2}{c}{Control}
				High	*Low*	*High*	*Low*
				\multicolumn{2}{c}{Block one}	\multicolumn{2}{c}{Block two}
Capital	High	Control	High				
			Low				
						\multicolumn{2}{c}{Block three}
Developmental	Low	Control	High				
			Low				

Source: Modified from Bélanger and Edwards (2007: 716, Figure 1).

much incentive to compromise with labour. Block three, finally, depicts irreconcilable opposition between the two; neither side has enough developmental concerns to pursue to make social compromises attractive.

The fruitfulness of combining property spaces is dependent on how wide-ranging each of them is. In the same way as in other types of expanding property spaces, you risk finding yourself in a situation of drowning in a typology that is too big to handle if one or both are very comprehensive.

Inserting process arrows

Property spaces express combinations of dimensions and properties, which have many advantages. However, one drawback is that it is not self-evident how to depict development, change and other processes. We have, though, shown some such possibilities in Table 6.5 on historical work forms, and process arguments are implicit in Etzioni's theory of organizations, Table 5.6. Another solution to this problem is to insert arrows into, or transcending, the property space, thereby indicating processes (cf. pp. 30–1). We will look at two examples, the first one with process arrows within the property space, the other with arrows going out from it. (A technical note: in the literature, property spaces are sometimes called tables, sometimes figures. We call them tables when they are only made up of rows and columns, including when process symbols are parts of a cell as in Table 6.5. When such symbols cross cells or

98 Tools for theorizing in social science

TABLE 6.9 Interpretation of Kolb's dimensions of learning

		Prehension	
		Concrete experience	*Abstract conceptualization*
Transformation	Active experimentation	Accommodative knowledge	Convergent knowledge
	Reflective observation	Divergent knowledge	Assimilative knowledge

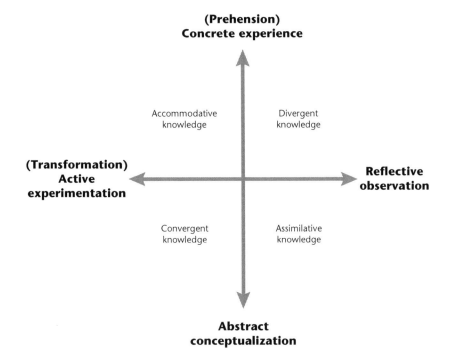

FIGURE 6.1 Interpretation of Kolb's dimensions of learning as processes

transcend the property space, for example, process arrows going out from it, we give it the title figure as in Figure 6.1.)

The first example is a simplified interpretation of a complex and influential theory about learning (Kolb 1984), starting with the transfactual question, 'what must exist for learning to take place?' Kolb's answer is that two processes are required, namely, on the one hand, a grasp of something, which he calls *prehension*, and on the other hand, a *transformation* of that understanding. In consequence thereof, he defines learning in this way: 'Learning is the process whereby knowledge is created through the transformation of experience' (1984: 38, emphasis removed). Only grasping or only transformation is not enough: both must be there for learning to arise. Further, there are two ways in which we can grasp something: one is through concrete experience of that from which we can learn, the other is through abstractly thinking about and conceptualizing it. In the same way, there are two types of transformation: active experimentation with the external world and internal reflection about it. In our interpretation, prehension can be regarded as a dimension, with the properties concrete experience and abstract conceptualization; in a similar way, transformation is a dimension, the properties of which are active experimentation and reflective observation (Table 6.9).

The types represent four different kinds of knowledge, produced by different combinations of the properties of prehension and transformation, respectively. This is, then, the resulting typology of knowledge:

- Accommodative knowledge results when experience is grasped by concrete experience and transformed by active experimentation.
- Convergent knowledge when grasped by abstract conceptualization and transformed by active experimentation.
- Divergent knowledge when grasped by concrete experience and transformed by reflective observation.
- Assimilative knowledge when grasped by abstract conceptualization and transformed by reflective observation.

These processes are, however, not clearly depicted in this property space. We need to do some changes to it to express the notion that these are not states but things altering their states. This is where process arrows enter the picture (Figure 6.1). In this design, the arrows indicate that there is movement in the relations between types of prehension and transformation that shapes knowledge and its different forms. In order to present the types of knowledge in Figure 6.1 as relations in processes, we have to put the properties of the dimensions in another order than in Table 6.9. Each property is now at the end of a two-way arrow, while the dimension is the arrow itself. Incidentally, do not feel that rearranging the property space in this way is wrong somehow. You are allowed to do anything you like with a property space, as long as it helps your theoretical creativity along. What you might be careful about is, though, breaking the logic of the property space; even if that can be a creative step, there is a risk that it results in conceptual flaws.

Already in Chapter 4 we discussed the importance of finding labels for types, and, thereby, giving them terms. Looking at Figure 6.1, we find that the types are indicated by terms: the four types of knowledge. When it comes to the process arrows, there is a further possibility, namely to assign terms to the arrows or parts of them. This is what Kolb does. The prehension arrow, which is about grasping, is divided into grasping via apprehension (the part that is about concrete experience) and grasping via comprehension (abstract conceptualization). The transformation arrow is divided into transformation via extension (active experimentation) and via intention (reflective observation). Finally, Kolb introduces process arrows between the properties: from concrete experiences to reflective observation, from reflective observation to abstract conceptualization and so on.

TABLE 6.10 Karasek's demand-control model

		Demands	
		Low	*High*
Control	Low	Passive job	High-strain job
	High	Low-strain job	Active job

Source: Modified from Karasek (1979: 288, Figure 1) and Karasek and Theorell (1990: 32, Figure 2-1).

To sum up the steps we can learn from this example: you start with a simple fourfold table (Table 6.9), but you are curious about the learning processes involved so you have to depict them. Therefore, you introduce process arrows, but in order to make clear what they mean, some technical changes to the table have to be made (turning it into a figure – Figure 6.1), through which the arrows become dimensions and their endpoints are properties. Then you assign terms to the arrows themselves and finally you draw process arrows between the properties. In this way, you have unwrapped Kolb's theory of learning by successively constructing property spaces representing it – or at least parts of it.

This first example of inserting arrows in property spaces deals with a case in which the arrows are kept within the table. For an example of arrows transcending the property space, we go to one of the most famous fourfold tables in research on the work environment. It was originated by Robert Karasek (1979), as we mentioned in Chapter 1. Let us remind you that before he presented his theory, there were two influential, but quite different, theories about working environments. The kernel of one of them was *demands* in work and how they could result in stress among employees. The other concentrated on employees own *control* and the extent to which they could make their own decisions in work. In both cases, there were empirical findings that the researchers could not explain. Karasek's great achievement was to bring these two theories together with the help of a seemingly simple property space. He regarded 'demands' and 'control' as two dimensions, each with the properties 'low' and 'high', and then he put them together in a fourfold table (Table 6.10).

The result is a typology of jobs or work environments: they can be passive or active, low-strain or high-strain. The basic idea is that qualities of work environment are a function of the specific combination of demands and control. Karasek labelled each cell with terms that were to describe those qualities. On this basis, it is possible to create a hierarchy of jobs from good to bad ones. The really good ones are those combining high demands with high control, that is the active ones. Thereafter comes a type of job that is fairly good as it also contains high control, namely low-strain jobs. Jobs characterized by low control are bad ones, and high-strain jobs are worse than passive jobs as they also contain high demands.

One important trait of the theory is highlighting the balance between demands put on a worker and the worker's possibilities to handle these demands through control. There are two types of relations involved. One is when demand and control diverge, which is the case when demands are relatively greater than the worker's control; the

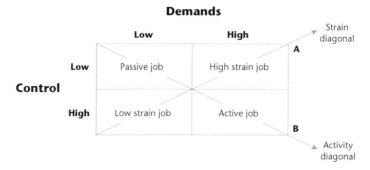

FIGURE 6.2 Karasek's demand-control model with strain and activity developments

Source: Karasek (1979: 288, Figure 1).

other is when they match each other. This idea makes it possible to formulate two hypotheses about developments (arrows A and B in Figure 6.2):

H_1: Arrow A symbolizes the process in which strain increases as demands increase: stress flourishes.
H_2: Arrow B indicates the opposite development, in which learning and other active processes expand: the worker flourishes.

The hypotheses are expressed through process arrows going through the matrix and out of the property space.

This property space and the process arrows that Karasek inserted indicated the solution to the problems that the theories about stress and decision latitudes, respectively, were riddled with. Later, there was another expansion of this property space; in fact, it doubled. The expansion took place by introducing a third dimension, namely the social support the worker can find at the workplace from workmates and superiors (Karasek and Theorell 1990: 68–71) – but that is another story.

In this section, we have shown two ways of theorizing through introducing process arrows. In the first, we reconstructed traits of Kolb's theory of learning, in the second, we showed how Karasek combined two existing theories into a new one and formulated hypotheses for empirical research. At the same time as arrows can make social processes clearer and thereby inspire theorizing, they carry the risk of over-burdening the property space. If you are not careful, your curiosity and need to play about with conceptual relations might result in confusion rather than clarity.

Creating scales

In our interpretation of part of Kolb's model of learning (Figure 6.1) there are process arrows. These could instead be designed as scales, expressing growing values of something, for example from a little to a lot, from 0 to 100, or from cold to hot. In the following example, two workplaces are compared when it comes to management and employee activities – one scale for each.

102 Tools for theorizing in social science

The point of departure is relations between management control at the workplace and employee behaviour as answers to this control (Bélanger and Thuderoz 2010). Management control can be divided into two types, subjection and responsibilization. Control by subjection means that the employee is expected to follow detailed orders about what to do in work. It is a form of direct control, for example in Taylorism. Control by responsibilization means that the employees have a bit more independence in work, often through teams with a certain amount of responsible autonomy. Employees' behaviour can also take two forms, commitment and opposition. Commitment to work 'is associated with employees' attitudes and behaviour regarding their craft, their occupation or professional abilities, and the use of this set of knowledge and skills in productive activities' (Bélanger and Thuderoz 2010: 146). Employee opposition to management can take many forms, from covert disrespect for management and cynicism about their work to overt militancy and rebellion.

These are, of course, analytical distinctions. In real organizational life, management uses both types of control simultaneously, while employee behaviour is both committed and oppositional at the same time (Karlsson 2012). There can, however, in each empirical case be differences in where the main emphasis on type of control and type of employee behaviour is placed. We can, then, regard management control as a dimension with the properties subjection and responsibilization, and employee behaviour as another dimension, the properties of which are commitment and opposition (Table 6.11). Now, we could go on in the usual way by trying to understand what the types mean and finding terms for them. We can also follow another route. One kind of expansion of a property space is to place the properties as axes of two crossing scales (Figure 6.3). Thereby, we relate the properties of management control to the properties of employee behaviour in a different way from the property space in Table 6.11. This table has been expanded by providing us with the opportunity to analyse the amount of management direct control in relation to responsible autonomy, and at the same time, relate this pattern to the amount of employee commitment and opposition.

The authors exemplify their use of this figure with two workplaces, showing quite different empirical patterns of combinations of management control and employee behaviour. (In this case, the scales are not the result of rigorous quantitative measurements, but qualitative judgements based on interviews and observations. Still, the technique can, of course, be used in statistical analyses.) In the first instance (Figure 6.4), which Bélanger and Thuderoz call *Presswork*, management's emphasis is

TABLE 6.11 Management control and employee behaviour 1

		Employee behaviour	
		Commitment	*Opposition*
Management control	Subjection		
	Responsibilization		

Expansion of property spaces in theorizing 103

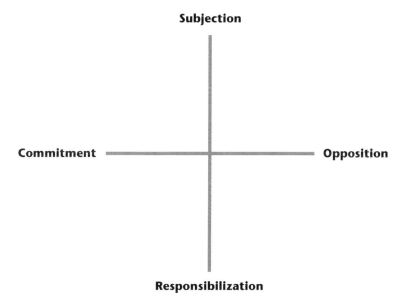

FIGURE 6.3 Management control and employee behaviour 2

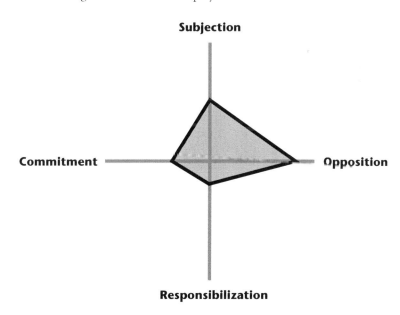

FIGURE 6.4 Pattern of management control and employee behaviour at *Presswork*

Source: Bélanger and Thuderoz (2010: 149, Figure 7.2).

much more on subjection through direct control of the employees than on responsible autonomy for them. This results in behaviour among employees being characterized to a higher degree by opposition to management than commitment to

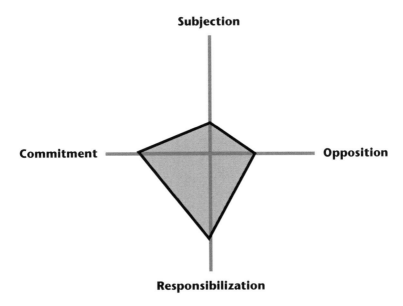

FIGURE 6.5 Pattern of management control and employee behaviour at *Tech*

Source: Bélanger and Thuderoz (2010: 151, Figure 7.3).

their jobs. All four properties are present, but there are marked differences in the degree to which they are there. These patterns cannot be expressed in the original fourfold table; in order to depict them, we had to expand that table through the use of scales.

The *Presswork* pattern can be compared to a workplace at a company called *Tech* with a quite different result (Figure 6.5). All four properties are present there too, but the proportions are quite dissimilar. Management control goes mainly through responsibilization, which results in commitment being the most extensive employee type of behaviour. Simultaneously, though, there is some degree of management subjection of employees combined with opposition on the employee side.

Notice that what we want to label when expanding a property space in this way is not the types in the form of cells, but the empirical patterns we find. Based on these patterns, the authors suggest that theoretically the *Presswork* figure shows an *industrial* pattern and the *Tech* figure a *post-industrial* pattern (Bélanger and Thuderoz 2010: 149–50).

Creating scales from property spaces moves them closer to the expository qualities of displays while keeping their logical abilities. At the same time, the risk of overburdening them is there. It could, for example, be tempting to combine Figures 6.4 and 6.5 in a single figure in order to make the comparison of the empirical patterns at *Presswork* and *Tech* more visible. Such a combination could, however, be counterproductive through becoming too complex.

Summary

In this chapter we have discussed the opposite operations compared to Chapter 5. Then it was reduction of property spaces, now it is expanding them. We started out with substruction, which means that a property space could be a reduction of a more comprehensive property space and the operation tries to reconstruct it. As an example we followed Lazarsfeld and Barton's substruction of Fromm's analysis of authority structures in the family. His typology of four authoritarian relations was shown to be a reduction of a property space with nine types of authority structures. Second, we discussed an example of finding more properties of dimensions of an existing property space, and third, instead adding more dimensions. Both concerned work forms in the history of human beings. A fourth possibility is to combine two existing property spaces in which we went back to examples from the former chapter on social compromise in capitalism. The fifth kind of expansion is a bit different, as it means introducing a new element, namely change processes symbolized by inserting arrows. We used two examples to illustrate this, one concerned arrows within the property space (Kolb's dimensions of learning), the other going out from it (Karasek's demand-control model). Finally, we discussed expansion by creating scales of the properties of a fourfold table.

A conclusion of the two chapters is that it seems wise to continuously let expansion and reduction of property spaces interplay with each other. Such interaction between the processes of expansion and reduction is usually a fruitful way of theorizing.

References

Barton, Allen H. (1965) 'The Concept of Property-Space in Social Research', pp. 30–53 in Paul F. Lazarsfeld and Morris Rosenberg (eds), *The Language of Social Research*. New York: Free Press.

Bélanger, Jacques and Paul Edwards (2007) 'The Conditions Promoting Compromise in the Workplace', *British Journal of Industrial Relations*, 45(4): 713–34.

Bélanger, Jacques and Christian Thuderoz (2010) 'The Repertoire of Employee Opposition', pp. 136–58 in Paul Thompson and Chris Smith (eds), *Working Life. Renewing Labour Process Analysis*. Basingstoke: Palgrave Macmillan.

Cohen, Gerald A. (1978) *Karl Marx's Theory of History: A Defence*. Princeton: Princeton University Press.

Elman, Colin (2005) 'Explanatory Typologies in Qualitative Studies of International Politics', *International Organization*, 59(2): 293–326.

Eriksson, Birgitta, Jan Ch. Karlsson and Tuula Bergqvist (2011) 'The Development of Attitudes to Work in Sweden', pp. 126–38 in Bengt Furåker, Kristina Håkansson and Jan Ch. Karlsson (eds), *Commitment to Work and Job Satisfaction. Studies of Work Orientations*. London: Routledge.

Finley, Moses I. (1981) *Economy and Society in Ancient Greece*. London: Chatto & Windus.

Karasek, Robert A. (1979) 'Job Demands, Job Decision Latitude, and Mental Strain: Implications for Job Redesign', *Administrative Science Quarterly*, 24(2): 285–308.

Karasek, Robert and Töres Theorell (1990) *Healthy Work. Stress, Productivity, and the Reconstruction of Working Life*. New York: Basic Books.

Karlsson, Jan Ch. (2004) 'The Ontology of Work. Social Relations and Doing in the Sphere of Necessity', pp. 90–112 in Steve Fleetwood and Stephen Ackroyd (eds), *Critical Realist Applications in Organisation and Management Studies*. London: Routledge.

Karlsson, Jan Ch. (2012) *Organizational Misbehaviour in the Workplace. Narratives of Dignity and Resistance*. Basingstoke: Palgrave Macmillan.

Karlsson, Jan Ch. (2013 [1986]) *Begreppet arbete*. Lund: Arkiv.

Kolb, David A. (1984) *Experiential Learning. Experience as the Source of Learning and Development*. Upper Saddle River: Prentice Hall.

Lazarsfeld, Paul F. (1937) 'Some Remarks on the Typological Procedures in Social Research', *Zeitschrift für Sozialforschung,* VI: 119–39.

Lazarsfeld, Paul F. and Allen H. Barton (1965 [1951]) 'Qualitative Measurement in the Social Sciences: Classification, Typologies, and Indices', pp. 155–92 in Daniel Learner and Harold D. Lasswell (eds), *The Policy Sciences*. Stanford: Stanford University Press.

PART II
Tools for writing social science

So far we have discussed analytical tools for theorizing – devices for thinking visually and systematically in order to develop theory, whether in quantitative or qualitative studies. But all these analyses, all this working out and constructing of concepts and theories, should result in writing essays, articles and books to let your teacher, fellow students, colleagues and the world know about your analyses. Becker puts it nicely:

> [I]ntellectual life is a dialog among people interested in the same topic. You can eavesdrop on the conversation and learn from it, but eventually you ought to add something yourself. Your research project isn't done until you have written it up and launched it into the conversation by publishing it.
>
> *(Becker 1986: 124)*

If your own curiosity should be satisfied in the research process, you have to rouse the readers' curiosity in the reporting process. If you play around with concepts through experimenting with their relations in displays and property spaces to satisfy your curiosity in the research process, you play around with relations between arguments at different levels in the reporting process to satisfy your audience's curiosity. In both the research process and the reporting process, it is important to get your ideas down on paper. You do not really know what you think until you have written it down. It is not until then that you can notice some of the gaps in your theoretical and argumentative ideas, but also their potentials. It is therefore not until in the reporting process that you need to start taking care of *how* things are written – that is that it is written in such a way that your audience can understand your message, your proposal of ? → !.

Few rules are needed for writing in the research process, but there is a wealth of whole books on how to do it in the reporting process. Still, this distinction is seldom noticed in books on academic writing. The closest we come is an akin and helpful distinction between writing for discovery and for presentation in which Mills (1977 [1959]: 205) stresses the importance of the interplay between the two types of writing. In writing for discovery, you try to make your thoughts clear to yourself, and when you think they are, you write for presentation to others. What usually happens then, Mills says, is that you find that the idea is not as clear as you imagined, which makes you start again writing for discovery – and so on. Like we said in Chapter 1, the research process and the reporting process go on at the same time, although you always need to know which process you are working in. They also have a common element in that you play about with relations in both. In the research process, you experiment with concepts and relations between them, in the reporting process, you play about with arguments for your proposal and relations between them.

A second likeness is that if constructing social theory is working on already existing theories in the research process, writing in the reporting process is mostly working on texts you have already written. Writing is primarily rewriting. It is easy when you start out as a student to think that you just 'write up' your ideas in the essay you are required to present to your teacher – and that is it. You soon learn differently, as experienced writers testify. So one of them says:

> 'I doubt whether I have ever published a chapter in which every paragraph has not been re-written . . . fully three times, and reconsidered, pen in hand, fully thirty; yet even now I rarely read a chapter of my own without seeing that it ought to be rewritten.'
>
> *(Henry Adams in Sica 2014: 3)*

And from a course on writing in which the students had practiced editing and rewriting a text, something that showed that they did not realize the following:

> [People] who write professionally, and write a lot, routinely rewrite as we just had. I wanted them to believe that this was not unusual and that they should expect to rewrite a lot, so I told them (truthfully) that I habitually rewrote manuscripts eight to ten times before publication. . . . Since . . . they thought that 'good writers' (people like their teachers) got everything right the first time, that shocked them.
>
> *(Becker 1986: 6)*

Our experience of writing this book corroborates these statements in full.

In this part we present a model, which we call the Model of Argumentation, for systematically writing scientific texts. How do you write such a text? How do you systematically pursue a proposal in your reports – be it essays, articles or books, be it reports of quantitative or qualitative studies? Often we have met the idea among doctoral students that a social science report should be written like a detective story. But such a story can be told in at least two different ways. One is like the Ellery Queen film series, in which the audience is continuously presented with clues as to who the murderer is – and towards the end, Ellery himself turns to us and says that we have been presented with all the clues and that we now should be able to disclose the murderer. The Model of Argumentation does not encourage us to write according to that idea of letting our audience figure out for itself what our ?→! is. It rather inspires us to write like it is a Lieutenant Columbo film, in which the viewers know from the start who the murderer is and the interesting thing is how Columbo's investigation step by step leads him to expose the murderer. Following this way of telling your story, you start out with explaining what your chain of reasoning, your proposal of ? → ! looks like. Then you systematically present your arguments for the proposal. Thereby you encourage your audience to follow your argumentation rather than guess at clues.

But will not the text you produce become unbearably boring when you write it by applying the Model of Argumentation, stressing logic and systematic argumentation? There has now and then been a debate in the social sciences on which style to use to be 'objective' and 'scientific' and if more 'literary' or even 'poetic' styles are to be preferred – or what Clifford Geertz (1988: 9) calls an author-evacuated and author-saturated text, respectively (for a short overview, see Swedberg 2014: 204–9). One of those debates took place between well-known sociologists including Kai Erikson (2008a, 2008b), Howard S. Becker (2008), Dorothy Smith (2008) and Ben Agger (2008). In this most informative exchange, they all seem to agree that *clarity* is the most important thing. In this light, the Model of Argumentation lays the foundation for clarity in your argumentation, but it does not determine the style of writing. The model is consistent with objective scientific as well as literary and poetic writing. There are many dimensions behind how you write, but you are always part of a culture of writing – you never write alone. Your discipline, the type of theory you are theorizing, the entity of the theory and numerous other things influence how you write. Our advice is to not regard the model and clarity in systematically presenting your argumentation as obstacles to good social science writing – whether by 'good' you mean objective, scientific, literary or poetic writing.

We start this part with a chapter (Chapter 7) about what in the science of rhetoric is called the rhetorical situation, a social structure you enter as soon as you start writing for an audience. We thereby concentrate on the subject matter of your report and especially how to use the Model of Argumentation to systematize your presentation. The model is a hierarchical tool to formulate your arguments through a chain of reasoning running through the whole report supported by a number of chains of argument, each of which in their turn is sustained by a number of arguments. In Chapter 8, we provide you with examples of how to use the model, first in writing and then in reading a social science text. The first part is devoted to a reconstruction of how we wrote Chapter 2 of this book, including how playing around with arguments made us realize when we had to rewrite according to a different principle from the one we had experimented with initially. Thereafter, we analyse the structure of Chapter 4 to show that the same model can help you to scrutinize the way the argumentation of a social science text is built up, by this means making it easier to understand the author's ?→!. Finally, Chapter 9 pulls the threads of the whole book together by following our research and reporting processes of a study of forecasts of working life and an article we wrote as part of that study. We exemplify (some of) the displays and property spaces we played around with in the research process as well as relations between different arguments with the help of the Model of Argumentation in the reporting process.

References

Agger, Ben (2008) 'Political Sentences: Anti-Intellectualism, Obscurantism and Polymorphous Perversity', *Sociological Inquiry*, 78(3): 423–30.
Becker, Howard S. (1986) *Writing for Social Scientists*. Chicago: University of Chicago Press.
Becker, Howard S. (2008) 'Above All, Write with Clarity and Precision', *Sociological Inquiry*, 78(3): 412–16.
Erikson, Kai (2008a) 'On Sociological Writing', *Sociological Inquiry*, 78(3): 399–411.
Erikson, Kai (2008b) 'Kai's Response to Howard, Hana, Ben, and Dorothy', *Sociological Inquiry*, 78(3): 437–42.
Geertz, Clifford (1988) *Work and Lives. The Anthropologist as Author*. Cambridge: Polity.
Mills, C. Wright (1977 [1959]) *The Sociological Imagination*. Oxford: Oxford University Press.
Sica, Alan (2014) 'Kind of, Sort of, Maybe', *Contemporary Sociology*, 43(1): 1–10.
Smith, Dorothy E. (2008) 'From the 14th Floor to the Sidewalk: Writing Sociology at Ground Level', *Sociological Inquiry*, 78(3): 417–22.
Swedberg, Richard (2014) *The Art of Social Theory*. Stanford: Stanford University Press.

7
THE MODEL OF ARGUMENTATION
Chain of reasoning, chains of argument and arguments

Writing in the reporting process involves rhetoric – not in the pejorative meaning the word often has in everyday use: 'That is just rhetoric! It is not true!' Instead, it can be regarded as an attempt to convince someone of something – or, more elaborately:

> [The] exercise of arguing in such a way as to make what one says plausible and accessible to one's hearer [or reader], to bring it home to him or her – in a manner which enhances the hearer's ability to make what one says an independent part of his or her own perceptions and decisions.
> *(Edmondson 1984: xiii)*

There can, of course, be misuses of rhetoric in social science writing (cf. Stones 1996: Ch. 7), but we discuss the rhetorical situation that always arises whenever you write for an audience. We have claimed that the subject of social science – social entities – is made up of relations and relations between relations. In consequence, social theory is constructed by statements identifying relations between examined concepts and theorizing is playing about with concepts and relations in order to produce such a theory. Accordingly, when you present your theory to an audience, it is important that your argumentation is systematically built up by relations between arguments at different levels to cover the relations between the concepts of the theory.

The rhetorical situation

There is a science studying rhetoric and it can be described like this: 'Rhetoric is the systematic study of the acts of communication by which people convince others of the reality or truth of their assertions' (Hunter 1990: 4). It has been found that a rhetorical situation arises whenever you enter the reporting process of writing something intended to be read by other people. The first thing about handling rhetorical situations is to be aware that there are such things and that you can influence them. The rhetorical situation contains a number of problems that you have to solve – and if you do not try to solve them, they remain problems. In essence, we have only one piece of advice on this matter: make yourself aware of the problems of the rhetorical situation so that you can try to unravel them consciously. There is no way of writing a scientific text that does not involve a rhetorical situation – there is no such thing as simply stating the facts.

There has been an extensive debate about the concept of rhetorical situation ever since Lloyd F. Bitzer (1968) first presented his analysis of it. He claimed that the rhetorical situation is an objective reality that individuals enter in certain types of speech or writings that determine their actions. This determinism has been criticized from the point of view that the rhetorical situation is entirely subjective, being created independently by each speaker or writer (Vatz 1973). We position ourselves between these extremes, acknowledging that there is a real rhetorical situation but that it can be influenced by individuals in interaction in the same way as any other social structure (Archer 1995; Elder-Vass 2010). You do enter the rhetorical situation when writing in the reporting process, but you can change the conditions of the situation by your actions – the rhetorical situation is an objective and a subjective entity at the same time constituted by the relation between author and audience (Consigny 1974; Garret and Xiao 1993; Gorrell 1997).

'Rhetoric' means communication in order to assure an audience that your message is valid, which is what a scientific text ultimately is about. You write – report research results – in order to convince other researchers (and sometimes also practitioners) that you have made an empirical discovery, refined an existing theory or formulated a new theory. The theory of the rhetorical situation conveys a number of problems in convincing someone of something, problems that we apply here to the specific rhetorical situation of writing a social science report. The main problems involved in such rhetorical situations are your purpose, your persona, your audience, your tone and the subject matter (Hult 1996: 113–16). All problems of the rhetorical situation are interconnected, which means that the solutions ought not to contradict each other – at least not very much. We regard the rhetorical situation as a whole that is more than its parts, but we analytically separate those parts in order to reflect on them.

Purpose

A scientific report should have an explicit purpose – that is advice on having an explicit purpose can be found in any textbook on writing such texts. We agree with that, and we can formulate it as making clear which question you are going to answer in which way in ?→!. The problem of the purpose of the rhetorical situation is, however, a different one. You enter the rhetorical situation with other purposes than your research aim. Maybe you want an exam that opens up new parts of the labour market, perhaps you wish to prove your brilliance to your colleagues, you could also be interested in being published in a specific journal with a high impact factor, or possibly you write in order to help an underprivileged group – for example, women or the working class – in a political struggle. All these possible purposes pose problems that do not go away if you leave them unsolved. Each problem requires that you do something about it.

If you write for an exam, there are rules you have to follow. Showing brilliance requires that you know what is regarded as brilliant among the colleagues you want to impress; most journals have instructions for authors, which a manuscript editor guards scrupulously, and political texts usually have to be written in a different style from academic texts. As Becker observes:

> You will write one way for the people you work with closely on a joint project [in our terms, in the research process], another way for professional colleagues in your subspecialty, still another for professional colleagues in other specialties and disciplines, and differently yet for the 'intelligent layman'.
>
> *(Becker 1986: 18)*

We want to add that the precondition for solving the rhetorical problem of purpose is that you have made clear to yourself what the problem consists of. Our advice is simple: make yourself aware of your rhetorical purpose, so you can handle it in a conscious way.

Persona

A 'persona' is the character a person has or wants others to believe he or she has. Becker (1986: Ch. 2) makes a distinction between four types of persona, which he has found in sociological writing. One is the 'classy' persona, which a student of his expressed as 'I am looking for a writing style that makes me sound smart' (1986: 31). Through using a very complicated language and strange words, this persona conveys themself as somebody who understands things better than others, and, therefore, should be assumed to be right. Another is the 'inside dopester', who heaps detailed knowledge about a strictly delimited topic, leading to acceptance as an expert. Then there is the authoritative persona, claiming that we sociologists or we political scientists or we economists know a lot of things that you lay persons are ignorant about. Still, they say, 'We must recognize . . .' and 'It is important that we realize . . .' and that 'one' has to do this and that. They are also fond of the passive voice, as it conveys that what they say is not their personal views but scientific fact based on their unique knowledge. Finally, there is the 'folksy' persona, who says 'We may know a few things others don't, but it's nothing special' (1986: 36) and to which Becker confesses that he strives:

> Such writers want to use their similarity to others, their ordinariness, to persuade readers that what they are saying is right. We write more informally, favour the personal pronoun, and appeal to what we-and-the-reader know in common rather than what we know and the reader doesn't.
>
> *(Becker 1986: 37)*

Hult also mentions a couple of possible personas in social science texts, and even though she does not define them, they are easy to interpret as dualisms or opposite ends of a continuum: 'objective and fair' versus 'heated and passionate' and 'sincere and persuasive' versus 'informative and rational' (Hult 1996: 114). There are probably more possible personas in social science writings, but our advice is again: make yourself aware of which persona you want to convey, so you can handle it in a conscious way when writing a social science report.

Audience

Hult (1996: 115) defines the audience as 'Those who are the most likely to read your writing.' In terms of the rhetorical situation, we could also put it as those who you *want* to read your writing. Of course, you have to adapt your way of writing to this audience, but this is a topic that we will not go into as it is covered in all handbooks on social science writing.

If you are at the beginning of your academic career – and sometimes also later on – it can be a difficult step to go from writing in the research process to doing it in the reporting process. You keep writing as if your audience knows almost as much about the topic as you do. You take a lot for granted, not elaborating your argumentation in full. We have all committed this sin. You can, however, avoid doing that by imagining an audience to which you have to explain every step of the argumentation and which will read your text with a quite sceptical air. When writing in the reporting process, we often imagine a person who has the very unpleasant habit of looking totally unconvinced when reading our texts. It can be quite useful to think of such a person when constructing your argumentation about ? → !. Of course, you can have a real person in mind, someone to whom you must explain exactly your way of reasoning. In any case you should always be aware that now you are not writing for your own benefit or for your closest colleagues, but for an audience that you want to convince.

Tone

There are, of course, different ideals of style in all types of writing – and so it is also *within* social science. One of us (Jan Ch. Karlsson) was, for example, present at one occasion when this became very clear. There were a number of professors from different disciplines in a meeting to review a number of students who wanted to become doctoral candidates. Most of us agreed that a certain student was the most suitable one, but one of the professors had a divergent opinion. The professor claimed that this student could not be expected to become a serious researcher as she presented and argued her research problems in a chatty and unscientific way. When we discussed this it turned out that the professor's impression emanated from the student writing 'I' when turning to the reader, such as 'So far I have described how I structured the interviews and now I continue to the interviewees.' Therefore, the professor got the impression of a less serious and unscientific tone – and without reflecting upon it, he translated this to the student being a less serious, chatty, unscientific person. The professor's own style ideal, it turned out, was that in writing social science texts the author should use the pronoun 'we' or preferably the passive form, such as 'So far a description of the structuring of the interviews has been provided and now we continue to the interviewees' (cf. Billig 2013). What we can learn from this simple story is that style and tone are important when writing for an audience. It is a problem that always exists in the rhetorical situation. As Patrick Dunleavy points out in a book on authoring a PhD:

> How your text uses terminology, the concepts and vocabulary it deploys, and the style cues that you signal as author – all these will be used by readers to try and classify you and your text, to understand where you are coming from, where your scholarly tribal affiliations really lie. If these cues do not fit with your self-classification in the professional scene, or what you later say and do, then readers will receive incompatible messages – and code them as confused authorial purposes.
>
> *(Dunleavy 2003: 90)*

Therefore, consciously choose a tone in the reporting process and adjust your writing to it. As the example illustrates, connections between the parts of the rhetorical situation showed that the ideal tone of the professor expressed a classy persona while that of the student represented a folksy one.

The subject matter

Your proposal, which is your question, your answer and the road between them (? → !), makes up the subject matter of your essay, article or book. In the rest of this chapter, we go into detail on how to build up this text of the reporting process. We present systematic ways of constructing the chain of reasoning, relating the chains of argument to the chain of reasoning, and relating arguments to the chains of argument to build up the structure of your report. This means that we suggest a tool that we have found to be helpful in the reporting process, both in our teaching and in our own writing of articles and books (including this one), which we call the Model of Argumentation. It is a fairly simple model of systematic presentation of relations between logical arguments in order to pursue a proposal. If rhetoric is an attempt to convince someone of something, argumentation is doing that by giving 'a set of reasons or evidence in support of a conclusion' (Weston 2009: xi).

The model can be used as an aid in understanding and dissecting research reports written by your colleagues, which we will discuss in the second part of Chapter 8. When it comes to the reporting process, it is more important as a tool for ordering the presentation of your proposal, something that we take up in the first part of that chapter. But we start with presenting the model.

The model

In consequence with the associations between social ontology (social entities are relations), epistemology (social theories are relations between concepts) and rhetoric (relations between arguments) that we have taken up repeatedly, it is a relational and hierarchical model with three levels (Figure 7.1): (1) chain of reasoning (CR); (2) chains of argument (CA); and (3) argument (A). A chain of reasoning is systematically built up from a number of chains of argument and each chain of argument is in the same way built up from a number of arguments. Let us take your writing an article as an example. The chain of reasoning contains the whole article, from the first word to the last. It comprises the proposal you are pursuing, the whole reporting process of ?→!. The chains of argument make up the parts that together form the chain of reasoning, while a number of arguments in their turn form a chain of argument. These relations are symbolized by the sign} (let us call it a curly bracket), which is extremely important as the relations in union build the whole structure of the argumentation; it is the cement keeping the model together.

When you are writing an article, start with formulating the chain of reasoning, the ?→!. This is the message you want to convey to the world – or at least to your audience, such as: 'Three structures are necessary for the reproduction of gender segregation in organizations, namely gender, power and division of labour' (cf. pp. 47–8). The same goes for when you read an article: start with trying to figure out the author's message, which is the chain of reasoning of the text, such as 'a missing classification of retail markets can be built on the dimensions customers' cost consciousness and style consciousness, resulting in mass style, boutique style, value fashion and other types of market' (cf. pp. 57–8). These examples are somewhat simplified as they do not take into account the empirical results, which naturally are incorporated in your proposition. But this is just to give you a first idea of what a chain of reasoning can look like. The important thing is that the chain of reasoning stretches through the whole article – it is the proposition, the result of the research process and the value of which you wish to convince your audience.

Now, the chain of reasoning cannot stand alone; it needs support in the form of chains of argument that together build up an argumentatively stable structure. It must have systematic backing, symbolized in Figure 7.1 as a curly bracket between each chain of argument and the chain of reasoning. A chain of reasoning is a whole, covering your message, but it can be divided into parts – each part being formulated as a chain of argument. The same principle applies to the arguments, argument$_1$ to argument$_n$, supporting each chain of argument.

The chain of argument$_1$ of the chain of reasoning, 'A missing classification of retail markets can be built on the dimensions customers' cost consciousness and style consciousness, resulting in mass style, boutique style, value fashion and other types of market' is, we suggest, 'The literature lacks a classification of retail markets', covering this part of the chain of reasoning: 'A missing classification of retail markets'. Table 7.1 shows part of the structure of the argumentation, although we have simplified the presentation compared to the model in Figure 7.1 to save space.

Chain of argument$_2$ is 'Two dimensions, customers' cost consciousness and style consciousness, can be used to construct the classification' covering the part of the chain of reasoning saying 'can be built on the dimensions customers' cost consciousness and style consciousness'. Chain of argument$_3$ is 'Combining the presence

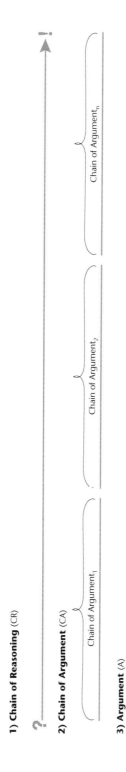

FIGURE 7.1 The Model of Argumentation for the reporting process

118 Tools for writing social science

TABLE 7.1 Example of the structure of an argumentation

> CR: *A missing classification of retail markets can be built on the dimensions customers' cost consciousness and style consciousness, resulting in mass style, boutique style, value fashion and other types of market.*
>
> CA_1: *The literature lacks a classification of retail markets.*
> A_1: *We have made a search of the literature on retail markets.*
> A_2: *No classification of such markets was found.*
> CA_2: *Two dimensions, customers' cost consciousness and style consciousness, can be used to construct the classification*
> A_1: . . .
> A_n: . . .
> CA_3: *Combining the presence and absence of the dimensions*
> A_1: . . .
> A_n: . . .
> CA_4: *The outcomes are mass style, boutique style, value fashion and other types of market*
> A_1: . . .
> A_n: . . .

and absence of the dimensions', covering 'resulting in'. And finally, chain of argument$_4$ is 'The outcomes are mass style, boutique style, value fashion and other types of market', covering the last part of the chain of reasoning. In this way, the chain of reasoning is related to a number of chains of argument, each supporting (the curly brackets) a specific part of it. Each chain of argument is, in its turn, built up by a number of arguments. Let us just take chain of argument$_1$ as an example: 'The literature lacks a classification of retail markets.' Argument$_1$ says, 'We have made a search of the literature on retail markets' and argument$_2$, 'No classification of such markets was found.'

Being hierarchical, the model can be moved between different levels of a research report (Figure 7.2). If you are writing a book, you construct your argumentation for the book as a whole, that is your chain of reasoning, whereby the different parts make up the chains of argument and each chapter is an argument. In the book you are reading now (check the table of contents), this means that the whole book, from the first word to the last, is a chain of reasoning, while Chapter 1, Part I, Part II and Chapter 9 are chains of argument, together making up this chain of reasoning. Finally, Chapters 2 to 6 are the arguments of the chain of argument Part I, while Chapters 7 and 8 are the arguments building up the chain of argument Part II. But you can also move the model to a lower level, such as a single part. Then the part becomes the chain of reasoning, the chapters' chains of argument and the main sections of the chapters become arguments. If we, for example, look at Part I of this book, it is then the chain of reasoning. *Part I Tools for theorizing in social science* and Chapters 2 to 6 are chains of argument, and such sections as 'Graphic representations' of Part I and 'What is a display?' of Chapter 2 are arguments. A final example is to move the model down to a single chapter (or an article). The chapter (or article) is then, of course, the chain of reasoning, while the main sections are the chains of argument and the

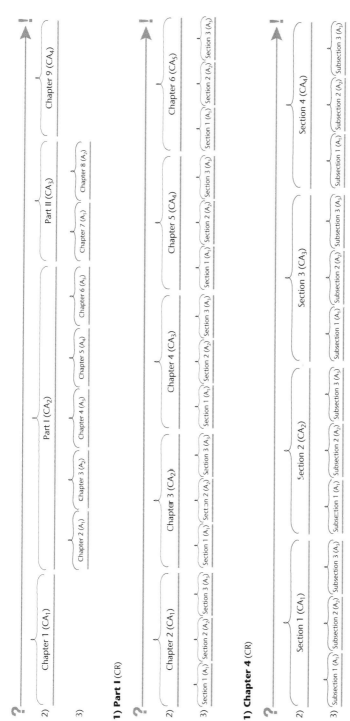

FIGURE 7.2 Detailed Model of Argumentation of the reporting process at different levels

sub-sections are the arguments. Look at Chapter 4, '*Basics of property spaces*', which is now the chain of reasoning. The sections '*Constructing a property space*', '*Housekeeping*', '*Labelling the types: terms*' and so on are the chains of argument, and each table and the text belonging to it are arguments.

The examples should also make it clear that your chain of reasoning, chains of argument and arguments ought to be mirrored in the disposition of the report. Why do you divide books into parts, chapters and sections? Why do you insert subheadings and sub-subheadings? Why do you divide articles into sections, sections into sub-sections and sub-sections into paragraphs? Because it is a way of showing your readers the structure of your argumentation. All the way from Chapter 1 down to a new paragraph in a sub-section of a chapter you indicate that here comes a new part of the argumentation of? →!. Dunleavy (2003) says that it is almost impossible for you as an author to keep control of every argument and even less so for a reader. Therefore, it is necessary to put in 'cues [in the text] provided by "organizers", especially the sections of the chapter and their associated armoury of headings, which should convey in condensed form a sense of the argument being made' (2003: 77). That is the job that divisions into sections and paragraphs, headings and subheadings do.

Summary

The rhetorical situation is a social structure to which you necessarily relate when you write a social science report, such as an essay, an article or a book. It contains a number of problems for you as a writer and we suggest that you take them on rather than ignoring them. If you disregard them, they still exist as problems; if you take them on consciously, you can solve them. The difficulties of the rhetorical situation are, first, your purpose of writing the text – please your teacher, impress your colleagues, get an article accepted, get a book published by Routledge. Make yourself aware what it is you want. Second, which persona you wish your text to impress on the reader – classy, authoritative, folksy, objective, passionate? Third, to which audience you turn, as each type of audience requires different ways of writing. Our advice is that you imagine a very sceptical readership, requiring you to argue every part of your proposal extremely clearly and systematically. Fourth, the tone you seek to accomplish is connected to your persona and the audience you turn to. Different styles of writing ooze different personas and appeal to different audiences. Finally, you have to make clear the subject matter of your proposal to yourself in order to be able to make it clear to your audience.

For help in the latter endeavour, we suggest the Model of Argumentation, which pictures relations between arguments at different levels. This is because a theory is constructed by relations between examined concepts and statements about social entities existing in the world and it is these relations you want to present to your readers in the form of your proposition of ?→!. The model contains three levels – chain of reasoning, chains of argument and arguments – and through relating them to each other (the curly brackets), you can build up your argumentation. The chain of reasoning runs through the entire text, it is the thesis you want your readers to be convinced of. Under the chain of reasoning there are a number of chains of argument supporting it. Each chain of argument systematically builds up a part of the chain of reasoning. Finally, each chain of argument is supported by a number of arguments, which together construct it.

We recommend that you apply the Model of Argumentation as a tool for revealing the argumentation of social theories you read and for building your own argumentation in social science texts you write. In the next chapter, we exemplify how you can do this, thereby giving you more detailed suggestions on how to use this tool.

References

Archer, Margaret S. (1995) *Realist Social Theory: The Morphogenetic Approach*. Cambridge: Cambridge University Press.

Becker, Howard S. (1986) *Writing for Social Scientists*. Chicago: University of Chicago Press.

Billig, Michael (2013) *Learn to Write Badly. How to Succeed in the Social Sciences*. Cambridge: Cambridge University Press.

Bitzer, Lloyd F. (1968) 'The Rhetorical Situation', *Philosophy and Rhetoric*, 1(1): 1–14.

Consigny, Scott (1974) 'Rhetoric and Its Situations', *Philosophy and Rhetoric*, 7(3): 175–86.

Dunleavy, Patrick (2003) *Authoring a PhD. How to Plan, Draft, Write and Finish a Doctoral Thesis or Dissertation*. Basingstoke: Palgrave Macmillan.

Edmondson, Ricca (1984) *Rhetoric in Sociology*. London: Macmillan.

Elder-Vass, Dave (2010) *The Causal Power of Social Structures. Emergence, Structure and Agency*. Cambridge: Cambridge University Press.

Garret, Mary and Xiaosui Xiao (1993) 'The Rhetorical Situation Revisited', *Rhetoric Society Quarterly*, 23(2): 30–40.

Gorrell, Donna (1997) 'The Rhetorical Situation Again: Linked Components in a Venn Diagram', *Philosophy and Rhetoric*, 30(4): 395–412.

Hult, Christine A. (1996) *Researching and Writing in the Social Sciences*. Boston: Allyn and Bacon.

Hunter, Albert (1990) 'Introduction: Rhetoric in Research', pp. 1–22 in Albert Hunter (ed.), *The Rhetoric of Social Research: Understood and Believed*. New Brunswick: Rutgers University Press.

Stones, Rob (1996) *Sociological Reasoning. Towards a Past-Modern Sociology*. Basingstoke: Macmillan.

Vatz, Richard E. (1973) 'The Myth of the Rhetorical Situation', *Philosophy and Rhetoric*, 6(3): 154–61.

Weston, Anthony (2009) *A Rulebook for Arguments*. Indianapolis: Hacket.

8

EXAMPLES OF USING THE MODEL OF ARGUMENTATION

You can apply the argumentative model both when you read a social science report and when you write one yourself. To demonstrate this, we reconstruct our own use of the model during the course of writing and rewriting Chapter 2 on the characteristics of displays. Hence, before you go on, we recommend that you have a quick look at that chapter, and then continue to consult it as you proceed. Later in this chapter, we illustrate how to apply the model when reading a social science report. We apply it to Chapter 4 of this book, which relates to the basic traits and tasks of property spaces, and, therefore, it is useful for you to consult this chapter too.

Before we get involved in the chapters, here are some words of simple advice from our own experience of using the Model of Argumentation that can be applied both when reading and writing social science texts. Start by expressing your proposition (or that of the author) for the whole book, chapter or article, by using a single sentence by way of a statement. Do not formulate this in a descriptive way, for example: 'The proposition of this book concerns how to theorize in the research process and how to build the argumentation in the reporting process.' Instead, it can be formulated like this: 'Displays and property spaces are tools for theorizing in the research process, whereas the Model of Argumentation is a tool for systematic writing in the reporting process.' This assertive sentence expresses the chain of reasoning used in the book, at least in a preliminary way. It can, of course, be changed during the process of writing, since you cannot predict how any chain of reasoning, chain of argument or argument might develop. You may find it necessary to modify or revise some parts of them along the way, which will usually have consequences for other parts. Even the version that goes to print is not always the final one, as you may want to change parts of your argumentation in the next edition of your book, or in a subsequent article. Although you never stop rewriting and playing about with arguments, you should still formulate preliminary endpoints. In the Introduction to Part I of this book, we presented the argument that displays and property spaces used in theorizing can be seen as preliminary endpoints. We think that this provides an important insight that may be helpful in the writing process. It can make things easier for you when you suffer from analysis paralysis or intellectual drought. It can also help you to limit yourself if you suffer from hubris or an unlimited flow of ideas that cannot fit into one single report – at least that is our experience. If you look upon your text and ideas as preliminary endpoints that must be made visual and explicit at various stages of the writing process, then these can have a positive impact both on your creativity and on your capacity to remain focused on your main thesis and arguments. This is in line with the philosophical idea that all scientific knowledge is fallible and corrigible (Danermark et al. 2002: 141–2).

The process of writing a social science text: an example

Writing Chapter 2 about the basics of displays was surprisingly demanding. Frankly, the reason was that we had not defined what a display was in a strictly conceptual sense when we started to write the chapter. We nurtured the idea that we wanted to present a complementary alternative to property spaces, by way of a device that could be used in a looser theoretical way than that provided by property spaces. Hence, in relation to the book as a whole, we agreed that this idea should be the purpose of Chapter 2 (and later also Chapter 3), while the purpose of the chapter itself was to present what a display is. Therefore, we initially formulated the chain of reasoning of the chapter as 'displays are tools used for theorizing with fewer constraints than property spaces'. Another aspect that we had to take into account when setting up the internal structure of Chapter 2 was the fact that the chapters about property spaces had, to a large extent, already been written when we started to write about displays. Therefore, we wanted to keep in mind the logic and the structure of Chapter 4, *Basics of property spaces*, when writing the new chapter. One consequence was that we decided to give it the corresponding title, *Basics of displays*. However, the structure of the chapter on displays is somewhat different from that of the chapter about property spaces, as displays have fewer constraints than property spaces. Consequently, the chapter was initially written in a rather explorative way with dead ends, loops, repositioning of chunks of texts and bits and pieces going straight to a document called 'the recycle bin', or simply deleted. Yet another aspect that formed the process of writing the chapter, as well as the book as a whole, was that we had agreed at an early stage that the purpose of the book was not to introduce a number of theories in depth, but instead to use them as examples of theorizing by putting displays and property spaces together – by playing about with them.

A common misunderstanding of the process of writing is that it is only about the writing itself. Paradoxically, writing is for the most part about removing or even deleting as part of rewriting. Since these operations are a rather painful activity, there is always the risk that a piece of text can develop into an excess of words lacking stringency and with unclear chains of reasoning and argument. We use a three-phase strategy to deal with pieces of text that we are unsure about. The first stage is to highlight those parts in yellow. You might be a bit uncertain about whether a specific section is just misplaced, or if it is totally irrelevant. It is not hard to highlight it yellow; after all, it is still there. The next time you read or revise the document, you might be better able to see the whole picture and the parts, and whether they make sense and are logical. You might end up moving the section to the place where it more suitably belongs, or you might put it as a footnote at the bottom of the page (but this cannot be done with longer passages). Now the part is removed from the main text, but it is not totally gone. You can still glance at it. Then, when you read or revise the text for the third, fourth or fifth time, and feel totally comfortable with the text as it is, move the footnote to the recycle bin or delete it. Whether you are the sole author of a text or not, always invite others to read and comment on it. We have the advantage of co-writing, and can therefore talk about the text and help each other to spot weaknesses and missing links. In terms of writing, when deleting text, it is easier to 'kill someone else's darlings than it is to kill your own'.

After we had decided to write about the basics of displays, and that the chapter should consist of a definition of displays and some arguments for their usefulness (chains of argument), we turned to the literature. We were simply interested in what other social science scholars had written about displays. We began with piles of books and articles on our desks, and almost blank pages on our computer screens, with just the chapter's title, *Basics of displays*, at the top of the page. We soon found that the literature on displays was scanty, especially on their use as tools for theorizing. There was also a wide variation in the ways in which different graphical formats such as models and figures were used. The first fragments of our written text relied heavily on displays as tools for sorting and analysing data, mainly due to the fact that displays are often to be found in method books. However, in our case, these written pages and chains of argument turned out to be dead ends for this chapter, since our topic was theorizing rather than how to analyse or categorize data. Therefore, we had to revise our first objective, which was to present how other researchers had defined and used displays. With regard to text written, this was the first piece that was moved to the recycle bin. It went straight there, with no yellow highlighting or relegating to a footnote. It was a major dead end, but, as such, it helped us to define and forge the scope of the book. It helped us to focus on it being a book about theorizing. Often, knowing what to write comes as a result of acquiring the knowledge of what not to write.

So, back to a blank page again, but this time we started to write about what a display is – from *our* point of view. That meant that we went back to our chain of reasoning – displays are tools for theorizing of a less bound kind than property spaces – which we had lost sight of when immersing ourselves in the literature. To reveal the basics, we needed to formulate a definition, in other words, an argument of what a display is. Therefore, we asked ourselves how a display can be used when theorizing, what its purpose is and what it can do. These questions resulted in the heading, '*What is a display?*', thus expressing a new chain of argument, and this was when the writing process restarted. Aptly, the simple displays presented in Figures 2.1 and 2.2 provided the catalyst for our writing. By scrawling on a whiteboard, we had been playing about with different concepts in order to find a fruitful definition. It was by so doing that the thoughts of relations and relata emerged. We then refined our thoughts and arguments by adding the literal definition: 'a scientific display is a graphical representation of relations and relata that answers one or more research questions or statements'. By forming our definition of the concept of displays, we were also able to be more specific about their strengths and potential when theorizing. We used a series of arguments to claim that, although displays can take on many different forms and can be used in a great variety of ways, they have certain common characteristics. We argued that, by way of a graphic format, a display should either answer one or more questions, or illustrate one or more statements or assumptions. It has to be relational, and it should connect two or more sets (relata) to each other. By giving a number of pedagogical examples, we also argued that relata and relations depend on each other in order to exist. We further picked up the argument from Chapter 1 that relations are essential in social science, that you have to be cautious and be aware of what kind of relation you have in mind when theorizing and that displays are also valuable for this purpose. In retrospect, we can note that, once we had settled on our definition, this section was rather easy and fun to write. It paved the way forward. When you get that feeling of knowing how to proceed with your writing, keep on writing in that direction.

However, once we had decided on the definition and put forward arguments for it, our flow of writing came to an abrupt end. We realized that we had to say something about graphical representation as it was a part of the definition of a display. As social scientists, we were not very familiar with this field. We started to read and write about various graphical representations in order to achieve the following: first, we looked for arguments that graphical representations other than text are useful when theorizing; and second, we wanted to distinguish displays from other graphical formats such as diagrams and symbols. Among the literature studied, we found and became inspired by Banks (2001), who stresses that social scientists should make use of the variety of visual formats at hand. We were especially enthused by his idea of a continuum of visual formats, going from plain text at the one end of the spectrum to plain pictures at the other end. As a result, we wrote a section where we used his gradation with a chain of argument addressing this continuum and gave it the subtitle '*Graphic representations*'. In this section, we showed various examples of how the representations can be visualized by using the relational social phenomenon of gender segregation as arguments. After we had written the section, we noted two things. First, that displays span the part of the continuum between diagrams and symbols, and they cannot be reduced to a specific format given in the continuum; second, when writing the chapters about property spaces, we had overlooked the fact that they are also graphic representations, and thus, they also had to be part of the continuum. Since property spaces are more bound than displays, we placed them between tables and diagrams.

This turned, however, out to be problematic. As a result of adding property spaces to the continuum, the whole section of the chapter became inappropriate. The chain of reasoning was about displays, but this new chain of argument concerned something else – property spaces. Thus, we tended to end up with two chains of reasoning: one on displays and the other on both displays and property spaces. We did not recognize this logical discrepancy at once, but did so when we had finished the other parts of the chapter, leaving us with a first rough draft. Generally, when you find two chains of reasoning in a text (whether it be a book, a chapter or an article), something is wrong. If your reasoning is constructed in a systematic way, then there should be only one chain of reasoning. Our solution was to move the whole section about '*Graphic representations*' to the introduction in Part I, as its chain of reasoning embraced all chapters concerning both types of theorizing tools. We also moved other parts from Chapter 2 to the Introduction, such as sections written to frame the usefulness of displays when theorizing. We found that these arguments were also applicable to the discussion about property spaces. It is quite a common activity in the writing process to move things around in order to find a logical fit between the chain of reasoning, the chains of argument and the arguments in each chapter and in the book as a whole.

The next section to write was entitled '*Building blocks of displays*'. The purpose of the section was to describe different types of display by their building blocks, so as to inspire our audience to start constructing their own displays. We argue that there is no convention on how to build displays other than the criteria stated in the definition. In the section, we provide the reader with an overview of basic building blocks; in other words, different ways of depicting relations and relata in order to theorize. Here we started off by giving several different examples of how to construct displays. We wrote and we wrote, but when the section became too long, we realized that we needed to do something about it. We began to highlight in yellow parts that we felt were redundant, or those that were taking the discussion too far from the main intent. When we reread the text, we decided that we had to cut down the number of examples. There were simply too many arguments, and some examples were too complicated; in other words, they were difficult to fit into any chain of argument. We went back to the literature in order to see if we could get some ideas on how to revise the section. Engelhardt's (2002) distinctions between different simple graphical formats according to their structural composition and relations turned out to be suitable for the task. We had his scheme in mind when looking over the construction of the argumentation again and his distinction helped us to move some of the yellow highlighted parts to the recycle bin, while others were turned into footnotes before ending up in the bin. Yet others remained in the section, but were rearranged in order to follow Engelhardt's distinctions between different, but essential, building blocks, such as spatial clustering, separation by separators, line-up, linking and containment. The outcome of this rewriting led to a reduced number of graphically illustrated and literally described *simple* graphical compositions. When writing this section, we realized from our own experience how easy it is to overdo displays. Therefore, we stress that the strength of displays lies in their potential to make complexity understandable. The examples in this section and the next section will reveal this.

The next section, '*Putting a display together*', was written by using the building blocks in the previous section to show how one can develop and combine them into a display as a way to encourage theorizing. In this section, we argue that one fundamental characteristic of a display is to show *how* relata are related to each other, which was also the chain of reasoning of the section (or its chain of argument in relation to the chain of reasoning of the whole chapter). By taking our point of departure in the building blocks from the above section, we could confine the examples to a manageable number and with a logic with which the reader would be familiar. Thus, we continued to argue that a display used for theorizing involves clusters, boundaries and connectedness as line-ups and links between relata in the form of concepts. We then started to describe a number of displays, showing various ways that relata can be connected and how this can have an impact on the understanding of the phenomenon being studied. We emphasized that, on the one hand you have to separate relata from each other, but on the other hand, you must connect them in various ways. In this part, despite the fact that we intended not to depict too many variations, we ended up with quite a number. Some of them were more developed than others and the chapter was getting too long. We then discussed how much we should write about each example. The dilemma that emerged was how to put the displays in a conceptual context that made sense without getting caught up in writing too much about specific theories. Thus, we had to remind ourselves that the purpose of this section was to get the reader to start thinking about how they can put a display together in order to understand social phenomena.

After this recap, we went through the section again, highlighting many passages with yellow, the result of which was extensive chunks of highlighted text. When we reread these passages, we realized that Chapter 2 should be followed by a chapter in which we could present some comprehensive examples on *how to use* displays in theorizing. Whereas the original chain of reasoning for the chapter only concerned their building blocks and how to relate them, we realized that we had again built up a second chain of reasoning, which could be formulated as follows: 'extending, interacting and stepwise are ways of using displays when theorizing'. Therefore, we split Chapter 2 into two parts, and constructed Chapter 3, '*The use of displays in theorizing*', on the basis of the new chain of reasoning. In relation to this, we rewrote almost all the yellow highlighted passages as chains of arguments and arguments. Hence, in this case, a considerable amount of the yellow highlighted text that had been sent to the recycle bin was, in fact, recycled and used in Chapter 3.

After the split of the chapter, it was easier to go back to the section on 'how to put a display together' and write according to our first idea using that chain of argument. As in the previous section, every example on how to put a display together is an argument. In the final edited version, which then became this section, we first describe dichotomies and then more diverse displays with three or more categories. We continue by showing how relata can be separated, ordered in time and separated into phases or viewed as a continuum. Then we present displays where the relationship between different entities can be understood and depicted in terms of one or more of the following: as insiders and outsiders, as core or periphery, and, where one relatum contains another, as separate or overlapping parts. Thereafter, we present separated and ordered relata, where the relationship between them is hierarchical as in pyramid-like displays. We finish the presentation by portraying various examples of linking different nodes to each other; as, for example, in line-ups when linking one to one, or one to many or many to many occurs in different types of network.

The penultimate text we wrote in Chapter 2 was the introduction section. We followed the common advice not to write the introduction first, since you cannot write the introduction until you know what to introduce. The purpose of this section was to capture the reader's interest and give them an idea of what to expect. Here we stated that the chapter would give the reader an idea of what a display is, what the building blocks of a display are and how one can put them together when theorizing; in other words, what had finally become the three main sections of the chapter (its chains of argument). In some cases, you can write a draft introduction, but then it becomes more of a frame of reference and guideline to yourself, which you can glance at once in a while to keep within the given objectives of the chapter. In reality, it is more a way of formulating the chain of reasoning rather than a full introduction. We point out that the chain of reasoning underlying the whole chapter is to argue that displays are tools that are useful in theorizing in the research process, since they can visualize relations between concepts and other relata in heuristic and unbound ways. To convince the readers about the value of using displays, and to get them to start playing around with relations and relata, we affirm that our intention is to show this in a pedagogical way by building on three main sections of the chapter.

Finally, we wrote the '*Summary*'. The purpose of the summary is to remind the audience of what they just read in relation to the objectives of the chapter. It might seem like we are writing the same thing over and over again, which is exactly what we are doing. At this stage, it would be wrong to come up with other ideas and arguments. Hence, surprises in summaries are prohibited. Therefore, we reiterate the explicit purposes of the chapter, which are to show and define what a display is, what its different building blocks are and how one can put a display together in order to foster theorizing. Once again, we emphasize the graphical format of a display, its relational character and its usefulness when answering questions or making statements about social phenomena. After the main body of the text of the summary was written, we went over the chapter again and added *bannisters* between the different sections. The purpose of these is to help the reader to navigate their way through the text. Basically, bannisters tell the reader where we are up to now in the argumentation and where we are going next. Our general advice is to be very generous with distributing bannisters throughout the text. They provide an important device for making the whole structure of the chain of reasoning, chains of argument and arguments clear to your audience. Thus, the last thing we wrote in the '*Summary*' was a bannister to point forward to Chapter 3, as that chapter now includes the next logical step based on the basics of displays that was presented in Chapter 2. In this sentence, we reveal that the following chapter will present three more extensive examples on how to use displays when theorizing. As you know by now, the text and the examples that constitute Chapter 3 were once highlighted yellow and then recycled from Chapter 2.

Some final words of warning when you apply the model. If you find only one chain of argument under the chain of reasoning, something is wrong. It means that the chain of reasoning and the chain of argument in practice are the same, or that there is another chain of reasoning above them of which they are both chains of argument. Conversely, if you find two chains of reasoning, this indicates that you should split the text into two chapters, two sections and so on, or reformulate one of them to become a chain of argument under the other as the chain of reasoning.

We have now described what the back and forth process of writing a chapter can look like and how you can come to a preliminary endpoint. We continue with our next topic, which is how one can use the Model of Argumentation when reading. In the following example, the model becomes more clearly visible and is more clean-cut than in the example of writing Chapter 2. Reading someone else's preliminary objectives is a different process from writing and developing your own.

The (preliminarily) finished structure of a text: an example

One way of using the Model of Argumentation presented in Chapter 7 is to apply it when reading a social science report, whether it is an article or a book. That means making an analysis of the argumentation by searching for the chain of reasoning, the chains of argument supporting it and the arguments building up each chain of argument. One of our PhD students once said that applying the model in this way is like opening the watch casing to make it possible to see the clockwork inside. Using the model is like laying bare the mechanisms of the article, the chapter or the book at the same time searching for the skeleton and driving force of the report. We illustrate this by discussing the structure of Chapter 4 of this book as it develops in light of the argumentative model.

The structure of Chapter 4, 'Basics of property spaces'

The chapter starts with an introduction. According to most handbooks in writing social science, introductions have two purposes. One is to make the reader interested enough to go on reading. We try to accomplish this through the example of a Global Positioning System (GPS). The other is to provide the reader with an idea of the content of the chapter through sketching out a frame to be filled in during the reading. In our terms, this frame consists of the chain of reasoning, which will be progressively completed with further detail by way of the chains of argument and arguments building up the chain of reasoning. Therefore, we state the chain of reasoning explicitly in the introduction (p. 55):

> We start this chapter on the basics of property spaces by presenting the way in which they are built up, or what constitutes them. Then we discuss three basic procedures for using property spaces in social science theoretical work: housekeeping, developing a terminology and elaborating on already existing theories.

After this bannister for the chapter, it is divided into five parts, plus a summary. This structure reflects the fact that the chain of reasoning of the chapter is supported by five chains of argument, each with its own subtitle. We indicate that a new chain of argument begins by putting in a new subtitle in the chapter. The whole system of chapters, together with their subtitles, is intended to familiarize the reader with the structure of the argumentation. Therefore, when using the model to read a report, you are well-advised to have a close look at the disposition of the report. If the authors have done a good job, the structure reveals the argumentative build-up of the text.

Constructing a property space

The first part has the heading '*Constructing a property space*'. From the chains of argument that support the chain of reasoning of the chapter, it is built around chain of argument$_1$. It can be formulated in this way (Table 8.1): 'There are three parts of a property space: a title, a frame and a matrix, the latter consisting of different types.' Five arguments build up chain of argument$_1$. To start with, argument$_1$ (A_1) says that it is possible to divide a property space into parts, which is a precondition for the chain of argument$_1$ to refer to parts of property spaces. According to argument$_2$ (A_2), the first part is the title, the function of which is to define which subject is covered by the property space. Argument$_3$ (A_3) tells us that the second part is a frame, which in its basic form consists of the dimensions X and Y of which each has the properties A and B. If you combine A and B of dimension X with A and B of dimension Y, argument$_4$ (A_4) claims you get the third part, a matrix. Finally, argument$_5$ (A_5) says that the content of the matrix is a typology consisting of logically and qualitatively different types.

The chain of argument$_1$ ends there, but there are still some pages of the section left. This indicates a rather important insight: some parts of the report can be outside the chain of reasoning, but they are still relevant and of interest for its topic. Such *digressions* usually have a message of their own without directly supporting the

TABLE 8.1 Chain of argument$_1$ of Chapter 4

CA_1: There are three parts of a property space: a title, a frame and a matrix, the latter consisting of different types.
A_1: A property space can be divided into parts.
A_2: The first is the title, which defines the subject of the property space.
A_3: The second is the frame, which in its basic form is made up of two dimensions (X and Y) with two properties (A and B) for each dimension.
A_4: The combination of A and B of dimension X with A and B of dimension Y results in the third part, a matrix.
A_5: The matrix consists of a typology with logically and qualitatively different types (1 to 4).

Using the Model of Argumentation 131

chain of reasoning. The digression therefore has a chain of reasoning of its own, separated from the chain of reasoning of the chapter. In this case, it is expressed in the first two sentences and the chains of argument are the two examples – retail fashion markets and prediction and explanation. One reason we chose Chapter 4 to illustrate the use of the argumentative model when reading is that it is somewhat more complicated in that it contains a second digression, which is the quality of 'lacking' in two-fold property spaces. It is such a short section that we did not feel it necessary to put in a subtitle. What is common for the two digressions, however, is that they are relevant for the subject of chain of argument$_1$, constructing a property space, without being part of the support for the chain of reasoning of the chapter. Sometimes authors indicate digressions by putting them in special 'boxes', and one author (Korczynski 2014) gives them the name 'side steps' because they are side steps from the chain of reasoning. The final paragraph, which begins, 'In the rest of this chapter . . .' is a bannister, the importance of which we mentioned earlier.

Housekeeping

The next section is called '*Housekeeping*', and has a much simpler structure (Table 8.2). First, there is an introduction to attract readers into continuing reading. Then, chain of argument$_2$ for the chain of reasoning of the chapter is introduced through a number of quotations and a presentation of the demands of logically exhaustive and mutually excluding classifications. It says that housekeeping of concepts is important, and, furthermore, that property spaces are good devices for doing just that. Only three arguments support this chain of argument. Argument$_1$ generally claims that theorizing requires that the researcher can keep orderliness in the conceptual set-up, while argument$_2$ points to property spaces as devices for this purpose. To close the argumentation, argument$_3$ says that this can be done through several ways of building up property spaces. Finally, there is, of course, a bannister to the next chain of argument.

By now, we feel that we have made our points concerning how to use the argumentative model when reading a social science text. We suggest that you start working on how to apply the model by analysing the construction of chains of argument and arguments, and perhaps also introductions, digressions and bannisters, in the rest of Chapter 4.

TABLE 8.2 Chain of argument$_2$ of Chapter 4

CA$_2$: Housekeeping of concepts is important and property spaces are good devices for doing that.
A$_1$: In theorizing, it is necessary to systematically keep track of concepts.
A$_2$: Property spaces can keep track of concepts (variables and values, codes and properties).
A$_3$: There are several examples of ways of depicting this technically.

TABLE 8.3 Chains of argument of the section '*Housekeeping*' of Chapter 4

CR: Housekeeping of concepts is important and property spaces are good devices for doing that.
CA_1: In theorizing, it is necessary to systematically keep track of concepts.
A_1: Several authorities have said that systematic handling of concepts is important.
A_2: One reason is that classifications should be exhaustive to be systematic.
A_3: Another reason is that they should be mutually exclusive to be systematic.
CA_2: Property spaces can keep track of concepts (variables and values, codes and properties).
A_1: Property spaces can systematically relate concepts to each other.
A_2: An example is to construct mechanisms influencing attitudes to work as property spaces (Table 4.5).
CA_3: There are several examples of ways of technically depicting this in a property space.
A_1: One way is to make an eightfold table with three independent variables (codes) (Table 4.6).
A_2: Another way is to add one more variable (code) (Table 4.7).
A_3: Table 4.7 can be constructed as a sixteenfold table (Table 4.8).

Moving the model down one level

There is, however, one more quality of the model we wish to illustrate, namely the possibility of moving it between levels of a text. So far, we have applied it to Chapter 4 as a whole. The chain of reasoning covers the full chapter and the chains of argument building it up each cover one section of the chapter. Let us now move the model down one level to the heading '*Housekeeping*'. When we do that (Table 8.3), the former chain of argument$_2$ now becomes the chain of reasoning for this section: 'Housekeeping of concepts is important, and property spaces are good devices for doing that.' Through this operation, the former arguments become chains of argument, which are: chain of argument$_1$ – 'In theorizing, it is necessary to systematically keep track of concepts'; chain of argument$_2$ – 'Property spaces can keep track of concepts'; and chain of argument$_3$ – 'There are several examples of ways of technically depicting this in a property space.' All three are built up by arguments that were not visible when we applied the model at the higher level. Incidentally, this layering of arguments is the reason for our advice not to start with arguments when using the model, but instead to search for the chain of reasoning – otherwise you risk finding nothing but arguments and miss the hierarchical quality of the argumentation. Ultimately, every sentence can become an argument.

Things look different at different levels. For example, we might notice that what seemed like a digression at the level of the chapter as a whole, is now part of the arguments for chain of argument$_1$.

Summary

The purpose of this chapter is to present two extended examples on how to use the Model of Argumentation. The first example illustrates how to apply the model when writing a scientific text, using Chapter 2 in this book as a point of departure. The second example demonstrates how to use it when reading a scientific text, using Chapter 4 as an example. In the first part of the chapter, focusing the writing process, we simply describe the process of writing by dissecting and depicting how the chapter in question materialized into its present form. We describe the twists and turns, the dead ends, the deleting and the recycling of texts and the occasional outburst of flow that characterized the writing process when searching for propositions, lines of arguments and the line of reasoning. We show how writing is about working our way towards preliminary endpoints, which means a combination of reading texts of others, our own creativity and writing and an ability to use the Model of Argumentation as a sorting and structuring mechanism in order to get there.

If the first part of the chapter can be depicted as a winding process, the second part is more of an instant X-ray picture where the model becomes clearly visible and distinct. The purpose of the second part is to show how to use the model when reading a finalized chapter by showing the argumentative skeleton of Chapter 4. We describe what to look for in order to find and analyse the argumentation, in other words, we highlight the chain of reasoning and chains of argument, and the arguments that are the foundation for each chain of argument. By having the model and its components in mind, we further stress how it can be used on different levels of a text, such as a whole book, a chapter or a section. We also show that there are parts of text outside the model that still are of importance for the topic and chapters, such as not necessary but still relevant digressions and bannisters.

References

Banks, Marcus (2001) *Visual Methods in Social Research*. London: Sage.
Danermark, Berth, Mats Ekström, Liselotte Jakobsen and Jan Ch. Karlsson (2002) *Explaining Society. Critical Realism in the Social Sciences*. London: Routledge.
Engelhardt, Yuri (2002) *The Language of Graphics: A Framework for the Analysis of Syntax and Meaning in Maps, Charts and Diagrams*. Amsterdam: Institute for Logic, Language and Computation.
Korczynski, Marek (2014) *Songs of the Factory. Pop Music, Culture, and Resistance*. Ithaca: ILR Press.

9
THEORIZING AND WRITING

We have presented toolboxes for theorizing and writing social science. First, the tools of displays and property spaces for theorizing in the research process, then, the tools of the rhetorical situation, especially the Model of Argumentation for writing in the reporting process. In this chapter, we pull the threads together through an example from our own research. We reconstruct parts of how we used the tools of displays and property spaces in the research process of a project on ideas of the future of work, as well as the application of the Model of Argumentation when writing an article on that topic (Bergman et al. 2010; reprinted in the Appendix to this chapter). Of course, in reality, we give the process a more orderly nature than the chaos we lived in and we have edited the memos we reprint to make them readable to people other than ourselves.

Research process and reporting process

In the chain from social ontology over social epistemology to social science rhetoric there is a tendency to put emphasis on relations. Social entities are what they are because of the relations they have to other social entities, and relations between those relations. Whatever we study in social science – be it classes, genders, identities, cultures, families, workplaces, ethnicities, rationality processes, individualization, globalization – they are made up of relations. There is therefore a tendency that we construct our knowledge of social things and processes as relations between concepts in our theories. Further, in the social science rhetoric of convincing readers of what we claim in our research reports, we build the propositions by relations between arguments about those concepts. And this is the way it should be. Normatively, we argue that when social theory is constructed, it should be in the form of relating examined concepts to each other as social science epistemology ought to follow from social ontology. In addition, writing in the social science reporting process should build on relating arguments about those concepts (through their terms) to each other. We talk about a tendency because not every social scientist follows these norms. There are, of course, those who do not embrace the ontology, epistemology or rhetoric we have put forward, but our impression is that most social researchers follow this logic – at least in their practice.

Towards the background of this ontology, epistemology and rhetoric, we define social theory as 'interrelated statements that claim that a certain entity exists in the world and often what this entity can do'. We also stress that those concepts are examined and reflected over, while their thought content is expressed through a specific word, a term. Therefore, theorizing is to construct a theory through concepts and labelling the concepts with terms. It is of some importance to notice that theorizing can be – and usually is – a question of small steps and quite modest changes to parts of a theory that you are working on. Theorizing is seldom a grand enterprise, rather, gradual conceptual changes.

Two phrases have turned up repeatedly in the preceding chapters, both on theorizing and on writing. One is to 'play about' or 'play around' with concepts, terms and arguments, the other to be 'curious' about something. This is not a coincidence. To put the expressions together, we could say that we want to highlight the importance of your curiosity as a driving force for playing about with thoughts, concepts, terms, arguments and their relations when theorizing and writing. Curiosity is generally regarded as a desire to know, to fill knowledge gaps (e.g. Litman 2005; Lowenstein 1994) and that is what you do in theorizing at the same time as you try to convince your audience that you have done so when writing. Play is sometimes considered as a rival to work as the main mechanism behind the development of human societies. It is not only *Homo Faber* (Man the Maker) but also *Homo Ludens* (Man the Player) that is involved. There is an important literature on the philosophy and sociology of play (Caillois 2001 [1958]; Huizinga 1955 [1938]; Shotter 1973), and we can learn a lot from it if we apply it to theorizing and writing. Huizinga says that play is a free activity, delimited within a special field and Caillois agrees: 'a basic freedom is central to play in order to stimulate distraction and fantasy' (2001 [1958]: 27). In this spirit, the tools we have presented in this book are tools to be used playfully to reach serious results in the field of social science theorizing and writing. In fact, Shotter (1973) explicitly talks about himself as 'an academic *playing* with ideas' and gives us this example:

> I thought that what I was doing yesterday would turn out to be really important; I worked on it all night in fact. Now I realize it was all quite useless, and I was mistaken . . . however, I was only playing with ideas to see where they'd lead . . . there was no guarantee, there could be no prior guarantee of their validity . . . I'll have to try another approach . . . Look at the problem this way . . . Hey, that's better, that seems promising . . . this could be really serious.
> *(Shotter 1973: 49–50)*

Creativity is immanent in play and playfulness fosters imagination and creativity – play tends to lead to creativity (Swedberg 2014: 195). Huizinga (1955 [1938]: 3) and

Caillois (2001 [1958]: 6) add that fun too is an essential element of play – and to us, this is a true observation: we think it is fun to play about with concepts and terms in theorizing and with arguments in writing reports. We cannot know in advance which course play will follow, or what the result will be – if any. At the same time, games of problem solving, as in theorizing, make up 'the most prevalent and pure forms' of playing (Caillois 2001 [1958]: 30).

The use of tools – such as displays, property spaces and the Model of Argumentation – require skills to handle them well and play is an important feature here (Reilly 1981: 60): 'We have long known that a plethora of skills gather incrementally around play. The intense participatory involvement of the player facilitates the acquisition of skills across the broad spectrum of art, crafts, drama, music, sports, games, and hobbies' – and, we like to add, in social science. Huizinga too stresses the intensity and absorption of engaging in play as well as the pleasure and fun of doing so. Play is rather a behavioural orientation than specific activities – all activities, including theorizing and writing, can be performed in a playful way (Mainemelis and Ronson 2006). Let your curiosity lead you to playing around with concepts, terms and their relations in displays and property spaces in the research process and arguments and their relations in the reporting process!

Displays

In the rest of this chapter we sum up what we have suggested about the use of displays and property spaces when theorizing and the Model of Argumentation when writing. We illustrate the reasoning with examples from a research project that we have been engaged in and in which we were curious about forecasts of working life. We were not interested in predicting the future working life, but in studying forecasts made in the literature. The following examples come from our theorizing in the research process and our writing in the reporting process, respectively. Writing when theorizing is, as we say, a way of thinking. You write in order to try out an idea as you can never be certain of its value for constructing theory until you have written it down. Grammar and syntax are less important at this stage. The possible use of the idea in theorizing is what is essential here. Much of what we wrote is therefore probably not understandable to other people. Thus, the examples are instances in the reporting process of authors carefully rearranging what really happened in the research process to make it comprehensible for readers.

In a continuum of graphic forms (Banks 2001), written text can be found at the bound extreme; here, grammar and syntax provide rules for how to write. Towards the middle of the continuum, we find tables and property spaces. You can play around with different dimensions and varying properties, but there are rules for how these can be combined to provide outcomes or types of a typology. Property spaces follow a specific logic as they are tools to systematize concepts in theorizing. Towards the unbound extreme are a great number of symbols that can be combined into displays. We define a display as a 'graphical representation of relations and relata that answers one or more research questions or statements'. The importance of displays

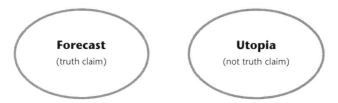

FIGURE 9.1 Forecast and utopia

lies in the possibility they provide to play around with relations between concepts in theorizing (and illustrating such relations through those who survive into the reporting process). There are few, if any rules of how to draw a display, it is only your creativity that limits what you can do with them.

At the beginning of the project about forecasts of working life, we thought that we needed some kind of terminology for sorting out different kinds of ideas about the future according to how they were expressed by their authors. We were interested in predictions and in order to distinguish predictions from other ways of relating to the future we were thinking of what the opposite could be – that is, non-predictions. So what are non-predictions about the future? In searching for an answer to this question, we played around with several displays, ending up with a simple display making a distinction between forecasts and utopias (Figure 9.1). The distinction was based on whether the author of a statement about the future claimed that it would in fact occur (which we called 'forecast') or if no such claim was raised ('utopia'). We should also explain that when we talked about truth claims, we did not intend anything necessarily pejorative. In parts of social science, it is regarded as a sin to raise truth claims, as anyone doing so is thought to use power – and using power is a sin. Instead, we simply meant what we said in the definition: the author claims that the forecast will come true.

In a memo about the term utopia we wrote:

> To the utopias we count Paul Lafargue's (1972 [1883]) visions based on the demand for 'the right to idleness' which he formulated in opposition to the parole 'the right to work'. And – to continue in the same vein – Bertrand Russell's (1960 [1932]) praise of idleness as a considerably more reasonable future attitude than industriousness. Both probably had political hopes, but there is nothing in their texts that even hints at their descriptions becoming real in a future society.

At this stage, our intention was to study only forecasts. The function of the distinction was to be able to winnow out utopias and concentrate on forecasts. We eventually discovered, however, that there were two types of forecasts (Figure 9.2). One of them lacked precision by not specifying mechanisms behind the future events or states described, while the other provided such causes. In memos we called the first type 'prophesy' and exemplified with forecasts in the Revelation of St. John the Divine and

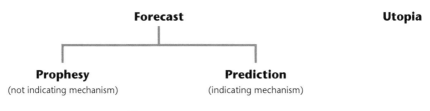

FIGURE 9.2 Two types of forecast

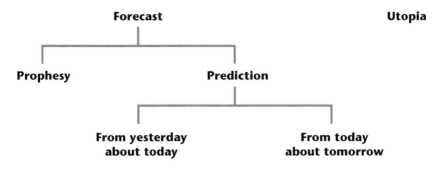

FIGURE 9.3 Two types of prediction

those made by the sixteenth century prophet, Nostradamus. The second type, which indicated such mechanisms, we gave the label 'prediction'. Now we had more forecasts that we could sort out, namely prophesies, keeping predictions for further study.

One of the examples of predictions we wrote about in memos was John Maynard Keynes' (1972 [1930]) argumentation behind his concern about what will happen to his grandchildren when all work has been automated but they still are indoctrinated to wishing to work:

> One formulation directly puts this forecast in the category of prediction, namely when he [Keynes] says (1972 [1930]: 322) that he wants to go 'to what is going on under the surface – to the true interpretation of the trend of things'. Keynes observes, then, a tendency, that is a mechanism in action, in technology to replace human labour, why this will end; at the same time he sees an innate tendency in the culture to value work so highly that it has created a need in people to work. It is this future dilemma his article defines.

All forecasts and utopias have a time dimension – and thereby so do prophesies and predictions – in that they make statements about events and states further on in time from when they are made. As we thought we were only interested in predictions, we let a display restrict itself to this type of forecast (Figure 9.3) – something we had to revise in more complicated displays later on in the research process. We made a rough grouping in those predictions made yesterday about today, which in our case meant around the year 2000, and those made today about tomorrow.

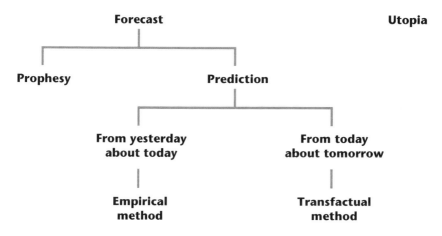

FIGURE 9.4 Two types of methodologies for studying predictions

In our methodological reasoning in connection with this theorizing, the distinction logically leads to a discussion of different approaches to them (Figure 9.4): empirical or transfactual method. We reasoned that when it came to questions about predictions from yesterday about today, we could look for the answers in existing data. Predictions have an empirical side in forecasting events and states and can therefore be compared to what in fact has occurred. In a memo we wrote:

> It is in principle possible to empirically test yesterday's predictions about today. That possibility has probably never before had such good preconditions to be realised as it has now. One reason is that the amount of forecasts that can live up to demands on a prediction probably is bigger now than ever. Another that there probably never before has existed such extensive and varying empirical material against which the statements can be tested.

The empirical method can not, however, be applied to predictions from today about tomorrow. There are, as we expressed it, no data from the future. Instead, we wanted to apply transfactual argumentation and retroduction. In memos on the method we referred to this definition:

> Retroduction [is] a thought operation involving a reconstruction of the basic conditions for anything to be what it is, or, to put it differently, it is by reasoning we can obtain knowledge of what properties are required for a phenomenon to exist. Transfactual or transcendental argument is a form of retroduction implying that one seeks these qualities beyond what is immediately given.
> (Danermark et al. 2002: 206)

More concretely, we wrote about examining the relation between the prediction's empirical description and the postulated mechanisms, studying whether the latter reasonably could lead to the predicted empirical pattern. Thereafter it would, we argued, be possible to go on to an analysis of which other effects these mechanisms could have in the same context. And also, what could happen in a different context. Finally, we wrote memos about the possibility of applying the transfactual method to yesterday's predictions about today. If they turned out to be empirically correct, it would be important to study what had this effect – and if they were empirically erroneous, it was as important to study what in the suggested mechanisms and the play between them in a certain context led to a different empirical outcome than the predicted one.

So far we had used a series of displays to delimit our research project on forecasts about working life like this: it was to be about predictions, not about utopias or prophesies, while making a distinction between two types of predictions on the basis of their chronology, leading to different methodologies. It is an example of what we in Chapter 3 called stepwise theorizing using displays. Let us go on to property spaces we constructed in the same project.

Property spaces

Like displays, the field covered by a certain property space is defined by its title. Without the title most displays and property spaces can easily be misunderstood. However, in contrast to displays, property spaces have a systematic form in two ways. First, there is a frame with a minimum of two dimensions with two properties on each that are combined with each other through a rule-bound logic. Second, the combinations thereby make up a matrix of logical outcomes forming a typology. That is why we say that displays have a free form and property spaces a bound form.

Several commentators have held that constructing property spaces makes the lives of social scientists less difficult. One basic way of doing that is to use them as housekeeping devices. They can help you to reveal logical errors in your conceptual set-up such as not being exhaustive or mutually excluding. They also assist you in keeping track of concepts and relations between them in your theorizing. Although there are many possible sources of terms to cover your concepts – for example, in vivo codes and everyday expressions, social science theories and fiction, poems and songs – the possibility to combine terms from the frame can often be a fruitful first step. If it is possible to find expressive terms, it can be regarded as an indicator of the property space being a rewarding one in your theorizing. The basic way of using property spaces is to develop an existing theory further. It can be one that you find in the literature, but, probably more often, it is the theory you have produced at the present stage of your theorizing. You play around with the concepts you have so far, through combining them in different ways, positioning them as dimensions, properties or types in a number of property spaces. Often these exercises result in the emergence of new concepts or new relations between concepts.

When you have constructed a property space, its power as a tool for theorizing has not been exhausted. Two procedures are possible: reducing it and expanding it.

The first means that you join types to diminish their number; the second that you find ways to increase their number. We have suggested a set of techniques to reduce a property space, namely rescaling, indexing, logic reduction, empirical reduction, theoretical reduction and pragmatic reduction. We have also indicated some ways of expanding a property space and they are substruction, adding properties of existing dimensions, additional dimensions, combining property spaces, inserting process arrows and creating scales. Note, you need to be aware that each operation involves risks.

Expansion and reduction can also be related to each other, something that is described by Bailey (1994) in this way:

> Substruction [in our terms expansion] is used when the researcher is presented with too few types and wishes to construct either the full typology, or at least some of the other missing types in the typology. Reduction solves the opposite problem. It is needed when one has too many types, and manageability is thus a problem. Although one would not generally first use substruction to construct a full typology and then use reduction to return to the original types, nevertheless these procedures can be used together. One might first use substruction to construct the full typology, and then use reduction to construct different types than the original ones.
>
> *(Bailey 1994: 28)*

Related to the displays we have shown so far, and later on in the project on forecasts of working life, we wanted to make a more systematic classification, and, therefore, we used the tool of property spaces. We had also abandoned the purist idea of only analysing what we at that point called predictions. We had found an empirical pattern in the literature that we later described as the 'absence of futurist studies in working life related journals, and the absence of work-life matters in future studies' (Bergman 2015: 3–4). It was simply the case that very few working life scholars made predictions (in our meaning of the term) and very few futurists predicted working life.

Therefore, we made a fresh start – confirming Merton's words about the 'false starts, mistakes, loose ends, and happy accidents' (1967: 4) cluttering up the research process – utilising the several dimensions that we already had to play around with from the displays. We were still curious about forecasts of working life – forecasts from yesterday about today and from today about tomorrow. To get an overview of these forecasts, we needed some new kind of typology to order the articles and books making them. Eventually, we went back to dimensions that we had played around with in displays and which we thought could be used in constructing a typology of forecasts:

(X) Truth claim: the author says that the forecasted states or events will in fact occur.
(Y) Explanatory claim: the author identifies mechanisms producing the forecasted states or events.

TABLE 9.1 Explanatory claims and truth claims

		Truth claims	
		Yes	No
Explanatory claims	Yes		
	No		

But what would the properties be? As you know, one possibility is always to try the common strategy to split each dimension into a positive and a negative side. Making and not making explanatory claims and truth claims, respectively. We did so and for each dimension formulated two properties:

A   The dimension is present.
B   The dimension is absent.

Putting the presence or absence of truth claims and explanatory claims in relation to each other, we constructed the property space found in Table 9.1. We did not regard these dimensions in themselves as mechanisms, that is, we did not put forward theoretical assumptions of the kind saying that the existence of truth claims influenced the existence of explanatory claims, or that one of the dimensions was an independent and the other a dependent variable. They were simply classificatory devices, resulting in a typology.

With this property space as a point of departure, we found in the literature more detailed suggestions concerning the positive properties of each dimension. When it comes to making truth claims, the famous futurists, Herman Kahn and Anthony J. Wiener (1969: Ch. 1), make a number of distinctions between different types of projections or forecasts. One is a simple continuation of an existing trend, which they call a naive projection, and is close to but not the same as a surprise free projection. Further, there are most probable and absolutely probable ones. There are, then, degrees to which possibilities can be actualized in the future. In this part of the frame of the property space, we therefore got the properties 'making naive truth claims', 'making surprise free truth claims', 'making most probable truth claims', 'making absolutely probable truth claims' and 'not making truth claims' (Table 9.2).

Further, an author can analyse different combinations of mechanisms and thus define a number of scenarios rather than a single forecast (Inayatullah 2002). The explanatory claim is then not for a single outcome, but several possible outcomes depending on the combination of mechanisms. In this part of the frame, we thereby got 'making truth claims of a single outcome', 'making truth claims of one of several alternative outcomes' and 'not making truth claims'. However, we found – to use Bailey's words – that manageability of this expanded property space became a problem. It turned out to be too complicated to assist theorizing. It did not help us to distinguish different types of forecasts in any meaningful way. Instead, we went back to our original idea and thereby reduced it to a fourfold table again (Table 9.3).

TABLE 9.2 Types of forecasts 1

		Making truth claims				Not making truth claims
		Naive	Surprise free	Most probable	Absolutely probable	
Making explanatory claims	Single outcome					
	Several outcomes					
Not making explanatory claims						

TABLE 9.3 Types of forecasts 2

		Truth claims	
		Yes	No
Explanatory claims	Yes	Prediction	Science fiction
	No	Prognosis	Utopia/dystopia

Source: Modified from Bergman et al. (2010: 859, Figure 1).

It is difficult to know in advance whether the content of the types of a property space is fruitful for classificatory or other theorizing purposes. One strong indicator is, however, whether you can find captivating, meaningful terms for them. In our case, we gave the types the terms prediction, prognosis, science fiction and utopia. The concepts that these terms cover are, then, defined in this way:

- A prediction is a forecast that is claimed to occur in the future and that contains an explanation of the forecasted states or events.
- A prognosis is a forecast that contains a truth claim, but no explanatory claim.
- Science fiction is a forecast without truth claims but which contains explanations of the forecasted states or events.
- A utopia/dystopia lacks both truth and explanatory claims.

Here we could make fruitful distinctions and later point out examples of each type – which is also why this property space survived the research process into the reporting process, as we will take up in the next section.

All those terms existed before we constructed the property space, but its fruitfulness is indicated by the terms not being related to each other in this way before. In the article, we also gave causes for the use of each term and exemplified each type with a specific forecast. Another confirmation of some fruitfulness occurred after the publication of the article in that it has been referred to by other researchers quite frequently, including using the fourfold table to structure the content of a special issue on the future of tourism (Yeoman and Postma 2015). Next, we move on to the subject of writing.

Writing

We make a distinction between writing in the research process and in the reporting process, emphasizing that it does not depict a chronological order but a matter of a difference in the aim of writing. In the research process, you write in order to make your ideas clear to yourself, in the reporting process, to make your ideas clear to an audience. We suggest that the Model of Argumentation can be used as a tool for systematically presenting the result of your theorizing to an audience. The statements of your theory can be hierarchically arranged from the overriding chain of reasoning (CR) expressing the proposal ?→!, over the chains of argument (CA) supporting different parts of the chain of reasoning, to a number of arguments (A) bearing up each chain of argument. The curly brackets (}) in the model indicates the importance of each level being supported by the underlying levels: chain of argument$_1$ to chain of argument$_n$ make up the backing for the chain of reasoning, while each chain of argument is based on a series of argument$_1$ to argument$_n$.

Part of the reporting process of the project on forecasts of working life was writing an article based on the property space in Figure 9.3. In the article, we needed an argument telling our prospective audience why it was worth bothering to read it. As we have said before, filling gaps in former research is a very common argument of that kind – at least if you can make it plausible that it is an interesting gap. Therefore, our argument ran like this: when studying the literature on forecasts, we have found that there are two kinds of typologies, one is epistemological and deals with the methods used to make forecasts and the other is normative and takes up questions about what future is desirable or undesirable. None of the existing typologies helps us along, as we want a more ontological approach; we are interested in the way in which different authors portray the nature of the social world they forecast. We therefore have to supplement the existing typologies with one built on ontological dimensions. One basic ontological concept is truth, another explanation – so our argument went. If our reporting process was to mirror our research process, this was not strictly accurate. In reality, we had first constructed the property space and only later studied the literature containing typologies of forecasts. But writing in the reporting process is not about the chaos of the research process, it is about arguing the proposal that became the result of the research process, the ?→!.

Further, it was of some importance in the reporting process that we could present expressive terms for the concepts of the matrix, that is, the types of the property space, not only of the frame. We felt that 'prediction' and 'prognosis' filled that function, but we had trouble with the other two types of the matrix. After some oscillating between the research and the reporting processes, we decided on 'science fiction' and 'utopia/dystopia'. Here is an example of a memo written in the research process that became decisive for one of those terms and which also entered the reporting process:

> I've been hunting around for a term for the concept 'explanatory claim but no truth claim'. It should of course be a word that somehow indicates the future, but a specific type of forecast about the future. Or if we can explain why we chose that term. (If it also produces ideas of the future in the minds of readers it is only a further advantage.) And now I think I have found such an explanation. I was leafing through a book on utopianism and organization [Parker et al. 2007] and came across this: there is a word that signifies 'A form of speculative fiction suspended somewhere between utopias, fantasy and sociology'. One definition is that 'it involves systematically altering technological, social or biological conditions and then attempting to understand the possible consequences' [2007: 247]. That means a search for explanatory claims in a classical sense, which the authors also talk about as involving 'thought experiments'. At the same time there is no indication that this word carries with it the idea that these consequences will come true. The word is *science fiction* and I think it is going to work.

If you detect a note of triumph in this memo you are quite right. It was written by Ann Bergman, who is a devoted science fiction reader and it was a special joy for her to get that term into the property space. And eventually we all agreed that it was going to work. This memo was also the input to solve a further problem in the research process. In most of the literature, science fiction and utopia are regarded in such a way that the latter is part of the former – utopia is a kind of science fiction. We found, however, that although the property 'explanatory claims' was applicable to science fiction it was not to utopia/dystopia. This genre generally lacked not only truth claims but also explanatory claims and we thereby found that the terms covered two qualitatively different concepts.

In writing the article and presenting the final property space (Table 9.4), we had to find examples of each type in order to make it more understandable to readers – and ourselves. We tried out several suggestions in memos, going back and forth between the research and the reporting processes. We mentioned earlier that there is a lack of forecasts of working life, which made the task especially difficult. Concerning the two outcomes of 'making truth claims', prediction and prognosis, examples were suggested at a rather early stage as they were famous books in futures studies: Kahn and Wiener (1969) and Toffler (1980). We had, however, considerable problems in finding examples of works of the dimension 'not making truth claims'. We therefore had quite an extensive discussion of whether it would be acceptable in a social science article to use examples from fiction. In one of our deliberations, our co-author Jonas Axelsson's interest in political ideas in combination with Ann Bergman's knowledge of science fiction turned up Ayn Rand's (1992 [1957]) *Atlas Shrugged* as an excellent example of the outcome science fiction: a book making explanatory claims but not truth claims and in which working life played a prominent

TABLE 9.4 Types of forecasts 3

	Making truth claims	Not making truth claims
Making explanatory claims	Prediction Example: Kahn and Wiener, 'The Year 2000'	Science fiction Example: Rand, 'Atlas Shrugged'
Not making explanatory claims	Prognosis Example: Toffler, 'The Third Wave'	Utopia/dystopia Example: Vonnegut, 'Player Piano'

Source: Bergman et al. (2010: 859, Figure 1).

role. This convinced us that it was more important to convey the content of the types through expressive examples than where these examples came from. Fiction, our verdict was, is acceptable. The final example, utopia/dystopia, was easy to find when we had made that decision: Kurt Vonnegut's (2006 [1952]) masterpiece *Player Piano*.

In the research process, we wrote extensive memos on each one of them (and to some extent on rivals) but in the article we gave more concentrated descriptions of the content of each example and explained why we had chosen it. As social scientists, we are more used to discussing conceptual texts than pure literature, which resulted in some extra difficulties in writing about Rand and Vonnegut – and when it comes to Vonnegut's book, the question was raised whether we would dare to write anything at all about what we regarded as such a great novel. (To be a bit more on the safe side, we mentioned in footnotes examples of works in social science that could be regarded as science fiction and utopia/dystopia, respectively.) Let us briefly show how we justified the place in the property space we assigned one of the social scientists and one of the fiction authors. Futurists, Herman Kahn and Anthony J. Wiener, use the word 'speculation' in the subtitle of their book *The Year 2000*, but they obviously regard futurology as a science. Their truth claims are quite sophisticated and formulated as alternative possible outcomes of complicated trends, but they are there. Mechanisms producing the development are also pointed out, building on theories presented by, among others, Pitirim Sorokin and Carroll Quigley. Kahn and Wiener's book is therefore a good example of the meaning of the concept expressed by the term prediction: it makes both truth claims and explanatory claims.

A player piano is a self-playing instrument for pre-programmed music – and the title of Kurt Vonnegut's first novel. It is set in a future society in which technology has taken over almost all human work. People do not control the machines any more; they are controlled by the machines and live under a constant threat to their humanity. The machines especially try to cut people off from nature. The hero, Dr Proteus, joins a resistance movement to fight super-technology. Vonnegut does not, however, say that this society will in fact come into existence, nor does he expound how it came about. He makes no truth claims and no explanatory claims. The book is a dystopia.

Let us finally just touch on how the article is structured according to the Model of Argumentation (Table 9.5). We formulated the chain of reasoning of the article

TABLE 9.5 The structure of the *Futures* article

CR: *Classifications of forecasts are mainly epistemological or normative but an ontological classification can be made based on the dimensions truth claim and explanatory claim, which in combination results in the types prediction, prognosis, science fiction and utopia/dystopia.*
Part 1
CA_1: *An example of an epistemological typology.*
CA_2: *Another example.*
CA_3: *Two examples of similar normative typologies.*
CA_4: *Another example.*
Part 2
CA_1: *The field of the ontological typology is forecasts.*
CA_2: *One dimension is truth claim.*
CA_3: *The other is explanatory claim.*
CA_4: *Each has the properties making and not making the claim.*
Part 3
CA_1: *The outcome making both explanatory and truth claims is a prediction.*
CA_2: *An example is Kahn and Wiener's book,* The Year 2000.
CA_3: *Making explanatory claims but not truth claims is science fiction.*
And so on . . .

(Appendix) like this: 'Classifications of forecasts are mainly epistemological or normative but an ontological classification can be made based on the dimensions truth claim and explanatory claim, which in combination results in the types prediction, prognosis, science fiction and utopia/dystopia'. We will not go into the level of arguments, only some chains of argument (readers who want to amuse themselves with finding arguments are welcome to do so). The first part of the chain of reasoning, 'classifications of forecasts are mainly epistemological or normative' is supported by four chains of argument. Chain of argument$_1$: an example of an epistemological typology (Slaughter); chain of argument$_2$: another example (Börjeson et al); chain of argument$_3$: two examples of similar normative typologies (Robinson and Masini, respectively), chain of argument$_4$: another normative example (Höjer and Mattsson).

The second part of the chain of reasoning is that 'an ontological classification can be made based on the dimensions truth claim and explanatory claim'. Here too there are four chains of argument. Chain of argument$_1$: the field of the ontological typology is forecasts; chain of argument$_2$: one dimension is truth claim; chain of argument$_3$: the other is explanatory claim; chain of argument$_4$: each has the properties making and not making the claim. The final part of the chain of reasoning is 'which in combination results in the types prediction, prognosis, science fiction and utopia/dystopia'. Chain of argument$_1$: the outcome making both explanatory and truth claims is a prediction; chain of argument$_2$: an example is Kahn and Wiener's book, *The Year 2000*; chain of argument$_3$: making explanatory claims but not truth claims is science fiction; – and so on. We do not think there is any need to prolong this example any further. By now you should have an idea of how to use the Model of Argumentation when writing social science reports.

Summary

In this chapter, we have given you some glimpses from our research and reporting processes in a project on futures studies of working life. It is far from a complete account of these processes, but it should have provided you with some insights of the research process and the reporting process of this case. We started out with praising the attitude of playing around with concepts and terms when theorizing, in which displays and property spaces are helpful tools. We also emphasized the importance of your own curiosity as the driver of your research. Without curiosity and play, theorizing risks becoming dull and sterile.

We then provided you with an example of theorizing about forecasts of future working life, using displays that stepwise developed a terminology. Then we showed how this terminology inspired further theorizing in the form of a property space that was first expanded and then reduced in order to find an ontological typology of futures studies. Finally, we showed the construction of an article about this typology according to the Model of Argumentation.

References

Bailey, Kenneth D. (1994) *Typologies and Taxonomies. An Introduction to Classification Techniques*. London: Sage.

Banks, Marcus (2001) *Visual Methods in Social Research*. London: Sage.

Bergman, Ann (2015) 'Back to the Future: Not Looking into the Future but at Futures', *Nordic Journal of Working Life Studies*, 5(1): 3–8.

Bergman, Ann, Jan Ch. Karlsson and Jonas Axelsson (2010) 'Truth Claims and Explanatory Claims – an Ontological Typology of Futures Studies', *Futures*, 42(8): 857–65.

Caillois, Roger (2001 [1958]) *Man, Play, Games*. Chicago: University of Illinois Press.

Danermark, Berth, Mats Ekström, Liselotte Jakobsen and Jan Ch. Karlsson (2002) *Explaining Society. Critical Realism in the Social Sciences*. London: Routledge.

Huizinga, Johan (1955 [1938]) *Homo Ludens. A Study of the Play-Element in Culture*. Boston: Beacon Press.

Inayatullah, Sohail (2002) 'Reductionism or Layered Complexity? The Future of Futures Studies', *Futures* 34(3-4): 295–302.

Kahn, Herman and Anthony J. Wiener (1969) *The Year 2000. A Framework for Speculation on the Next Thirty-Three Years*. London: Macmillan.

Keynes, John Maynard (1972 [1930]) 'Economic Possibilities for Our Grandchildren', *Collected Writings*, Vol. IX. London: Macmillan.

Lafargue, Paul (1972 [1883]) *La Droit à la Paresse*. Paris: Maspero.

Litman, Jordan J. (2005) 'Curiosity and the Pleasures of Learning: Wanting and Liking New Information', *Cognition and Emotion*, 19(6): 793–814.

Lowenstein, George (1994) 'The Psychology of Curiosity: A Review and Reinterpretation', *Psychological Bulletin*, 116(1): 75–98.

Mainemelis, Charalampos and Sarah Ronson (2006) 'Ideas Are Born in Fields of Play: Towards a Theory of Play and Creativity in Organizational Settings', *Research in Organizational Behavior*, 27: 81–131.

Merton, Robert K. (1967) *On Theoretical Sociology*. New York: The Free Press.

Parker, Martin, Valérie Fournier and Patrick Reedy (2007) *The Dictionary of Alternatives. Utopianism and Organization.* London: Zed Books.
Rand, Ayn (1992 [1957]) *Atlas Shrugged.* New York: Signet.
Reilly, Mary (1981) 'Defining a Cobweb', pp. 57–116 in Mary Reilly (ed.), *Play as Exploratory Learning. Studies of Curiosity Behavior.* London: Sage.
Russell, Bertrand (1960 [1932]) *In Praise of Idleness and Other Essays.* London: Allen and Unwin.
Shotter, John (1973) 'Prolegomena to an Understanding of Play', *Journal for the Theory of Social Behaviour*, 3(1): 47–89.
Swedberg, Richard (2014) *The Art of Social Theory.* Stanford: Stanford University Press.
Toffler, Alvin (1980) *The Third Wave.* London: Collins.
Vonnegut, Kurt (2006 [1952]) *Player Piano.* New York: Dial Press.
Yeoman, Ian and Albert Postma (2015) 'Developing an Ontological Framework for Tourism Futures', *Tourism Recreation Research*, 39(3): 299–304.

APPENDIX

FROM BERGMAN, ANN, JAN CH. KARLSSON AND JONAS AXELSSON (2010) 'TRUTH CLAIMS AND EXPLANATORY CLAIMS – AN ONTOLOGICAL TYPOLOGY OF FUTURES STUDIES', FUTURES, 42(8): 857–65

Futures studies as object

Among futurists the debate is lively about the possibilities of making forecasts, the rationale of foretelling the future, the methods used as well as the consequences of engaging in these activities [1, 2, 3]. Looking into how futures studies and their methods are described and systemized by the futurist scholars themselves it seems, however, to us that the epistemological matters and/or the normative concerns are given the most attention and that the ontological questions are quite rare. Often there are distinctions more or less in line with for example Slaughter's [4] scheme that divides the research into how the studies are conducted in terms of an *empirical/analytic* tradition with a strong positivist influence; a *critical/comparative* tradition, which is a more socially critical tradition; an *activist/participatory* tradition, which is often linked to different movements and to activism; and finally a *multicultural/global* tradition where there is a strong influence of non-western futurists. Within the dimension of the epistemological issues we can also include an extensive number of classifications that rest on different techniques. Following the path of scenario studies, Börjeson et al. [5] make an ambitious attempt to develop a typology from a user's perspective that covers different types of scenarios and scenario techniques. In their typology there is also a clear normative side since the leading argument is that scenarios should be useful for someone in some way. As users or stakeholders can have many different interests, Börjeson et al. [5] develop different categories of scenario studies relating to categories of interest groups, where a question constitutes the base for the categories. The questions are formed from a user's standpoint and are: *what will happen?* which is connected to predictive scenarios; *what can happen?* which is connected to explorative scenarios; and *How can a specific target be reached?* which is connected to normative scenarios.

Following the normative and technical track we find classifications as for example Robinson's [6, 7] and Masini's [8] which also rest on aspirations to conduct futures studies that are built upon scenario techniques that are normative in terms of trying to map out the feasibility and the consequences of desired futures. In other words: if this is what we want – is it possible to get there and in that case how? Behind these questions lie an assumption that there is a 'fundamental uncertainty' regarding what is going to happen in the future. Robinson [6] states that this fact makes the use of forecasting somewhat problematic since it is a method of predicting the likelihood that some futures can develop given certain circumstances, such as the existence of specific structures and processes. Instead he advocates backcasting, since it does not rest upon predictive truth claims and the analysis includes conditional predictions about a number of feasible and desirable outcomes. Also Höjer and Mattsson [9] belong to the category of futures scholars that see backcasting as a fruitful alternative to forecasting. They argue that the way the forecasting approach extends trends and tendencies in society into the future is too shallow an analysis. What we need is a deeper understanding of how different mechanisms interact and the consequences of this interaction. Here we can trace an ontological reasoning which also includes explanatory claims, which are one of the keystones in our model for classification of various futures studies.

Looking at futures studies along a historical dimension one can say that there has been a shift from what Inayatullah [10] calls single point forecasting – as precise predictions – to scenario planning – which is embracing not only one outcome, but several – and then further to foresight and backcasting to map out complexity, layered causal powers involved in social processes and outcomes. According to Strand [11] forecasting in terms of predictions is seen as a naive scientific activity among futures scholars today. In line with Blackman [12] he further declares that futures studies rather are a tool and an aid to make as good and more informed decisions and choices when trying to manage the processes of change, than an engine for making predictions. In agreement with Slaughter [4] and Kristóf [13], he states that since uncertainty is always present, the main task is to understand the past and the present, i.e. words try to understand the causal links and their consequences but at the same time keeping in mind that this is causality in an epistemological sense and not in an ontological one. We agree on the 'uncertainty factor', but at the same time we would like to question why being epistemologically cautious has to be linked to a rejection of ontological matters. On the contrary, the philosophy on which we build our reasoning – critical realism – is characterized by epistemological cautiousness and ontological boldness [14].

Ehliasson [15] claims that futures studies have to be evaluated on their own merits, it is impossible to claim the same quality, in terms of sophistication and transparency, of futures studies as of social science in general. The question is not if the forecast is good or bad or wrong or right, rather it is about whether it is good enough. Nevertheless, in this article we are presenting our attempt to contribute to this matter – not by judging a forecasts' quality, but by deciding what kind of forecast it is. The examples given above reveal that the main ideas behind the classifications are not resting on the same principles as our typology. Even though different modes of explanatory claims and truth claims are considered in the various types of categorisations it seems to us that the questions of epistemology and of normative concerns are given priority as a sorting mechanism. In our contribution, however, we want to emphasise ontological matters. It is within the ontological dimension the possibilities for different future realities lie, and we therefore need to take this into account when classifying futures research.

A typology and its use

The point of departure for the typology is the term *forecast*, meaning simply a statement about future events or states. And it is future in relation to when it was made, which means that there are forecasts from yesterday about today and from today about tomorrow. The typology provides a classification of forecasts and it is applicable independently of their chronology. We build the typology with the help of two ontological dimensions, of which one is 'truth claim'. We do not give that term the pejorative connotation it has in post-modernistic and other radical relativistic theories. We do not, then, regard it as a sin to make truth claims. The meaning of the term is simply that the author of a statement about the future also explicitly claims that what is forecasted in fact is going to happen. Statements can be classified according to if they make truth claims or not. A statement that is said to make truth claims can, further, be more or less definitive. An example is a forecast that does not postulate a single outcome but a number of possible outcomes, e.g. scenarios, depending on which mechanisms are active and in what way they are active: If the mechanisms M_1 and M_2 are activated the result is future F_1, but if mechanisms M_3 and M_4 are activated the result is future F_2. We include these more complicated statements about future events or states – statements about a loose coupling between mechanisms and outcome – as belonging to the category 'makes truth claims'.

This discussion about mechanisms brings us to the second dimension of the typology, 'explanatory claims', i.e. whether the author of a statement explicitly indicates mechanisms as causes behind the events or states that are forecasted. With 'mechanism' or 'generative mechanism' we mean anything that 'makes something happen in the world' [16]. A couple of examples: according to Habermas [17] the fact that people can use language in a rational way depends on three mechanisms, namely that we can use it representatively (distinguish between what is and what seems to be), expressively (distinguish between what the individual is and what he or she pretends to be), and to develop common values (distinguish between what is and what ought to be). And Bauman [18] finds that the causes behind the Holocaust are made up of a combination of a mechanism that he calls a 'gardening culture' and developed bureaucratic hierarchies with fixed roles that create a distance between actions and their consequences. Mechanisms are, then, what we refer to when we explain a phenomenon. Consequently, statements can be classified not only on the basis of whether they make truth claims, but also of whether they make explanatory claims.

In the typology there are, then, two ontological dimensions with two values on each, which result in four possible outcomes (Table A.1): forecasts with truth claims that indicate mechanisms (predictions); with truth claims, but without indicating mechanisms (prognoses); without truth claims, but indicate mechanisms (science fiction); and without both truth claims and mechanisms (utopias/dystopias). We regard the cases of the typology as ideal types [19], i.e. we use them as yardsticks of different statements on the future. That is the way

TABLE A.1 Types of forecasts

	Making truth claims	*Not making truth claims*
Making explanatory claims	Prediction Example: Kahn and Wiener, '*The Year 2000*'	Science fiction Example: Rand, '*Atlas Shrugged*'
Not making explanatory claims	Prognosis Example: Toffler, '*The Third Wave*'	Utopia/dystopia Example: Vonnegut, '*Player Piano*'

in which we can try to determine what is a prediction and what is a prognosis, science fiction and a utopia.

In the following we present an example of each outcome in order to exemplify its use, i.e. a prediction, a prognosis, a science fiction story and a utopia/dystopia. Concerning the examples of forecasts we have chosen examples with connections to the economic and working life since our research about future studies are mainly concentrated on these aspects of social life.

Prediction

Predictions usually have scientific ambitions and are more precise than in the other outcomes, as they indicate mechanisms and tendencies behind the events and states. Moreover they contain explicit truth claims. As an example of predictions we choose the book *The Year 2000. A Framework for Speculation on the Next Thirty-Three Years* by Herman Kahn and Anthony J. Wiener [20]. Kahn is the more famous of the two authors (and we have already mentioned him above) – he is known as a rather daring practitioner of futures studies/futurology. Maybe his most remarkable research result is an unusually 'optimistic' view of nuclear war. A nuclear war would, argues Kahn, cause human death on a large scale (Kahn talks about 'megadeath', death of millions of people) but humanity, as a species, would still survive despite the massive destruction caused by nuclear weapons. Human flourishing is a possibility even after a nuclear war [21].

It is possible to question if *The Year 2000* really contains predictions in a strict sense. Kahn and Wiener [22] sometimes use modest descriptions of their enterprise – for example, they call their work 'speculative'. But the book contains much detailed scientific reasoning; it seems clear that the authors believe in a *science* about the future (futurology) and not only speculation about possible future events. When Kahn and Wiener use the word 'speculative' about their enterprise, they point out that they do not present *definitive* statements about what is going to happen; they present a spectrum of possible outcomes. But a statement about possible outcomes can be characterized as 'making truth claims'. Hence we can in Kahn and Wiener's text see the first component in our definition of 'prediction'. It can be noticed that Kahn and Wiener [23] make distinctions between 'surprise-free', 'most probable' and 'absolutely probable' actualizations of possibilities when they discuss future events.

The second component in predictions is 'explanatory claims'. Certain mechanisms behind historical development are indeed pointed out by Kahn and Wiener. They use for example ideas from Pitirim Sorokin [24] regarding the dynamics in historical developments. Kahn and Wiener also use concepts borrowed from Carroll Quigley [25]. Quigley theorized about 'instruments of expansion' as essential in human history. One powerful instrument of expansion in human history is slavery, according to Quigley. Kahn and Wiener argue that the most important instrument of expansion after the world wars can be called 'modern management and production techniques' and this instrument has replaced the earlier instrument of expansion – industrialism [26]. When Kahn and Wiener use concepts from Sorokin and Quigley to explain large scale dynamics in human history, they are indicating mechanisms behind coming events. And this means that also the second component of predictions can be found in *The Year 2000*.

Kahn and Wiener's book discusses many aspects of the futuristic year 2000. One important aspect is working life. Fundamentally, Kahn and Wiener believe in the idea of the post-industrial society. A post-industrial society is, among other things, a society in which service-oriented economic activities dominate over activities in the primary or secondary economic sectors. The authors believe that the post-industrial society will lead to an increased amount of leisure. Kahn and Wiener [27] make a comparison between the Western world anno 2000 and the Roman Empire:

> It is interesting to note that when Augustus came to power the free citizens of Rome had 76 holidays a year. When Nero died, not quite a century later, they had 176 holidays a year. In our world, if productivity per hour goes up by 3 or 4 per cent a year (or by a factor of three or four by the year 2000), it is not likely that all of this increased productivity will be used to produce more. As in the Roman Empire, much may be taken up in increased leisure.

One consequence of the leisure orientation in the year 2000 is a renaissance for the mainly non-working 'gentleman' as a lifestyle. We are here talking about the archetypical English gentlemen, who had much time and resources for development of humanist interests. But in this area we can also see differences between Western Europe and North America, argues Kahn and Wiener. In Europe we have much stronger gentleman-traditions than in North America. We have remaining hereditary nobilities, monarchies, et cetera. Hence it is easier to wake up old values from the gentlemen's leisure culture in Europe than in America [28].

Leisure orientation sounds perhaps good and comfortable, but Kahn and Wiener also see serious problems in the coming post-industrial society. One such problem is alienation. The technological development will cause feelings of estrangement among humans. It is highly probable that new technology will lead to increased human feelings of being an 'alien' among artefacts. Kahn and Wiener [29] see new medical technology as especially threatening in this respect.

Our conclusions about Kahn and Wiener's book can be summarized as follows: *The Year 2000* contains predictions. Kahn and Wiener make both truth claims and explanatory claims. Kahn and Wiener's belief in a science about future events makes even the modest claims in the book predictive.

Prognosis

Prognoses are characterized by not being rooted in an explanation – they do not make explanatory claims about future events and states. They do, however, raise claims that the forecast really will occur. A common form of prognosis is to extrapolate empirical, usually statistical trends. They can be very sophisticated, but the basis is that the development will continue to follow the direction that data points out. (In medicine there is a quite different meaning of the term, which we disregard here.) We also regard argumentations in which there is a loose coupling between mechanisms and outcome as prognoses. We choose Alvin Toffler's famous book *The Third Wave* as an example [30]. To turn to Toffler when talking about futures studies seems to be natural – he is a writer who is often discussed and referred to in this context. But to call his study a prognosis is perhaps more controversial. It is not easy to decide whether Toffler makes predictions or prognoses. But since he stresses the unscientific character of his book – he writes [31]: 'social forecasts (. . .) are never value-free or scientific' – we conclude that the study mainly consists of prognoses. That he makes truth claims is apparent in the following words about the content of his book [31]: 'this work is based on massive evidence and on what might be called a semi-systematic model of civilization and our relationships to it'. So even if he does not try to reach the peaks of scientific systematics, he has the ambition to reach a *science-like* clearness in his study about the future. Further, it can be argued that the metaphoric use of the word 'wave' indicates extrapolation from a specific trend with a specific direction. This operation is typical in the making of a prognosis.

The first wave was the Neolithic revolution, the second consists of the Industrial revolution – and the third wave, argues Toffler, is a Post-industrialization in which new, advanced technology makes new civilization patterns possible. A prognosis is, as mentioned, a forecast which contains truth claims but not explanatory claims. When Toffler leaves his discussion about the two first waves and enters into the coming third, he makes truth claims about the future.

Toffler has many ideas concerning work and economic life in the future; his book is like a fountain of new concepts and fresh reasoning. Here we focus only on three of his work-related concepts. The first is the concept of 'the electronic cottage'. In the second wave people mainly worked at special workplaces – factories, offices et cetera. In contrast, the third wave makes it possible for people to work in their homes. The new technology offers such possibilities. Toffler [32] writes with clear sight, long before the expansion of Internet

> When we suddenly make available technologies that can place a low-cost 'work station' in any home, providing it with a 'smart' typewriter, perhaps, along with a facsimile machine or computer console and teleconferencing equipment, the possibilities for home work are radically extended.

In third wave society people will live in 'electronic cottages' – and this fact promotes wellbeing and quality of life. In some way it is a step back to the pre-industrial way of living where the economic and the household units were held together. Toffler sees positive effects on different levels. On a community level we will see much more stability, and more of interpersonal belonging. The electronic cottage strengthens *Gemeinschaft*. In the new society we will for example see more stable marriages and lower divorce rates. On an environmental level the cottage minimizes pollutions caused by car traffic et cetera.

Stability is not everything, however, in the third wave society. A second work-related concept in Toffler's book points in a totally different direction. Toffler has an idea of the coming society as 'the accelerative economy'. In the third wave the economy runs faster and faster. Trends in consumption become more ephemeral, products become more short-lived, and workers have to accept fast changes in their relation to working life. It will be an economy with more short term job contracts and more flexibility. Toffler talks about a 'high-adrenalin business environment'; and the high doses of adrenalin have effects concerning rationality: 'Under these escalating pressures it is easy to see why so many businessmen, bankers, and corporate executives wonder what exactly they are doing and why' [33]. It is not clear, however, how Toffler consistently can combine focuses on both coming stability and coming instability.

The third concept we briefly want to mention is 'prosumer'. We are used to make a distinction between production and consumption, but Toffler challenges these common concepts and the distinction between them. The third wave will generate a middle ground between production and consumption – prosumption. The electronic cottage, the strengthened *Gemeinschaft* and other decentralizing trends lead to a type of demarketization, according to Toffler. Since people during the third wave live in more intimate networks, they will exchange more goods outside the market. All this leads to a more diffuse line between leisure and work. In the third wave society it will be increasingly difficult to judge if an activity is characterized by production or consumption [34].

To summarize: Toffler's famous book seems to contain a prognosis. He is making truth claims but not explanatory claims. The metaphorical use of the concept 'wave' indicates extrapolation from trends, which is typical in this type of forecasts.

Science fiction

We call the combination of not making truth claims and indicating mechanisms behind the descriptions science fiction. What has led us to the term is a common definition, which stresses that this literature makes explanatory claims; science fiction, it says, 'involves systematically altering technological, social or biological conditions and then attempting to understand the possible consequences' [35]. At the same time works in this category do not, then, make claims that their descriptions will be actual events or states.

We choose *Atlas Shrugged* by the Russian-American author Ayn Rand as an example of science fiction [36]. It's not an obvious choice since *Atlas Shrugged* is not the typical technology-oriented science fiction story – but as an example of a more social scientific SF-literature the book is extremely interesting and relevant. And we are not alone in classifying *Atlas Shrugged* as science fiction – The Rand-expert Chris Sciabarra [37] sees *Atlas Shrugged* as SF (but also as more than SF).[1]

Rand was a writer and a non-academic philosopher who constructed a whole philosophical system called Objectivism, which lies behind every word in *Atlas Shrugged*, her magnum opus. *Atlas Shrugged* is one of the longest novels ever written (1069 pages) and one of the greatest bestsellers. Aristotle is one of her most important philosophical heroes and Objectivism can be characterised as 'Aristotelian individualism' and her philosophical system is extremely individualistic. Her political ideal is unbound egoism and capitalism [37]. According to Rand it is the geniuses who are the engine of world history. It is their creativity that makes the world go round, and makes it possible for 'ordinary people' to survive and flourish. Without genius human history would be totally miserable. Rand honours all types of geniality – the genius of the artist but also the brilliance of the successful businessman. All humans that are great, independent and rational creators are worthy of praise, according to Rand. Her vision of the ideal human being has some resemblance to the Nietzschean *übermensch*.

As mentioned before, science fiction contains explanatory claims; SF-stories point out mechanisms behind events in a narrative way. Since *Atlas Shrugged* to a large extent is a narrative way of promoting a theory (Objectivism), it is relatively simple to point out mechanisms. The specific mechanisms in *Atlas Shrugged* are the productive potentials possessed by extraordinarily creative individuals.

The book shows the indispensability of creative genius for the world's material and spiritual wealth. The book describes what happens when great creative people stop working and begin a strike. The story takes place in a future USA, characterized by extensive state interventions which threaten the whole society; the people behind the strike hide in the mountains of Colorado and create a sort of capitalist utopia there. In the narrative we meet a lot of persons. Since Rand is not a master of nuance, we find on the one hand really good guys, and on the other hand really bad guys. The inventor John Galt and the industrialist Hank Rearden are examples of good guys who are strong, creative, rational egoists. They bear the world on their shoulders, as Atlas did in the legend.

At the end of the book Galt holds a radio speech, and this speech covers over 55 pages in *Atlas Shrugged*. Galt says the following about the motive behind the strike (1957:924–925):

> We are on strike against self-immolation. We are on strike against the creed of unearned rewards and unrewarded duties. We are on strike against the dogma that life is guilt. There is a difference between our strike and all those you've practiced for centuries: our strike consists, not of making demands, but of granting them. (. . .) We have granted you everything you demanded of us, we who had always been the givers, but have only

now understood it. We have no demands to present to you, no terms to bargain about, no compromise to reach. You have nothing to offer us. *We do not need you.*

We see here Rand's extreme individualism. The creative persons of the world can with good conscience treat the non-creative persons with indifference. A creative and rational person is self-sufficient, according to Rand's philosophy. The ordinary 'mass' of men and women needs the creative genius, but the creative genius needs nobody. Therefore, of course, the strike of the creative individuals is catastrophic for mankind.

Rand is very interesting when it comes to views on work and productivity. She is also much undiscovered among social scientists. Rand's philosophy can be described as some sort of 'inverted Marxism'. Like Marx she holds a high view of work and productivity. Sciabarra [37] writes: 'For Marx, as for Rand, persons are rational, productive beings with inherent potentialities. Both thinkers viewed labour as causally efficacious, as enabling the actualization of specifically human powers and needs'. But unlike Marx she is interested in the few, in the elite, instead of the masses of workers.

Concerning Rand we want to conclude: *Atlas Shrugged* is science fiction. The book contains explanatory claims but not truth claims. The story is SF since it is future oriented, and since it is embodying a specific theory about causal mechanisms in the world (Objectivism).

Utopia/dystopia

Utopias (or dystopias), finally, are put forward without pretensions of being true and neither do they show why things are going to be the way they are said to be. The word utopia, or *outopia*, means 'no place' which seems to us to be a good term for forecasts that neither want to tell truths nor point out causes. It is another thing that authors of utopias often want to offer critical truths about the society in which they live, and perhaps also indicate mechanisms behind a social development that they want to give warnings about. 'Utopias are', Gray and Garsten [40] emphasize, 'intimately tied to the historical and social milieu in which they arise'. A dystopia is entomologically an anti-topia, but we keep the usual connotation that utopias have a positive and dystopias a negative profile. This is, however, not an absolute classification. The original utopia by Thomas More from 1516 hardly stands out today as a society in which very many would look forward to live.

We choose Kurt Vonnegut's famous novel *Player Piano* [41] as a dystopian example.[2] This choice seems to us to be a rather uncontroversial one as it is quite common to describe Vonnegut's work as dystopian in character. But before going further, we must ask the question: can *Player Piano* be described as science fiction instead? Vonnegut's first words in the Foreword can make one confused concerning the answer whether the book is a dystopia or an SF-novel. He writes in the foreword [43]: 'This book is not a book about what is, but a book about what could be'. Could these words introduce a science fiction story as well as a dystopia? The focus on causal mechanisms in SF leads to a partial focus on 'what is' in this genre. The indication of mechanisms in SF-literature seems to implicate a sort of causal connection between 'our time' and 'future time'. SF tells not only about our future, but also about the way to the future. This causal link between 'now' and 'future' seems to be absent in utopian/dystopian literature. According to this reasoning a dystopian (or a utopian) story neither makes truth claims nor indicates mechanisms behind future events. All it does is give a picture, or present a narrative, of a dark or bright future. A utopia or a dystopia is a forecast but the most non-scientific form of forecast since both truth claims and explanatory claims are absent.

The chosen novel was published in 1952 and is Vonnegut's first one. Vonnegut is well known for dark and satirical narratives and *Player Piano* is a typical Vonnegut story in this respect. It is written against the background of World War II and in a time of rapid modernization and technologization of Western everyday life. The theme of the novel is the threat that comes from a high level of mechanization. The story is about a very technological society, which has almost taken away the needs for human work, and the possibilities for actualizations of human activity. And it is certainly a very dark *picture* of a possible future for the modernized world; it is a narrative or a 'picture' without truth claims or explanatory claims.

This fictive society is like a player piano, a piano that mechanically and automatically plays melodies. The machines are no longer in the hands of humans, the humans are instead in the hands of the man-made machines. The machines have taken over almost every human task. People need not do any cleaning any more, for example, as the technological society in this story offers self-cleaning houses. Prima facie a world without cleaning can be characterized as a rather pleasurable world, but Vonnegut shows inherent threats in such absences of human tasks and responsibilities. Humanity cannot capitulate before its own artefacts.

The novel takes place in a future USA and the main character is Dr Paul Proteus, citizen of the city Ilium. Vonnegut [44] describes the city in the following words:

> Ilium, New York, is divided into three parts.
>
> In the northwest are the managers and engineers and civil servants and a few professional people; in the northeast are the machines; and in the south, across the Iroquois River, is the area known locally as Homestead, where almost all of the people live.

Paul Proteus is seriously plagued by ambivalence. On the one hand he feels committed to the machine-dominated, hyper-technological society since his father was one of its founders; on the other hand he is unhappy with the situation and thinks that the machines have become tyrants and a threat to human life. He dreams about totally different conditions – his inner mental life contains revolutionary secrets. Vonnegut [45] writes:

> Doctor Paul Proteus was a man with a secret. Most of the time it was an exhilarating secret, and he extracted momentary highs of joy from it while dealing with fellow members of the system in the course of his job. At the beginning and close of each item of business he thought, 'To hell with you'.

Proteus tries to connect his own critical thoughts to critical voices in the world literature [45]:

> He had never been a reading man, but now he was developing an appetite for novels wherein the hero lived vigorously and out-of-doors, dealing directly with nature, dependent upon basic cunning and physical strength for survival – woodsmen, sailors, cattlemen . . .

He wants to establish a direct contact with the wild untamed nature – a contact which all technology, all machines, in his society try to prevent.

The high-technological society causes alienation and a revolutionary movement called 'Ghost shirt society' emerges. This movement fights against progress and technology and wants again a society where the hope for human beings lays in their bare humanity, not in their technology and machines. Proteus joins the anti-technological movement and in a letter he writes in a revolutionary tone [46]: 'I propose that men and women be returned to work as controllers of machines, and that the control of people by machines be curtailed'. The Ghost shirt society sees similarities between themselves and struggling Native Americans. They fight against an enemy more modern than themselves, with the help of old wisdom and ancient spiritual values.

In sum: *Player Piano* is a dystopia. The book contains neither truth claims nor explanatory claims. As a typical dystopia the book makes no causal connection between 'now' and 'future'. It is not explained how it all went wrong.

Discussion

When discussing forecasts in relation to social science, it is not very controversial to mention predictions and prognoses, but perhaps not self-evident to take up science fiction and utopias. One of the reasons we include the types of works that can be found in the right hand column of the typology is that they have been important for futures research, not least for the creation of scenarios [47]. Further, in organization theory it has been pointed out that these types of forecasts have been useful for theoretical development [48]. In science fiction and utopias/dystopias the scenario technique is mixed with fantasy and literary creativity in a way that is not legitimate in social science. There are, however, traits that are similar. For example, science fiction – like utopias and dystopias – is often based on contrafactual and transfactual propositions [49], which is also a basic scientific way to argue [50]. Further, they are often built around scientific concepts, especially concerning technology, time and space; usually this concerns how something that already exists on a smaller scale has had a great breakthrough in the future [51, 52, 53] and how different political, economic and social systems have gone through dramatic changes [54, 55, 56, 57]. Livingston [47] also points out that science fiction and utopias/dystopias, like other types of forecasts, can have effects functioning in accordance with Merton's [58] argument on self-fulfilling and self-denying prophesies respectively: they influence partly those formulating the prophesies, partly the society they are directed towards. By depicting possible negative and positive scenarios of the future, preconditions are created for reflections on, attitudes towards and actions to promote change or prevent certain phenomena. Henshel [59] calls this the prediction dilemma, which means that the prediction can change the course of events and thereby work as a self-alternating prophesy. To the extent that one has the intention to judge the results of forecasts, i.e. what in fact happened, the discussion about self-alternating prophesies is central. In this case science fiction and utopias/dystopias can have a greater effect on social development then predictions and prognoses, but it is effects of the forecast itself and has nothing to do with the eventual explanatory claims. A forecast can then, independently of truth claims, work as a self-fulfilling or self-denying prophesy.

We are aware that the typology might raise other questions. Probably they mostly concern two areas, both related to the drawing-up of borderlines. One has to do with what is included in and what is excluded from the model, i.e. what can be regarded as a forecast. It concerns, then, operationalisations or practical applications of this concept. Here questions of what is usually the object of forecasting are also raised – including what is commonly absent from forecasts. It is of interest not only to map which topics that are often forecasted, but also which are seldom or never treated. A hypothesis is, for example, that technology belongs to the former category while gender division of work in the family belongs to the latter.

The other question concerns inherent logic and the internal boundaries, and how we categorize specific works in relation to the four ideal types. It has turned out that it is mainly in the vertical dimension of the typology that this problem turns up. If we look at the left hand column an example is this: it can be possible to identify a number of mechanisms in a certain work, but in spite thereof it happens that it is far from clear how the interaction between these mechanisms result in the outcome described. This is a case of what we earlier talked about as a loose coupling between mechanisms and outcome. The result is that it in some cases can be difficult to decide whether the forecast is a prediction or a prognosis. In the right hand column an example of a problem of categorization is that science fiction often is a utopian or a dystopian narrative, and vice versa. The two categories tend to overlap – and, as we just pointed out, the distinction is not absolute. Further, it is not always possible to treat a specific work as a coherent whole when it comes to truth and explanatory claims. One and the same work can, for example, contain both prognoses and predictions. Still, the typology gives us the possibility to systematically play with the different ideal types, studying both how works can be sorted into them and how different types of forecasts can be present in a specific work.

There are, then, a few careful deliberations that must be made in the use of the typology as a classifying mechanism, but we think it is a valuable point of departure for analyses of forecasts. The typology has a general value in providing the possibility to classify forecasts according to their qualitative character on ontological dimensions. We think that the relative simplicity of our typology is of great epistemic value when it comes to navigating in the difficult terrain of futures studies. Finally, we want to underline that when we talk about the quality of the forecasts we do not imply their qualitative *worth*, but their qualitative *place* in the dimensions of the typology. This does not entail such judgements as predictions necessarily being 'better' than imaginative dystopias in forecasting the future, only that they have different qualities.

Looking into the field of futures studies of today, the forecasts appear mostly to be a means – i.e. something that are intended to have more or less preferable or desirable effects on society – more than an end – i.e. a precise prediction stating an outcome without taking account of what is desired. This tendency of using forecasts as tools to contribute to a desired society we take as a call to consider the ontological dimension. It is here rather than in the epistemological dimension we see the potential of different futures as realities. Nevertheless, given that our fallible and corrigible knowledge about the world is our chance to understand it – we recognize futures studies along with social science in general as important mechanisms for change. Even though post-modern criticism can be seen as a healthy injection of awareness against scientific arrogance, we want to reclaim the trust of science as being a useful tool in the making of a better society. Neither fatalism nor the postmodern tendency of regarding everything that is not critique as crap seems as attractive alternatives. Futures studies with their normative and sometimes action oriented design is one device for this. However, as for science in general there is need for a continuous investigation and evaluation of their theoretical and empirical adequacy and their impact on society. Habermas's [60] declaration that the modern project is not yet completed can be understood as a faith in science as something useful since it actually can say something about society and thereby influence the way it develops. One way of taking futures studies seriously is by identifying what ontological claims forecasts are resting on.

Conclusions

We have tried to show how a typology based on the author raising truth claims and explanatory claims respectively, can be used in order to systematically classify different types of forecasts.

By examining yesterday's forecasts about today and today's forecasts about tomorrow regarding how they relate to truth claims and explanatory claims, four ideal types can be discerned: predictions, prognoses, science fiction and utopias/dystopias. We have exemplified the use of the typology with an oeuvre within each category. They are examples of works illustrating the different ideal types and not necessarily in total correspondence with the hypothetical abstraction that the ideal type in itself provides. Still, the characteristics that we point out are, we think, fruitful for analyzing futures research.

Toward the background of the examples we have brought out, we can see a number of questions that will be actualized in the coming work of applying the model to forecasts. A first one is the extent to which futures studies can be evaluated on the same grounds as traditional science. This is something that should be related to how the claims raised in an oeuvre is evaluated, as the object of futures studies has not happened yet; it can only be formulated as a possible, probable or perhaps desirable event or series of events.

When we have used the model more extensively, we also will be able to analyze in more detail how different works and singular forecasts of different works can give us a picture of how the types of truth claims can be manifested in literature and research in the area. This is, however, an empirical question, which cannot be answered until we have made more wide-ranging analyses of forecasts. Systematic studies of how truth claims are formulated are thereby an important part in our continued use of the typology and the mapping work that this implies. Going on to the second dimension, explanatory claims, we expect it to be a bit easier to handle than the truth claims, as they usually are more explicitly expressed in the theoretical as well as analytical parts of (futures) research. Thereby it is perhaps not as difficult a task, although a laborious one, to identify the causal chains expected to lay behind the forecasts. We expect the main merit of the typology to be that it makes it possible to relate truth claims and explanatory claims to each other; and by doing so it will also be possible to understand causal processes and their – intended as well as unintended – consequences in an ontological sense.

Notes

1 For readers feeling uncomfortable with literary examples in a social scientific article we will briefly indicate a social science example in this category, namely Piore and Sable's [38] plea for flexible specialisation. The authors clearly point to the mechanisms that make the second industrial divide – revival of craft technology – possible, namely the crises of the industrial society with saturated mass markets, lack of innovation power, high unemployment and economic decline. But at the same time the future society of flexible specialization is just a thought experiment [39], it is an abstract model, used by Piore and Sabel in a politically prescriptive rather than an empirically descriptive way. They raise explanatory claims, but no truth claims – in our terminology their book is a work of science fiction.

2 It is easy to understand utopia/dystopia as a typically *literary* category, but according to our definition theoretical works in social science could also be characterized as utopian/dystopian. If the work in question is future oriented and neither contains truth claims nor explanatory claims, we can call it utopian/dystopian. Lyotard's book *The Postmodern Condition* [42] could, for example, be seen as utopian/dystopian since it is about the future but contains no truth claims or explanatory claims.

References

[1] H. Kahn, The alternative futures approach, in: F. Tugwell (Ed.), *Search for alternatives: Public policy and the study of the future*, Witrop Publishers, Cambridge, Mass., 1973.

[2] M. Marien, Top 10 reasons the information revolution is bad for us. *The Futurist* 31 (2002) 261–281.

[3] S. Strand, Forecasting the future: pitfalls in controlling for uncertainty, *Futures* 31 (1999) 333–350.

[4]   R.A. Slaughter, Professional standards in futures work, *Futures* 31 (1999) 835–851.
[5]   L. Börjeson, M. Höjer, K-H. Dreborg, T. Ekvall, G. Finnveden, Scenario types and techniques: Towards a user's guide, *Futures* 38 (2006) 723–739.
[6]   J. Robinson, Energy backcasting: a proposed method of policy analysis, *Energy Politics* 10 (1982) 337–344.
[7]   J. Robinson, Future subjunctive: backcasting as social learning, *Futures*, 35 (2003) 839–856.
[8]   E. Masini, Rethinking futures studies, *Futures* 38 (2006) 1158–1168.
[9]   M. Höjer, L-G. Mattsson, Determinism and backcasting in futures studies, *Futures* 32 (2000) 613–634.
[10] S. Inayatullah, Reductionism or layered complexity? The future of futures studies, *Futures* 34 (2002) 295–302.
[11] S. Strand, Forecasting the future: pitfalls in controlling for uncertainty, *Futures* 31 (1999) 333–350.
[12] C. Blackman, From forecasting to informed choices, *Futures* 26 (1994) 3.
[13] T. Kristóf, Is it possible to make scientific forecasts in social sciences? *Futures* 38 (2006) 561–574.
[14] B. Danermark, M. Ekström, L. Jakobsen, J.C. Karlsson, *Explaining society. Critical realism in the social sciences*, Routledge, London, 2003, Ch. 1.
[15] K. Ehliasson, Futures studies as social science: An analytic scheme and a case study, *Futures* 40 (2008) 489–502.
[16] B. Danermark, M. Ekström, L. Jakobsen, J.C. Karlsson, *Explaining society. Critical realism in the social sciences*, Routledge, London, 2003, 206.
[17] J. Habermas, *The theory of communicative action*, Polity, Cambridge, 1984.
[18] Z. Bauman, *Modernity and the Holocaust*, Polity, Cambridge, 1991.
[19] M. Weber, 'Objectivity' in social science and social policy, in Max Weber: *The Methodology of the Social Sciences*, Free Press, New York, 1949/1904, 89–90.
[20] H. Kahn, A.J. Wiener, *The year 2000. A framework for speculation on the next thirty-three years*, Macmillan, London, 1969.
[21] H. Kahn, A.J. Wiener, *The year 2000. A framework for speculation on the next thirty-three years*, Macmillan, London, 1969, 329.
[22] H. Kahn, A.J. Wiener, *The year 2000. A framework for speculation on the next thirty-three years*, Macmillan, London, 1969, 1.
[23] H. Kahn, A.J. Wiener, *The year 2000. A framework for speculation on the next thirty-three years*, Macmillan, London, 1969, 38.
[24] P.A. Sorokin, *Social and cultural dynamics*, Bedminister Press, New York, 1962.
[25] C. Quigley, *The evolution of civilizations*, Macmillan, New York, 1961.
[26] H. Kahn, A.J. Wiener, *The year 2000. A framework for speculation on the next thirty-three years*, Macmillan, London, 1969, 41–48.
[27] H. Kahn, A.J. Wiener, *The Year 2000. A Framework for Speculation on the Next Thirty-Three Years*, Macmillan, London, 1969, 189.
[28] H. Kahn, A.J. Wiener, *The Year 2000. A Framework for Speculation on the Next Thirty-Three Years*, Macmillan, London, 1969, 213–214.
[29] H. Kahn, A.J. Wiener, *The Year 2000. A Framework for Speculation on the Next Thirty-Three Years*, Macmillan, London, 1969, 212.
[30] A. Toffler, *The third wave*, Collins, London, 1980.
[31] A. Toffler, *The third wave*, Collins, London, 1980, 21.
[32] A. Toffler, *The third wave*, Collins, London, 1980, 213.
[33] A. Toffler, *The third wave*, Collins, London, 1980, 247.
[34] A. Toffler, *The third wave*, Collins, London, 1980, Ch. 20.
[35] M. Parker, V. Fournier, P. Reredy, *The dictionary of alternatives. Utopianism & organization*, Zed Books, London, 2007, 247.
[36] A. Rand, *Atlas shrugged*, Signet, New York, 1957/1992.
[37] C.M. Sciabarra, *Ayn Rand: The Russian radical*, The Pennsylvania State University Press, University Park, PA, 1995, 115.
[38] M.J. Piore, C.F. Sabel, *The second industrial divide. Possibilities for prosperity*, Basic Books, New York, 1984.

[39] M.J. Piore, C.F. Sabel, *The second industrial divide. Possibilities for prosperity*, Basic Books, New York, 1984, 258.
[40] C. Grey, C. Garsten, Organized and disorganized utopias. An essay on presumption, in: M. Parker (Ed.), *Utopia and organization*, Blackwell, Oxford, 2002, 10.
[41] K. Vonnegut, *Player piano*, Dial Press, New York, 1952/2006.
[42] J-F. Lyotard, *The postmodern condition*, University of Minnesota Press, Minneapolis, 1984.
[43] K. Vonnegut, *Player piano*, Dial Press, New York, 1952/2006, Foreword.
[44] K. Vonnegut, *Player piano*, Dial Press, New York, 1952/2006, 1.
[45] K. Vonnegut, *Player piano*, Dial Press, New York, 1952/2006, 137.
[46] K. Vonnegut, *Player piano*, Dial Press, New York, 1952/2006, 302.
[47] D. Livingston, The utility of science fiction, in: J. Fowles (Ed.), *Handbook of futures research*, Greenwood Press, Westport, Conn., 1978, pp. 163–178.
[48] E.g. M. Parker (ed.) *Utopia and organization*, Blackwell, Oxford, 2002.
[49] J. Määttä, *Raketsommar. Science fiction i Sverige 1950–1968*, Ellerström, Lund, 2006.
[50] B. Danermark, M. Ekström, L. Jakobsen, J.C. Karlsson, *Explaining society. Critical realism in the social sciences*, Routledge, London, 2003.
[51] I. Asimov, *I, robot*, Bantam, New York, 1991.
[52] A.C. Clarke, *A space odyssey*, Orbit, London, 1998.
[53] C. Sagan, *Cosmos*, Random House, New York, 1980.
[54] A. Huxley, *Brave new world*, Chatto & Windus, London, 1932.
[55] R. Bradbury, *Fahrenheit 451*, Grafton, London, 1987.
[56] G. Orwell, *1984: A novel*, New American Library, New York, 1950.
[57] U.K. Le Guin, *The dispossessed. An ambiguous Utopia*, Harper & Row, New York, 1974.
[58] R.K. Merton, The self-fulfilling prophesy, in: R.K. Merton, *Social theory and social structure*, The Free Press, Glencoe, Ill., 1957, pp. 421–436.
[59] R.L. Henshel, Self-altering predictions, in: J. Fowles (Ed.), *Handbook of futures research*, Greenwood Press, Westport, Conn., 1978, pp. 99–123.
[60] M. Passerin d'Entrèves, S. Benhabib (eds), *Habermas and the unfinished project of modernity*, MIT Press, Cambridge, Mass., 1997.

INDEX

absence 58, 65, 67, 79, 81, 85, 90, 118, 141–2, 158
abstract xiii, 4, 8, 17, 19, 26, 27, 50, 76, 82, 83, 98–9, 161
Ackroyd, Stephen 4, 15, 88, 106
age 27, 32–5, 59, 60, 62–4, 75
Agger, Ben 109, 110
Åhlberg, Mauri 21, 24
alienation 4, 80, 154, 158
Anderson, Jonathan 40, 41
argument xii–xiii, 1–3, 9, 12, 13, 14, 20, 21, 27, 37, 87, 97, 107, 108, 110, 111, 115, 116, 120, 122–33, 134–48, 150, 159; chain of 10, 13, 14, 83, 116, 118–20, 122, 124, 125–7, 129–32, 144, 147
argumentation xii, 1, 2, 12, 14, 15, 22, 57, 79, 80, 81, 82, 87, 108–10, 111, 114, 115, 116, 121, 122, 126, 128, 129, 130, 132, 133, 134, 136, 138, 139, 144, 146, 148, 154
Argyris, Chris 43–5, 54
article xii, 1, 7, 9, 15, 107, 108, 115, 116, 118, 120, 122, 129, 134, 141, 144–7
Asplund, Johan 22, 23
Atkinson, John 35, 41
audience xiii, 1, 7, 9, 11, 12, 13, 14, 25, 32, 107, 108–9, 111, 112, 114, 115, 120, 126, 128, 135, 144
availability 7, 36
Axelsson, Jonas 145, 148, 150

Bailey, Kenneth D. 22, 23, 55, 61, 72, 74, 88, 141, 142, 148

Banks, Marcus 17–20, 23, 125, 133, 136, 148
bannister 128, 130, 131, 133
Barber, Elinor 11, 16
Barsalou, Lawrence W. 27, 41
Barton, Allen H. 22, 23, 61, 73, 76, 88, 89, 90, 91, 105, 106
Becker, Howard S. 15, 20, 22, 23, 85–7, 88, 107, 108, 109, 110, 113, 121
Bélanger, Jacques 83, 88, 97, 102–4, 105
belief 3, 154
Bergman, Ann 7, 15, 36, 41, 46–8, 54, 134, 141, 143, 146, 148, 150
Bergqvist, Tuula 72, 105
Billig, Michael 115, 121
Bitzer, Lloyd F. 112, 121
book 1, 10–11, 17, 107, 108, 112, 114, 115, 118–20, 122, 124, 129
bound 12, 14, 17, 18, 22, 26, 55, 71, 124, 125, 128, 136, 140
boundary 29–30, 85
Brown, Kenneth 40, 41
Bunge, Mario 2, 15, 19, 23, 47, 54

Caillois, Roger 135–6, 148
capital 6, 8, 50–3, 83, 87
capitalism 6, 8, 80, 83–5, 96, 105, 156
capitalist 66, 93
casino 77–8
category 32–3, 62, 76, 138, 151, 152, 156, 159, 161
chapter 108, 118–20, 123–9, 129–32
circle 19, 29, 30, 32, 35–6
class 3, 4, 6, 7, 8, 37, 59–60, 65–6, 77–8, 113

classification 6, 33, 55, 61–2, 65–6, 70, 85, 96, 115, 116–17, 131–2, 143, 147, 151–2, 160
cluster 29, 32, 37–8, 77, 126, 127
Cohen, Gerald A. 92–3, 94, 105
Collier, David 22, 23, 56, 65, 69, 72
commodity 5, 79, 80
concept xii–xiii, 1–2, 3–9, 11, 13, 17, 19, 21–3, 27, 32, 37, 38, 45, 55, 57, 64–5, 68–9, 76, 79, 81–2, 83, 111, 120, 123–5, 131–2, 134–6, 140, 143, 145
conceptualization 3–4, 7, 17, 65, 98–9
connection 1, 5, 11, 12–14, 21–2, 25, 27, 28, 30, 32, 36, 39, 49, 51, 67, 78, 112, 115, 125, 127, 157
containment 29, 30–1, 35, 37, 126
continuum 14, 17–20, 33–4, 114, 125, 136
contradiction 6, 7, 50–3, 57, 66, 74, 79, 90, 92, 93, 94, 112
core–periphery 35, 127
corrigibility 4, 15, 25, 123, 160
craft 5, 102, 136, 161
creativity xii, 1, 5, 11, 13, 22, 25–6, 34, 57, 79, 82, 99, 123, 135, 137, 159
curiosity 1, 5, 8, 9, 15, 22, 25, 42, 43, 46, 60, 101, 107, 135–6
curly bracket 116, 118, 120, 144
customer 3, 39–40, 57–8, 93, 116, 118

Danermark, Berth 2, 3, 4, 5, 15, 49, 53, 54, 59, 72, 82, 88, 123, 133, 139, 148, 162
data 7, 9, 10–11, 21, 25–6, 43, 47, 65, 124, 139, 154
deduction 10–11, 82
detective story 108–9
diagram 18–19, 20, 21–2, 26, 35, 61, 125
dichotomy 32–5, 68–9, 75, 81, 127
differentiation 32–3, 34, 35, 37, 47–8, 75, 78, 80
digression 130–1, 132, 133
dimension 13, 14, 18, 20, 21, 27, 44–5, 48, 55–71, 75–7, 78, 80, 81, 83–4, 86, 89, 91–2, 94–6, 97–9, 101–2, 116, 118, 130, 136, 138, 140–2, 144, 145, 147
drawing 1, 9, 17, 18, 20, 21, 44, 100, 137
Dunleavy, Patrick 115, 120, 121
dystopia 143–7, 152–3, 157, 159–61

Edwards, Paul 15, 69–71, 72, 83–5, 88, 97, 105
Elman, Colin 22, 23, 76, 77, 78, 79, 87, 88, 89, 91, 105
empirical 4, 5, 9, 11, 20, 21, 33, 35, 47, 56, 58, 61, 62, 69, 71, 74, 79–82, 86, 87, 90, 91, 92, 93, 94–5, 96, 100, 101, 102, 104, 112, 116, 139–40, 141, 150, 154, 160, 161
employee 3, 5–6, 7, 32, 35, 38, 39–40, 49–50, 52–3, 62, 66, 68, 69, 75–6, 79, 83, 87, 100, 101–4
employer 5, 7, 9, 32, 39–40, 49–51, 53, 79, 83, 93
Engelhardt, Yuri 17, 23, 26, 29, 30, 41, 126, 133
entity 2, 3–4, 19, 34, 38, 109, 112, 135
epistemology xii, 12–13, 14, 115, 134–5, 144, 147, 150–1, 160
Erikson, Kai 109, 110
Eriksson, Birgitta 62, 72, 96, 105
essay xii, 1, 9, 107, 108, 115, 120
Etzioni, Amitai 79–81, 82–3, 87, 88, 97
exit 68–9
explanation 2–3, 5, 8, 28, 42, 47, 59, 81, 131, 141–3, 144–7, 151–61
explanatory claims 141–3, 145–7, 150–61
exploitation 5, 8

fallibility 4, 5, 47, 82, 123, 160
family 7, 32, 36–7, 38, 61, 90, 95, 105, 159
Faulkner, Robert R. 85–7, 88
fiction 65, 140, 145–6
figure, definition 97–8
Finley, Moses I. 91, 105
Fleetwood, Steve 3, 15, 88, 106
flexibility 35, 66–8, 155, 161
forecast 15, 109, 136–9, 140–3, 144–7, 148, 150–61
friendship 26, 28, 38
Fromm, Erich 90–1, 105
futures studies 141, 145, 148, 150–1, 153, 154, 159–61

Geertz, Clifford 109, 110
gender xiii, 3, 4, 33, 62–3, 64, 81, 134, 159, segregation 7, 18–20, 27, 29, 35, 43, 46–9, 54, 59–60, 116, 125
Glaser, Barney G. 23, 65, 72
Goldstone, Robert 27, 41
Gouldner, Alvin 69–71, 72
graphic 14, 17–20, 21–2, 25, 26, 28–30, 31, 32, 35, 37, 40, 42, 118, 124–6, 128, 136

Hall, Richard 57–8, 73
Hempel, Carl G. 59, 73
hierarchy 14, 19–20, 37, 38–9, 47, 79, 100, 109, 116, 118, 127, 132, 144, 152
Hirschman, Albert O. 68–9, 73
Hochschild, Arlie Russell 8–9, 15

Index

Huberman, A. Michael 21, 24, 26, 41, 56, 73
Huizinga, Johan 135, 136, 148
Hult, Christine A. 112, 114, 121
Huzell, Henrietta 6, 15
hypothesis 2, 68, 82, 100, 159, 161

image 11, 13, 17, 19, 20
induction 10–11

Jónasdóttir, Anna G. 8, 15

Kahn, Herman 142, 145, 146, 147, 148, 153–4
Karasek, Robert 6–7, 15, 100–1, 105
Karlsson, Jan Ch. 4, 6, 15, 49–53, 54, 68, 72, 73, 76, 88, 91, 105, 106, 114, 133, 148, 150
Keynes, John Maynard 138, 148
knowledge 3, 4, 5, 11, 25, 27, 38, 43, 45, 46, 49, 60, 82, 98–9, 113, 114, 123, 124, 128, 134, 135, 139, 160
Kolb, David A. 98–9, 100, 101, 105
Korczynski, Marek 40, 41, 131, 133

labour 3, 5–6, 8–9, 18, 32, 35, 36, 43, 47–8, 50–3, 65–6, 75–6, 78–9, 83–5, 87, 92–7, 112, 116, 138, 157
Lafargue, Paul 137, 148
language 2, 3, 4, 17, 65, 113, 152
LaPorte, Jody 23, 72
Larsson, Patrik 6, 15
Layder, Derek 5, 12, 16, 65, 73
Lazarsfeld, Paul F. 22, 23, 61, 73, 88, 89–91, 105, 106
learning 5, 43–6, 54, 98–100, 101
line-up 29, 30–1, 32, 34, 37–8, 126, 127, 128
link 21, 25, 29, 30–1, 32, 38–9, 44, 49, 126, 127–8
literature xiii, 10, 21, 38, 68, 72, 97, 116, 118, 124–5, 126, 136, 140, 141, 142, 144, 145, 146
Litman, Jordan J. 135, 148
logic 8, 11, 13, 21, 22, 23, 25, 29, 32, 56, 58, 59, 60, 61–3, 68, 70–1, 74, 78–9, 85–6, 87, 92, 93, 94, 104, 109, 115, 123, 124, 126, 127, 128, 130, 131, 136, 139, 140–1
Lowenstein, George 135, 148

management 45, 70–1, 83, 101–4, 153
manager 6, 19, 38, 40, 66, 68, 69, 158
Marx, Karl 8, 78, 88, 157
Maslow, Abraham 37, 39
means of production 78–9, 92–3, 94

mechanism 2, 4, 7, 11, 42, 46, 48, 52–3, 62–3, 81, 85, 129, 132, 133, 135, 137–8, 139–40, 141–2, 146, 151, 152, 153, 154, 156, 157, 160
memo 12, 134, 137, 138, 139, 140, 144–5, 146
men 7, 8, 18, 19–20, 36, 47–8, 81–2
Merton, Robert K. 2, 11, 16, 141, 148, 159, 163
method xii, 5, 10, 11, 22, 26, 32, 56, 62, 124, 139–40, 144, 150, 151
Miles, Matthew B. 21, 26, 56
Mills, C. Wright 61, 73, 108, 110
Mitchell, G. Duncan 2, 16
music 4, 62, 76–7, 85–7, 136, 140, 146

network 21, 29, 30, 38–9, 128, 155
Nostradamus 138

O'Brien, Mark 26, 27, 41
ontology xii, 12–13, 14, 115, 134–5, 144, 147, 148, 150–2, 160–1
Oppenheim, Paul 59, 73
organization 3, 18–19, 35, 37, 43–5, 47, 49–53, 66–8, 79–81, 87, 97, 102, 116, 145, 159

persona 14, 112, 113–14, 115, 120
picture 17, 18, 19, 20, 21, 25, 29, 125
play 1, 7, 9, 14, 66, 70, 85, 87, 91, 101, 107, 108, 109, 111, 122, 123, 135, 136, 137, 140, 141, 146, 148, 152, 157, 158, 159, 160
Podolny, Joel 27, 41
positivism 59, 150
power 8, 27, 28, 31, 45, 47–9, 53, 61, 80–1, 82, 83, 84, 96, 116, 137
Pratt, Michael G. 69, 73
prediction 59, 122, 131, 136–47, 150–4, 159–61
preliminary endpoint 21–2, 122–3, 129, 133
presence 58, 65, 67, 79, 81, 90, 116, 118, 142
problem 6, 7, 14, 43, 50, 92, 97, 101, 112, 113, 114, 115, 120, 136, 141, 142, 145, 151, 160
process arrow 97, 99–101, 141
prognosis 143–7, 152–5, 160
prophesy 137–9, 159
proposal 11–14, 22, 42, 107–9, 115, 116, 120, 144
proposition 25, 116, 120, 122, 133, 134, 159
publish 107, 108, 112, 120

qualitative 19, 21, 22, 26, 35, 37, 40, 56, 60, 61, 77, 102, 107, 108, 130, 145, 160
quantitative 7, 18, 19, 21, 22, 35, 56, 60, 61, 62, 65, 76, 77, 102, 107, 108
Quigley, Carroll 146, 153, 162

Ragin, Charles C. 62, 73, 81–2, 88
Rand, Ayn 145, 146, 149, 156–7
reader xii, xiii, 1, 9–10, 11, 12, 13, 107, 111, 113, 114, 115, 120, 126, 127, 128, 129, 130, 131, 134, 136, 145
reading 14, 18, 109, 114, 118, 122, 129, 131, 133
reasoning 17, 21, 32, 33, 43, 59, 60, 81, 83, 114, 136, 139, 151, 153, 155, 157; chain of 13, 14, 92, 109, 111, 115–33, 144, 146, 147
rectangle 31–3
Reilly, Mary 136, 149
relata 13, 14, 20, 21, 22, 25–9, 32–5, 38–40, 44–9, 54, 125–8, 136
relatum 27, 28, 35, 44, 47, 48
reporting process i, xii, 2, 9, 10, 11–12, 13, 14, 15, 22, 25, 27, 28, 30, 31, 32, 107, 108, 109, 110, 111, 112, 114, 115, 116, 117, 119, 122, 134–6, 137, 143–5, 146
research process i, xii, 1, 2, 5, 6, 9, 10–11, 12, 13, 14, 15, 21, 25, 26, 27, 28, 31, 32, 44, 55, 57, 60, 72, 107, 108, 110, 113, 114, 116, 122, 128, 134–6, 138, 141, 143, 144, 145, 146, 148
research question 12, 14, 26, 42, 74, 85, 125, 136
retail 5, 57, 58, 116, 118, 131
retroduction 139
rewrite xiii, 14, 31, 108, 109, 122, 123, 126
rhetoric i, 12, 13, 14, 108, 109, 111–15, 120, 134, 135
risk 29, 74, 76, 77, 79, 82, 85, 89, 91, 94, 96, 97, 99, 101, 104, 123, 132, 141, 149
Rueschmeyer, Dietrich 61, 73
rule 9, 22, 31, 32, 55, 61, 62, 69–71, 107, 113, 136, 137, 140
Russell, Bertrand 137, 149

Sayer, Andrew 3, 16, 59, 73, 76, 88
Scagnoli, Norma 21, 24
Schön, Donald 43–5, 54
science fiction 143–7, 152, 153, 156–7, 159, 160, 161
Seawright, Jason 23, 72
self-employed 65–6, 76, 78
separation 29–30, 32, 33, 35, 36, 48, 126
separators 29, 31, 126

serendipity 11
serf 91–3
Shotter, John 135, 149
sign 18–19, 25, 116
Simmel, George 40, 41
slave 79, 91–4, 153
Smith, Dorothy 109, 110
social theory i, xii, 1–15, 17, 21, 26, 32, 55, 57, 62, 64, 65, 72, 82, 108, 111, 134, 135
sociology xiii, 4, 11, 22, 135, 145
Sorokin, Pitirim 146, 153, 162
statement 2, 3, 5, 13, 14, 22, 25, 26, 27, 28, 35, 40, 95, 108, 111, 120, 122, 125, 128, 135, 136, 137, 138, 139, 144, 152, 153
Stinchcombe, Arthur 23, 24, 61, 73
stratification 37, 47, 48
Strauss, Anselm 65, 72
structure 6, 14, 18, 25, 34, 46, 47, 48, 49, 66, 76, 83, 90, 91, 105, 109, 112, 114, 115, 116, 118, 120, 123, 128, 129, 130, 131, 144, 146, 147, 151
Swedberg, Richard 5, 9, 10, 16, 65, 73, 109, 110, 135, 149
Swieringa, Joop 45, 54
symbol 3, 17, 18, 19, 20, 25, 28, 29, 30, 31, 32, 80, 89, 93, 97, 101, 105, 116, 125, 136

table, definition 18, 97
technology 36, 89, 138, 146, 154, 155, 156, 158, 159, 161
tendency 13, 134, 135, 138, 160
tenure 81, 82
term 1 6, 8, 9, 11, 12, 13, 21, 32, 56, 58, 60, 64–70, 72, 84, 86, 89, 93, 96, 99, 100, 102, 120, 135, 136, 137, 140, 141, 143–8, 152, 154, 156, 157; definition 3
textual 17, 18, 20, 31, 49
Theorell, Töres 6–7, 15, 105
theorizing, definition 5
theory, definition 2
thought experiment 145, 161
thought operation 3, 139
Thuderoz, Christian 102–4, 105
Tilly, Charles 33, 41
time 7, 9, 28, 30, 31, 34, 37, 40, 45, 60, 78, 83, 95, 108, 124, 127, 138, 157, 158, 159
title 56, 59, 63, 71, 83, 84, 98, 123, 124, 125, 126, 130, 131, 140, 146
Toffler, Alvin 145, 149, 154–5
tool i, xii, 1, 5, 7, 9, 12–15, 17, 21, 22, 23, 25, 26, 27, 29, 32, 33, 35, 42, 55, 56,

57, 61, 64, 68, 71, 72, 74, 77, 78, 94, 107, 109, 115, 121, 122, 123, 124, 126, 128, 134, 135, 136, 140, 141, 144, 148, 151, 160
trade union 49–54
transfactual 97, 139, 140, 159
triad 39, 40, 48
triangle 19, 29, 30, 37, 39, 40
trichotomy 33
truth claim 137, 141–3, 145–7, 150–61
typology 14, 22, 56, 60–1, 62, 66, 72, 78, 87, 89, 90, 91, 92, 93, 94, 95, 97, 99, 100, 105, 130, 136, 140, 141, 142, 147, 148, 150–2, 159–61; definition 56

utopia 137–40, 143–7, 152–3, 156–7, 159, 160, 161

van den Broek, Diane 57–8, 73
variable 7, 18, 27, 55, 56, 60, 62, 65, 131, 132, 142
Verdinelli, Susanna 21, 24

visual format xii, 26, 27, 29, 125
voice 68–9, 113, 158
Vonnegut, Kurt 146, 149, 157–9

wage labourer 53, 79, 92–3, 95
Wajcman, Judy 69–71, 72
Wheeldon, Johannes 21, 24
Wiener, Anthony J. 142, 145, 146, 147, 148, 153–4
Wierdsma, Andre 45, 54
women 3, 7, 8, 15, 18–20, 32, 36, 47, 48, 113, 157, 159
worker 6, 7, 8, 40, 53, 61, 62, 66, 67, 69, 70, 71, 75, 76, 78, 84, 85, 87, 95, 100, 101, 155, 157
workplace 38, 46, 68, 69–71, 83, 84, 87, 96, 101, 102, 104, 134, 155
Wright, Eric Olin 6, 7, 9, 16, 65–6, 73
Wright, Martyn 88
writing i, xii, xiii, 1, 2, 5, 9–15, 17, 21, 30, 31, 33, 40, 43, 57, 107–9, 111–16, 118, 120, 122–9, 133, 134, 135, 136, 144–7